Mom's Updated Recipe Box

2nd Edition

300 Family Favorites Made Quick and Healthy

Donna L. Weihofen, R.D.

Adams Media
Avon, Massachusetts

Published by
Adams Media, an F+W Publications Company
57 Littlefield Street, Avon, MA 02322. U.S.A.
www.adamsmedia.com

ISBN: 1-59337-275-2

Printed in Canada.

J I H G F E D C B A

Library of Congress Cataloging-in-Publication Data
Weihofen, Donna L.
Mom's updated recipe box / by Donna L. Weihofen.—2nd ed.
p.   cm.
ISBN 1-59337-275-2
1. Cookery. I. Title.

TX714.W327 2005
641.5—dc22
                          2004019233

This publication is designed to provide accurate and authoritative information with regard to the sub-
ject matter covered. It is sold with the understanding that the publisher is not engaged in rendering
legal, accounting, or other professional advice. If legal advice or other expert assistance is required,
the services of a competent professional person should be sought.
                    — From a *Declaration of Principles* jointly adopted by a Committee of the American
                              Bar Association and a Committee of Publishers and Associations

Many of the designations used by manufacturers and sellers to distinguish their products are claimed as
trademarks. Where those designations appear in this book and Adams Media was aware of a trademark
claim, the designations have been printed with initial capital letters.

Cover illustration by Ken Jacobsen.

This book is available at quantity discounts for bulk purchases.
For information, call 1-800-872-5627.

Acknowledgments

My gratitude and thanks go to my lifelong friend Mary Risgaard for her expert, yet practical cooking advice and for testing many of the recipes on her family and friends.

Many thanks also to my husband Ray, my children, Wayne, Vicki, Wendy, and son-in-law Steve for helping me choose only the very best recipes. After writing two other cookbooks, it was my daughter Vicki who told me, "This is the book I am waiting for." It is in *Mom's Updated Recipe Box* where she can find all the best of the old recipes she loved to eat as she was growing up. Now she can make them herself.

Contents

Chapter Ten
Vegetables

Chapter Eleven
Breads

Chapter Twelve
Sauces and Salsas

Introduction

$\mathcal{M}$om's home cooking was something special. She and the other neighborhood moms used those wonderful recipes that had been passed along from one generation to the next. We have fond memories of simple family suppers, holiday feasts, picnics, potlucks, and after-school treats. Delicious? It sure was! Lo-cal? Not very much! Lo-fat? Don't even think about it! Could Mom's recipe box use an update for our lifestyle in the new millennium? That's what this little book is all about.

Mom's Updated Recipe Box, 2nd Edition, is full of those traditional recipes you'll want to prepare for both family and friends. Each recipe was adapted to eliminate the "not-so-healthy" ingredients or cooking techniques and still retain the great tastes that you remember. When necessary, modifications were made so that the preparation would be simpler and/or quicker than the traditional recipe without compromising the appearance or the flavor. None of them requires a professional chef. This is home cooking that we've tested in a home kitchen to make certain you will succeed the first time you try each recipe. The book is also full of cooking and baking tips that will help those with all levels of experience in the kitchen.

This is a fun cookbook, now with fifty new favorites that are just as evocative—and just as healthy—as the original 250. Family and friends will be asking you to share your recipes. And how about the kids? They'll grow up, spread their wings, and leave home to do their own thing. And one day, they'll be on the other end of the phone saying, "Hey, Mom! How do you make that great-tasting pot roast of yours? I want to try it."

I hope these recipes will bring pleasure to your family dinners and become incorporated into your family's traditions. Enjoy the food and enjoy the memories!

Notes about the Book

The calories and nutrient information for each recipe are derived from a computer analysis (Master Cook 4.0—Sierra Home) based on information from the USDA. Every effort has been made to check the accuracy of these numbers. It is important, however, to note that there are numerous variables in making these calculations. All analyses should be considered approximate.

Fiber content of each recipe is listed as low (less than 1 gram per serving), medium (1–3 grams per serving), high (3–4 grams per serving), or very high (more than 4 grams per serving). Measurement of fiber is not an exact science. In fact measuring the amount of fiber in food can vary as much as 50 percent from one research report to another, depending on the method of analysis used. Dietary fiber contains the parts of plant materials that are resistant to human digestive enzymes. Dietary fiber is considered to be the sum of indigestible carbohydrate and carbohydrate-like components of foods. Cereal grains, vegetables, fruits, legumes, seeds, and nuts are the major sources of dietary fiber. Processing these foods, such as grinding or cooking, can affect the physical properties of the food, but the fiber remains.

Cooking and Baking Tips

Kitchen Tools

Cooking is so much more enjoyable if you have the right tools and equipment. Start collecting the most essential ones and make a birthday or holiday gift "wish list" for everything you would like to have. Visit a good kitchen store when making your list.

• Invest in good knives.
• Kitchen shears are handy for cutting dried fruit, marshmallows, pizza, biscuits, and many other foods. Make sure they can be washed in the dishwasher.
• Pick out four different colored cutting boards and use each one for a different type of food. For instance, use a green one for cutting vegetables, orange for fruits, red for meat, and a wooden one for breads. It is safer because it prevents cross contamination between meat and other foods.
• To prevent the cutting board from moving around while cutting, put a damp cloth underneath the board.
• If you have casserole dishes or bowls that are not labeled with a size, fill the bowls with water and pour the water into measuring cups to figure out each bowl's capacity. Mark the capacity on the bottom of the bowls with a permanent marker.

Organizing

• Store utensils that you use often in an attractive jar or container on your counter near the stove. You will never have to dig in a drawer for them.
• Alphabetize your spices and seasonings so they will be easy to find. Choose a cupboard in the cooler area of your kitchen. Do not store spices in the cupboard above the stove.

Oven

• Check your oven temperature with an oven thermometer. Some ovens heat higher or lower than the setting would indicate, which could ruin a lot of recipes.

Meal Prep

• If you are preparing more than one or two dishes at a time for a meal, write out your menu and keep it on the counter while working. It helps you keep focused and prevents you from forgetting to prepare or serve an item.
• If you often prepare meals with several recipes, buy several kitchen timers to set for each dish you are cooking.
• When you cook for company, write out the menu with the names of the guests and the date. File it away. You may find it

helpful if you invite the same people back a year later and you don't want to repeat the same menu.
• Don't worry about a mess in your kitchen while you are cooking. It will all be cleaned up eventually. Maybe you can even get someone else to do the dishes.

Leftovers
• Store leftovers in clear glass or plastic containers so they are easy to identify and you are reminded to use them quickly. It is also helpful to put a date on leftovers and opened cans of foods and beverages.

Grocery List
• Keep an ongoing grocery list on a notepad. Whenever you are running low on a standard item, write it down. Make a house rule: Whoever uses up the last of something adds the item to the list. If everyone in the family is "trained" to do so, you will never run out.

COOKING TIPS

Cooking and Frying
• A spatter lid made with fine mesh is handy when frying food to prevent fat spatters from getting all over your stove. It works differently from a pan cover because the spatter lid lets the steam escape. This is important if you are frying food to get a nice brown crust.

• To prevent a pot on the stove or a casserole dish in the oven from boiling over, off-set the cover slightly to allow a small amount of steam to escape. A small object such as a thin wooden skewer can also be placed between the cover and pan to allow steam to escape.

Onions and Garlic
• When a recipe calls for cooking or sautéing onions and garlic, always cook the onions first. Cook the onions until they are translucent (shiny and opaque) and then add the garlic. Cook the garlic for only 1 or 2 minutes. Do not allow the garlic to brown. If it browns, it will become bitter and the flavor will ruin your dish. If it browns, throw it out.

Cheese
• When using regular cheese in cooked dishes, add the cheese at the end of the cooking process. Do not overcook.
• Grate semi-firm cheese such as Cheddar when the cheese is cold. Very hard cheese such as Parmesan is easier to grate at room temperature. If you need a lot of Parmesan, grate it in the food processor.
• One-fourth pound of cheese will make 1 cup of grated cheese.

Sauces
• For a no-fail cheese sauce, use a processed cheese. These cheeses have been processed with heat and they have special emulsifiers added. They melt easily and do not get stringy.

• When a recipe calls for reducing a sauce, you need to cook it long enough to evaporate some of the water so the sauce becomes thicker and more flavorful.

• When reducing a sauce, add salt and other seasonings at the end of the cooking process. If you add it before reducing, the flavor could become too intense.

• Egg yolks add a smooth texture and moisture to sauces. The natural emulsifiers in egg yolks hold water and fat together. Egg yolks are the secret ingredient in creamy, smooth sauces and custards.

• Cornstarch and flour when cooked with a liquid form gels that can be thick enough to cut with a knife. They are clear when hot, but get cloudy when cold. The sauce can separate when frozen.

• Root starches like arrowroot and tapioca make gels that freeze well. They are clear when hot and they remain clear when cold, but they do not get thick enough to cut with a knife.

• When making a white sauce or any sauce thickened with flour or cornstarch, use a wooden spoon to stir it constantly as it thickens. Also have a wire whisk handy in case the sauce begins to get lumpy. Keep stirring and reduce the heat until you have it back under control.

• Cornstarch is a fine white flour made from corn kernels. Always mix cornstarch with a cold liquid to form a thin paste before adding to a hot mixture.

• A sauce thickened with cornstarch is not as stable as a flour-thickened sauce. It may break down with long cooking in high heat. It may also break down with excessive stirring.

• For thickening purposes, substitute ½ tablespoon cornstarch for 1 tablespoon flour.

• When using flour as a thickener, mix flour with cold water in a shaker before adding it to the hot cooking mixture. A shaker works much better than trying to mix the flour and water together with a spoon.

Oils

• In place of the commercial nonstick oil sprays, invest in special spray bottles available in kitchen supply stores. You can fill your own bottles with good quality oils. They are great for spraying directly on foods for flavor. They can also be used for greasing cooking and baking pans.

• Extra-virgin olive oil is the oil that comes from the first pressing of the olives. The color is green and it has a fruity taste. The flavor depends on the type of olive and the growing conditions. It is the oil of choice for salad dressings or to use directly on food. It has a low smoking point so it should not be used in a heated cooking process.

• Virgin olive oil is the oil from the second pressing of the olives. It has less flavor than the extra-virgin.

• The last pressing of the olives is labeled 100 percent olive oil. It still has the same amount of good monounsaturated fat but it has little flavor. The 100 percent olive oil has a higher smoking temperature so it should be used when sautéing or frying foods.

• Keep both extra-virgin and 100 percent olive oils on hand to use for different purposes.

• The word "light" on an olive oil bottle does not mean it is lower in calories. It just means that the flavor is less intense. All oils, butter, and regular margarine have about 100 calories per tablespoon.

Pasta

• When cooking pasta, always add it to rapidly boiling water. Keep the water gently boiling as the pasta cooks. This will prevent the pasta from sticking together.

• Taste pasta for doneness. It should be served al dente or slightly firm. Mushy pasta will ruin your dish.

• When pasta is done, pour it into a colander in the sink. If you are not going to serve it immediately, chill it under cold running water. Set it aside until the meal is ready. Pour hot or boiling water over the pasta to quickly reheat.

• Leftover cold pasta keeps well in the refrigerator.

• Recipes usually call for 4 ounces or 1/4 pound of pasta per serving for a main course. Because the density of pasta differs, 1 cup of dry pasta can weigh anywhere between 2 and 4 1/2 ounces. Four cups or 1 pound of macaroni-style pasta makes about 9 cups of cooked pasta. One pound of spaghetti makes about 7 cups of cooked spaghetti.

Rice

• Choose the variety of rice that suits your recipe. Long-grain rice will be light and dry with separate grains. It is a good choice for side dishes or salads. Short-grain rice tends to stick together when cooked. It is a good choice for rice pudding. Brown rice takes longer to cook but is high in fiber.

• One cup of raw rice will make about 3 cups of cooked rice.

• If using rice to prepare a cold salad, add the dressing ingredients to the rice right after it is cooked. Mixing rice with the moist dressing will prevent the rice from turning hard as it cools.

• Wild rice is really not a rice but rather a form of grass seed. It needs to be washed before cooking.

Soups

• Homemade soup often tastes better the day after it has been made. Make it the day before serving and refrigerate it.

• Place a leaf of lettuce in a pot of soup while cooking to absorb some of the grease. Remove the leaf and discard.

• Any fat from homemade soup will rise to the top. After it cools it will become hard. Remove it with a fork and discard it. (Do not pour any liquid or hard fat into the sink drain or garbage disposal.)

• To help "de-gas" dried beans, add 1 teaspoon of baking soda to the soaking water of the beans. Pour off that water and add fresh water when ready to cook.

• No need to soak dried beans overnight. Instead, cover beans with water and bring to a boil for 2 minutes. Remove from heat, cover pan, and let stand for at least 1 hour. Drain this water, add fresh water, and continue making the soup or bean dish.

To thicken a soup:

• Remove part of the vegetables and purée them. Return puréed vegetables to the soup.

• Use an immersion blender to partially purée some of the vegetables in the soup.

• Add a mixture of cornstarch and cold water. Add small amounts to the boiling soup. Stir constantly. Add it until soup reaches the desired consistency.

- Add rice, barley, or pasta and cook until it is done.
- Add instant mashed potato flakes.

• To add more flavor to a bland-tasting soup, add some chicken or beef bouillon or soup base.

• Add dried herbs to soups and stews early in the cooking process but add fresh herbs late in the cooking process.

Taste It First

• Always taste food during cooking and at the end of the cooking process. Adjust seasonings for your taste.

• After food is chilled, the flavor is less intense than it was when the dish was hot. If the food is served cold, you may need to add some extra seasonings.

Eggs

• When an egg cracks while boiling, add a tablespoon of vinegar to the water to help keep the whites in the shell.

• The green discoloration around the yolk in a hard-cooked egg is a reaction of the iron in the yolk and sulfur in the white. This reaction is more likely to occur when eggs are cooked longer than necessary. The green color may not look good but it is harmless.

• For hard-cooked eggs that are easy to peel, use eggs that are at least ten days old. Very fresh eggs are difficult to peel.

• Mark hard-cooked eggs with a permanent marker so you know which eggs are the cooked eggs in the refrigerator.

• To prevent egg yolks from crumbling when slicing hard-cooked eggs, wet the knife before each cut.

• When poaching eggs, add a tablespoon of vinegar to the poaching water. This will help set the whites so they will not spread.

Gelatin

• Recipes that call for gelatin usually advise you to soften it. Mix the gelatin in a small amount of cold liquid (1 tablespoon in 1/4 cup liquid) for 2 to 3 minutes. To dissolve the gelatin, gently heat it on low heat, stirring constantly. It will be completely dissolved when you can no longer see small crystals in a spoonful of the mixture.

• When making a gelatin salad, some fresh fruits cannot be added because they have an enzyme that will soften the gelatin structure. They include raw pineapple, honeydew melon, papaya, kiwi, and figs.

• If you want to add fruit to a gelatin salad that has already set up, microwave it on low power until it softens. Add the fruit and refrigerate until firm.

Whipping Cream

• Whipping cream beats up best in a thoroughly chilled, tall, narrow bowl with cold beaters. Beat just until thick. Beating the cream too long will cause it to separate into curds (butter) and whey.

Ice Cream

• When mixing ice cream and crème de menthe for a grasshopper drink or dessert topping, use mint ice cream and less alcohol. The mixture will be thicker and will freeze better. (Alcohol lowers the freezing temperature.)

Coffee

• When making coffee, always use cold water. Add ½ teaspoon of sugar to coffee grounds to reduce the bitter flavor. You will not taste the sugar.
• Store coffee grounds in the freezer to retain the fresh flavor.

Candy

• An accurate candy thermometer is essential in candy making. Test your thermometer by making sure it registers 212°F in boiling water.

BAKING TIPS

Getting Started

• Double-check your recipe to make sure you have all the ingredients before starting to cook or bake. Neighbors get tired of loaning eggs.
• Line up all ingredients before you begin a recipe and put each one away after you have used it. This makes cleanup go faster, and you will never have to wonder if you left something out.

Measuring

• Measure all of the dry ingredients before the wet ones so you can use the same measuring spoons and cups.
• You can use either light brown or dark brown sugar in most recipes. The dark brown sugar will give a slightly more noticeable molasses flavor.

• When measuring brown sugar, pack it firmly into a dry measuring cup.
• To measure dry ingredients, such as flour or sugar, spoon them into a dry measuring cup and level it off with the straight edge of a table knife. If you scoop the measuring cup into the flour canister, the flour packs in too tightly and there will be too much flour in the recipe.
• For liquids, use a glass or plastic measuring cup. Fill the cup to the desired amount, then place the cup on the counter. Check the amount at eye level for accuracy.
• Dip the spoon or measuring cup in hot water before measuring shortening or butter. It will be easier to get the fat out of the cup.

Fats and Oils

• Soft margarine or reduced calorie margarine cannot be substituted for regular margarine, shortening, or butter in a recipe. Whipped fats are 30 to 50 percent air and light fats contain extra water.
• Substituting margarine for butter or shortening may change the quality of a baked product. This is especially true if the first ingredient listed on the label of the margarine is an oil.
• Rinse your bowl in hot water before adding and creaming butter and sugar. The ingredients will cream together more easily.
• Soften a stick of butter or margarine for baking by microwaving for 1 minute on 20 percent power.

Honey

• When measuring honey, syrup, or molasses, use the same cup you used for measuring the shortening or spray the cup with vegetable oil. The thick honey will come out more easily.
• Since honey is sweeter than sugar and has more liquid, you can substitute sugar for honey in a recipe by adding 1 1/4 cups sugar and 1/4 cup more liquid for each cup of honey.

Flour

• All-purpose flour is good for general cooking. You only need cake flour if you bake finely textured cakes and pastries. Bread flour has more protein and gluten so it rises a little better but all-purpose flour works well for breads too.
• Self-rising flour has about 1 1/2 teaspoons baking powder and 1/2 teaspoon salt added per cup of flour.

Mixing

• To keep a bowl steady while you mix or whip ingredients, place it on a damp towel or cloth.
• When using a mixer, choose a bowl that is large enough to prevent splatters.
• Follow recipe directions when mixing flour into a batter. For most quick breads and desserts, the batter should not be over-stirred after the flour has been added. Excessive stirring or beating develops the gluten in the flour and toughens the baked product.
• The secret to making tender muffins without tunnels in the middle is to mix liquid ingredients in one bowl and dry ingredients in another bowl. Make a "nest" in the middle of the dry ingredients. Pour the liquid in the nest and stir gently with a spoon. Stir only until the dry ingredients are moistened. Do not stir until completely smooth. The batter should still look lumpy.
• In cakes, muffins, and quick breads, sugar and fat are tenderizers while flour and eggs provide the structure.

Oatmeal

• When a recipe, such as oatmeal cookies, calls for oatmeal, you can use either regular old-fashioned oatmeal or quick-cooking oatmeal.

Baking Powder and Baking Soda

• Quick breads are leavened with baking powder, baking soda, or eggs. Always preheat the oven and prepare pans before starting to make the batter. The baking powder and baking soda begin to release gas the minute they are moistened. Once the wet and dry ingredients are combined, the batter should be baked.
• Baking soda (sodium bicarbonate) produces carbon dioxide gas when combined with liquid acid ingredients such as buttermilk, yogurt, or molasses.
• Recipes usually call for 1/2 teaspoon baking soda for every cup of liquid.
• Buy a new box of baking soda every six to eight months and place the opened older box in the refrigerator to keep it smelling fresh.
• Baking powder is a combination of baking soda, an acid like cream of tartar, and a moisture-absorbing product like cornstarch. The words "double-acting" on the box mean that it releases some of its gas when it gets wet and the rest when exposed to heat.

- Buy baking powder in small cans because it can lose some of its rising power if kept for more than six months. Check it out by putting a teaspoon in a cup of hot water. If it bubbles strongly, it is still good.
- For cakes, quick breads, and muffins, recipes generally call for 1 teaspoon baking powder or 1/4 teaspoon baking soda for each cup of flour.
- Too much baking powder or baking soda in a recipe causes a dry, crumbly texture. If the bread or other baked product over-rises, the product will probably end up falling. Too little baking powder or baking soda will produce a heavy, gummy bread.
- If you are out of baking powder, you can substitute 1/4 teaspoon baking soda, 1/4 teaspoon cornstarch, and 1/2 teaspoon cream of tartar for 1 teaspoon baking powder.

Buttermilk

- Buttermilk appears rich and creamy but it is actually low in fat or fat-free. It is the milk that remains after making butter. A culture is added to create the thickened milk with a slightly acid taste.
- If you would like to substitute buttermilk for regular milk in a muffin, bread, or cake recipe, add 1/2 teaspoon baking soda for each cup used. The alkaline (base) of the baking soda neutralizes the acid of the milk.
- A substitute for buttermilk can be made by adding 1 tablespoon lemon juice or vinegar to 1 cup of regular milk. Let stand for 10 minutes. Powdered buttermilk is available and it is handy to keep a box or can in the refrigerator.
- If a recipe calls for buttermilk, you can substitute plain yogurt.

Yogurt

- When a recipe calls for yogurt cheese or drained yogurt, place the yogurt in a very fine strainer and place the strainer over a jar or bowl. A coffee filter also works well. Refrigerate for several hours to drain off the excess liquid. Discard liquid. The yogurt will become thicker the longer it drains.

Eggs

- Always crack eggs one at a time into a small dish and then add to the batter you are preparing. If an egg is spoiled, you can throw it out before spoiling the whole recipe.
- When separating egg whites from the yolks, place each white in a separate cup or bowl before adding to the other egg whites. You can check each egg white for quality and remove any dots of egg yolk that may be present.
- Eggs are easier to separate if they are cold.
- For the best volume, bring egg whites to room temperature before beating. Use the appropriate size deep bowl as opposed to a large shallow bowl. The bowl must be clean and grease-free. Beat the egg whites first and then use the same beater for the rest of your recipe.
- To stabilize beaten egg whites for use in angel food cakes or meringues, add 1/4 teaspoon cream of tartar for every 3 egg whites.
- If you are beating egg whites to fold into another batter, beat them just until stiff peaks form. Overbeating will cause the egg and air structure to collapse.
- When folding beaten egg whites into a thick batter, take a small amount of the eggs and stir into the batter. Add remaining egg

whites and fold in gently. Use a large spoon or spatula. Cut through the middle; take the spoon and go down through the middle; bring the spoon up the side and fold the batter over. Turn the bowl slightly and repeat the process until the egg white is well distributed.

• Do not eat raw or undercooked eggs. Avoid recipes where the egg is not cooked. It may be possible to substitute commercial pasteurized whole eggs, powdered eggs, or liquid egg products in some of the recipes.

Chocolate

• Store chocolate chips, chocolate bars, and cocoa in a container to prevent contact with humidity or moisture. This will help prevent a gray discoloration. The gray film that may develop is called bloom. It might not look very good but the chocolate will melt fine and the bloom does not affect the taste in a baked or cooked product.

• Cocoa butter is removed from chocolate to form cocoa powder. In a recipe you can substitute 3 tablespoons unsweetened cocoa and 1 tablespoon butter for 1 ounce of unsweetened chocolate. Reduce the amount of flour in the recipe by the same amount of the cocoa you are adding.

• Melt chocolate over the lowest heat possible on your stove in a small nonstick skillet. Over high heat, the chocolate will separate irreversibly into cocoa butter and cocoa particles.

• Be careful to prevent any drop of moisture or even steam from coming into contact with chocolate as it melts. Any kind of moisture or liquid will cause the chocolate to become hard and lumpy. Do not add reduced-fat margarine to melting chocolate because margarine often contains water.

• If the chocolate becomes hard while melting, try adding 1 to 2 tablespoons of shortening for every 6 ounces of chocolate. Stir well over very low heat until it is soft.

• Chocolate may be melted in a large amount of liquid such as milk if there is at least 1/4 cup of liquid to 6 ounces of chocolate.

• Chocolate can be melted in a small zip-type plastic bag in the microwave. If you are drizzling chocolate on a dessert, snip the corner of the bag and let the melted chocolate drip from the hole. It is easy to clean up.

Baking Cookies

• Cookie dough will blend together more easily if all the ingredients are at room temperature.

• For rolled cookies, chill the dough. They will roll out more smoothly and stick less than warm dough. They will hold their shape better in the oven.

• Do not grease the cookie sheet unless the recipe calls for it.

• Cookies bake best with only one sheet of cookies in the oven at one time.

• When baking more than one large cookie sheet at a time, rotate them halfway through the baking time. This allows for more even baking.

• For great soft cookies, underbake them. Overbaking will result in drier crisp cookies. Remember that the cookies keep baking on the hot pans for a few minutes after you take them out of the oven.

• Adjust the baking time of your cookies depending on the baking pans you use. Dark sheets absorb more heat and may cause the bottom of the cookies to brown quickly and burn more easily. Air-bake pans will prevent burning. If your pans are very thin, you may try putting one pan on top of another.

• Always set a timer when baking. If you are working in another part of the house, carry the timer with you.

• Always check cookies at the minimum baking time so they don't overbake.

• When cookies do not spread enough, the dough may be over-mixed or the oven temperature may be too hot. When the cookies spread too much, there may be too much grease on the cookie sheet or the oven may not be hot enough. The ingredients in the recipe may also need to be adjusted.

• For small cookies that need to be dipped in powdered sugar or chocolate, use a meat fork to hold the cookies. There will be less mess on your hands.

• Cool cookies on racks. If cookies are very soft, let them remain on the cookie sheet until firm enough to transfer to the rack. When they are completely cool, place them in zip-type plastic bags.

• Cookies keep for months in the freezer and it takes only minutes to thaw them out for a quick treat or dessert.

Baking Pans

• When making bar cookies, use the pan size called for in the recipe. If a bar recipe calls for a 9" x 9" pan and you use an 8" x 8" pan, the bars will be thicker and probably will take longer to bake.

• Measure pans using the inside dimensions. It may be helpful to mark the size on the pan with a permanent marker. Compare pan sizes by multiplying the length by the width for rectangular pans. For instance a 9" x 9" pan has 81 square inches. That is closer to a 7" x 11" pan, which has 77 square inches, than it is to an 8" x 8" pan, which has 64 square inches.

• If you are increasing or decreasing the size of the recipe, make appropriate pan adjustments. Two 8" x 8" pans = one 9" x 13" pan. One 9" x 9" pan = one 7" x 11" pan.

• Line the bottom of a baking pan with aluminum foil for easy removal of bars.

• For a lighter, more tender crust on cakes or breads, use a shiny pan. Lighter shiny pans reflect the heat, whereas dark pans absorb the heat.

• Fill bread, muffin, and cake pans 1/2 to 3/4 full. This allows the product to rise without overflowing the pan.

• Water baths are used for custard or egg-type baked dishes. The smaller pan of custard is placed in a larger pan. Water is added to the outer pan. The water acts to insulate the custard pan and it diffuses the heat so the mixture will not separate.

Cakes and Bars

• When baking bars and cakes, be sure to spread the batter evenly to the edges of the pan.

• A cake is done when it shrinks away from the sides of the pan and springs back when lightly touched in the middle.

• After a cake is done, let it set in the pan for 5 to 10 minutes. The cake will firm up and the sides will loosen. Remove from pan and cool on a rack.

• When frosting a cake, tuck waxed paper under the cake. The paper will catch any extra frosting, leaving a clean plate when you remove the paper.

• Do you need a fast glaze for a cake or bars? Heat a can of prepared frosting in the microwave until it is very soft and pour it over the cake. This also works well if you have to frost a cake before it is completely cool.

• If you would like to impress family or friends with a dessert hot from the oven, mix up a bread pudding recipe. Refrigerate it for several hours or overnight and bake just before serving.

Pies

• To prevent the bottom pie crust of a cream pie from becoming soggy, sprinkle crust with powdered sugar or lightly press toasted, chopped nuts on the crust.

• For double-crust fruit pies, fold the top pie crust under the bottom crust before crimping. This will help keep the juices in during baking. It also helps to pierce the top crust to allow steam to escape.

• To prevent a pastry cloth from moving around on the counter when rolling out cookies or pie crust, wipe the counter first with a wet cloth and then lay the pastry cloth down.

Nuts

• Nuts stay fresher when stored in the freezer in airtight freezer bags.

• Toast all nuts, except pecans, before adding to recipes. This improves and intensifies their flavor. This also helps prevent them from sinking to the bottom in breads, muffins, or cake batters.

• Another tip to keep nuts and fruits from sinking to the bottom of a cake, muffin, or bread is to warm them in the oven and toss them with flour. Shake off excess flour before mixing them into the batter just before baking.

• Nuts can be toasted in a nonstick skillet over medium heat. Watch them carefully, stirring frequently. If you walk away, they will burn.

• Nuts and coconut can also be toasted in the oven. Spread them in a single layer on a baking sheet. Bake at 325°F for 5 to 15 minutes. Watch carefully and stir occasionally.

Raisins and Dried Fruits

• As a substitution for raisins in a recipe, try golden raisins, dried cherries, dried cranberries, or nuts.

• Raisins can be flavored and plumped in rum, brandy, or fruit juices before using them in a recipe.

• If a recipe calls for chopped dates, it is best to buy whole dates and cut them into the desired size. If you buy chopped dates, they are often coated with sugar and the recipe may need to be adjusted.

Breads

• For bread baking, a flour made especially for bread will give it a firm, coarse grain. Bread made with all-purpose flour will have a finer texture. Using milk instead of water in the recipe makes a more tender bread with a finer texture. Adding egg to the recipe will give the bread more flavor, color, and structure.

• Use an 8" x 4" loaf pan for a higher loaf or a 9" x 5" pan for a wider, flatter loaf. Grease the pans with shortening.

• When baking bread, a small dish of water in the oven will help keep the crust soft.

- To make a crisp loaf of bread, spread a little water on the bread while baking.

Oven Baking

- When using only one oven shelf for baking, position the shelf in the lower third of the oven. In baked products, the bottom crusts will be crisp and tops won't overbrown.
- When baking several items in the oven at one time, stagger the pans so that air can circulate. Do not position them directly over each other. Check occasionally to see that they are baking evenly. You may need to rotate them if one is baking faster than another one.
- Reduce the oven temperature 25°F when using glass or dark nonstick bakeware because they conduct and retain heat better than lighter-colored baking pans.

Cheesecake

- Cracks on the top of cheesecake may be prevented if you:
  - Place a pan of water on the bottom shelf of the oven to add moisture during baking.
  - Do not overbeat the cheese with the other ingredients because that adds too much air. The cake will rise too high and then it will collapse.
  - Bake it in a low oven (300°F).
  - Only open the oven door when ready to test for doneness.
  - Do not overbake. It can still be slightly soft in the middle when you take it out of the oven.
  - If your cheesecake does end up with cracks, decorate it with fresh fruit or sour cream.

Baking Time

- Always test the doneness of any food you bake in the oven 5 to 15 minutes before the end of the suggested baking time. This allows for differences in oven temperature and baking pans.

Storing Baked Goods

- Do not cover or place baked goods in a plastic bag until completely cooled. Otherwise the product will sweat from the steam and it will get soggy.

Don't Panic

- Try to make the best out of any cooking disaster. One time when I made a rhubarb pie and accidentally tipped it upside down onto the counter, I scooped it up into an attractive bowl and called it rhubarb cobbler.

MEAT, POULTRY, AND FISH

Storing and Thawing

- Store meat in the coldest part of the refrigerator. Place it on a plate or in a bowl to prevent meat juices from dripping onto other foods.
- Thaw meat in the refrigerator, not on the counter, to prevent dangerous bacterial growth.
- For quick thawing, place wrapped meat, poultry, or fish in a sink of cold water. Do not use warm or hot water because the outside of the meat will become too warm, allowing for the

growth of bacteria. The cold water will keep the outside safe yet it allows for thawing the inside.

• To get thin slices of raw meat or poultry, partially freeze the meat to make it firm and easier to cut.

• Do not completely thaw out frozen fish before cooking. This will prevent excessive moisture from escaping during cooking.

Hamburgers

• When shaping hamburgers, press the meat between plastic wrap or waxed paper to prevent getting the meat on your hands. You could also wear disposable plastic gloves.

Cooking Meat

• Generally, the cheaper cuts of meat take more time to cook and must be prepared using some liquid in a covered pan. Tougher cuts, such as beef chuck, are rich in natural gelatin, which melts during long, slow, gentle cooking. This is called moist cooking.

• Braising meat is used for less-tender cuts of meat. First the meat is browned and then a liquid is added. The pan is covered and it is either simmered on top of the stove or baked slowly in the oven until the meat is tender. This usually takes several hours. The braising liquid should bubble gently but should not boil. Boiling toughens the meat.

• Acidic ingredients, such as tomatoes and wine, added to meat while braising, help to tenderize meat.

• More expensive cuts of meat, such as sirloin steak, are usually tender. They can be prepared by frying, grilling, or broiling. This is called dry heat cooking.

• When broiling meat, spray the pan with vegetable oil.

• Prevent steak, bacon, and fish fillets from curling while they are frying by cutting slashes around the outside edges. Use a sharp knife or kitchen scissors.

• Avoid poking meat with a fork while cooking. The flavorful juices are lost in the process. Turn with a spatula or tongs that do not puncture the surface.

• Do not apply barbecue sauce or sweet glazes too early when broiling or grilling because they will burn quickly.

• When grilling outside, place the cooked meat on a clean, dry plate that has not been contaminated with raw meat.

Browning Meat

• Tips to brown meat, poultry, or fish:
  • Dry the outside surfaces with a paper towel. If the surface is wet, the meat steams in liquid instead of frying in oil.
  • Add oil to the pan and heat it before adding the meat.
  • Toss meat pieces in flour before browning.
  • To brown stew meat, use a pan large enough to avoid crowding. In a pan that is too small, the meat steams rather than browns. Avoid stirring the meat too often; allowing it to stick briefly to the pan causes the juices to caramelize, developing good color and flavor.
  • Sprinkle meat with a small amount of sugar.
  • Do not cover the pan during browning because steam would be produced.
  • Baste meats that will be grilled, broiled, or baked with a sauce that has some sugar or corn syrup in the recipe. The sugar caramelizes into a brown glaze.

- Sprinkle paprika on fish or poultry before baking.
- Brush meat with soy sauce, Worcestershire sauce, or Kitchen Bouquet.

Deglazing the Pan

• Deglazing the pan is accomplished by adding a small amount of liquid (water, broth, wine, or juice) to a hot pan after browning meat. Stir to loosen the browned meat pieces while the liquid comes to a boil.

Breading Meat

• The perfect pan for breading meat is a shallow pie pan.

• To coat meat or poultry with flour or bread crumbs quickly and with no mess, place the mixture in a resealable plastic bag and add the meat. Seal and shake the bag to coat evenly.

Marinating

• A marinade is a mixture of flavorful ingredients that usually contain some acid ingredients to tenderize the meat.

• When marinating meat, use a zip-type plastic bag. The meat stays in the marinade and can be turned easily. Cleanup is easy.

• If you intend to use a meat marinade to serve with the finished dish, it must be brought to a boil before serving. This will cook any meat juices that got into the marinade.

• Soak fish in milk for about 1 hour before cooking to remove the strong fish flavor.

• Lemon juice rubbed on fish before baking or grilling will enhance the flavor and keep the fish white.

Meat Thermometer

• Use a meat thermometer. Cutting into meat to check for doneness is not as accurate as a thermometer and meat juices will escape.

Serving Meat

• Before carving meat roasts or poultry, let them sit at room temperature for 10 to 15 minutes after removing from the oven. This allows the juices to be distributed evenly throughout the meat.

• Cut meat across the grain when ready to serve.

Perfect Gravy

• To make a perfect gravy:
  - Deglaze the pan with water or broth. Stir to loosen the browned meat pieces while the liquid comes to a boil.
  - Add the desired amount of water for the gravy.
  - Mix 1/2 cup of flour in a shaker with 1 cup cold water. Shake until smooth.
  - Bring liquid in the pan to a rolling boil.
  - Slowly add small amount of flour and water mixture. Stir constantly as you add it.
  - Bring mixture to a boil and check the thickness of the gravy. Keep adding flour and water until the desired thickness is reached.

- Reduce heat to low until ready to serve.
- Season with salt and pepper. Add chicken or beef bouillon if it needs more flavor.

Reheating
• When reheating stews and soups, first remove any congealed fat. If the stew or soup seems too thick, add a little water or broth during reheating. Taste and adjust seasonings.

FRUITS AND VEGETABLES

Make It Easy
• Buy precut produce such as cabbage, carrots, lettuce, and spinach to save time.

Washing
• Wash all fruits and vegetables thoroughly under cold running water.
• Wash lettuce and salad greens in cold water and spin dry or dry with a towel. Wrap in a dry paper towel and place in a zip-type plastic bag. Squeeze out air, seal, and refrigerate.

Storing
• It really is true that one rotten apple can spoil the whole bushel. When buying apples and other fruits in a bag or basket, separate them to remove any that are beginning to spoil. One spoiled piece of fruit speeds up the deterioration of the others.

Ripening
• To ripen a fruit such as a peach, pear, banana, papaya, or avocado, put the fruit in a perforated brown bag with an apple. The apple gives off a gas that helps ripen the other fruit.
• Some fruits never ripen after they are picked. They include berries, cherries, grapes, and citrus fruits.
• Fruits that ripen in color and texture but not in flavor or sweetness include melons, apricots, and peaches.
• Fruits that do not get sweeter after picking include apples, kiwi, and pears.
• Fruits that ripen nicely after they have been picked include avocados and bananas.

Cooking Pans
• Cookware made out of iron or aluminum can react with fruits and vegetables to produce off-colors.

Blanching
• To blanch vegetables and fruits, place them in a pan of rapidly boiling water for a very short period of time. Boil just until the flesh is slightly tender but not cooked through. The food then needs to be chilled quickly in very cold water to stop the cooking process.

Cooking with Fruits and Vegetables
• Do not add acids such as vinegar dressings or lemon juice while cooking green vegetables. They will lose their bright green color and become a drab olive green color.

- Most red and yellow fruits and vegetables maintain their color when cooked. There are some that lose their color, such as red cabbage, berries, and grapes. To prevent fading, add an acid ingredient.
- When using a slow cooker, cut vegetables in a uniform size so they cook evenly.
- Remove the lid of the slow cooker very briefly to stir the food. Lifting the lid releases heat and lengthens the cooking time.

Grilling Vegetables

- When you're using the grill for your meat, try grilling your vegetables too. Mix vegetables with a small amount of olive oil and seasonings of your choice. Place in a grill basket and grill until brown and tender.

Juicing

- One lemon yields about 3 tablespoons of juice. One orange yields about 5 tablespoons of juice.
- To squeeze the juice from oranges, lemons, or limes, bring the fruit to room temperature or place in the microwave for 15 to 30 seconds to warm slightly. Roll the fruit on the counter, pressing firmly. Cut open and squeeze.

Zesting

- To zest a citrus fruit, remove a very thin slice of the colored peel. Avoid going too deep and taking off the bitter white part. A zester tool works best. Put it on your wish list.

Apples

- To keep cut apples from browning, toss with lemon, lime, orange, or pineapple juice. A vinaigrette dressing will also keep them from turning brown.
- Apples that are good for both eating fresh and cooking include Cortland, Jonathon, McIntosh, and Winesaps. Choose Granny Smith apples for a tart, firm apple.
- There are 2 large or 3 medium apples in a pound.
- When making homemade applesauce, add sugar at the beginning of cooking if you like a chunky sauce. If you like a softer applesauce, cook the apples first and then add the sugar. Add a few red cinnamon candies for a special flavor and slightly pink color.

Asparagus

- Asparagus will snap off naturally at the tough end. Hold the spear with one hand at each end and snap.
- If asparagus is extra large with a tough stem, peel the stem with a vegetable peeler.
- Cook asparagus standing up in a covered pan of boiling water.

Avocado

- To prevent cut avocado from turning brown, brush or dip it with lemon or lime juice. Using these acid juices when making guacamole will enhance its color and flavor.

Bananas

• Dark, overripe bananas can be saved. Peel and place in a freezer bag until you are ready to make banana bread or cake.

Beets

• Do not peel beets before cooking. When boiled in water, the skin will slide off easily after cooking. Add a small amount of lemon juice or vinegar to the boiling water to keep the red color bright.

Berries

• Strawberries that are picked early in the morning or late in the evening will keep better than berries picked in the hot sun. Pick only ripe berries because they will not ripen after they are picked.

• Wash only the berries that you want to eat or use in a recipe. Store remaining berries in the refrigerator, unwashed, in a shallow pan covered with a towel. Damp berries will mold quickly.

• Adding sugar to berries will soften them and produce some juice.

• Always add frozen berries, such as blueberries, raspberries, and cranberries, to a muffin or cake batter while they are still frozen. This will prevent some of the color from bleeding out.

• Use a food processor to chop cranberries instead of a knife.

• A 12-ounce bag of fresh cranberries has 3 cups of whole berries.

• Fresh cranberries can be frozen right in the bag. Buy them when they are in season to use all year.

• Other washed berries can be frozen in a single layer on a cookie sheet. When frozen, place berries in a plastic freezer bag. Take out whatever you need and return the rest to the freezer.

Cabbage Family

• Vegetables in the cabbage family (cabbage, Brussels sprouts, cauliflower, broccoli, rutabagas, collards, turnips) become stronger and develop an unpleasant taste the longer they are cooked. Cut vegetables in smaller pieces and cook quickly in the shortest amount of time.

• One pound of cabbage yields 4 cups of raw shredded cabbage or 2 cups of cooked cabbage.

• To clean a head of cauliflower, soak it for a few minutes in salted cold water. This will bring out any bugs that may be hiding in the head.

• When cooking a whole cauliflower, remove the green stems and cut a deep X in the base to even out the cooking time. It will take 15 to 25 minutes to cook. Cook only until tender-crisp. Mushy cauliflower does not taste very good.

• The flowers of broccoli cook faster than the stem. To cook more evenly, cut slices in the stem. If stems are large, they can be peeled with a vegetable peeler.

• One pound of broccoli yields 2 cups of chopped broccoli.

Carrots

• The bitter thin peelings of large carrots should be removed by using a vegetable peeler. The peelings can also be removed by boiling them for 2 to 3 minutes, chilling quickly in cold water, and rubbing the skin off with your fingers.

- One pound of carrots yields 3 cups of chopped or 2½ cups shredded carrots.
- Most small bite-size carrots do not come out of the ground that way. They are cut from large carrots. They do not need to be peeled.

Celery
- If celery is excessively stringy, snap a stalk in half and pull strings off.

Mushrooms
- Wash mushrooms under cold running water but do not soak in water. Drain and blot dry.

Onions and Garlic
- To prevent your eyes from tearing when cutting onions, put the onions in the refrigerator for 2 hours before cutting. This prevents the volatile oils from being released when cutting the onions. These oils mix with the natural fluid in your eyes to produce mild sulfuric acid, which causes tearing.
- To decrease the strong taste of raw onions, soak cut slices in cold water for several hours with a dash of lemon juice. Remove onions, drain, and pat dry.
- There are 4 medium onions in a pound. This makes 2 to 3 cups of chopped onions.
- Store any raw chopped onions or pieces of raw onion in a glass jar in the refrigerator. Just wrapping onions in plastic is not enough to keep the aroma from escaping. Keeping them in a plastic jar causes the plastic to pick up the onion smell.

- Remove onion and garlic smells from your hands and cutting board by rubbing with lemon juice.
- Scallions are the same thing as green onions. Shallots are small bulbs that are purchased dry.

Peas
- If a cooked dish calls for peas, add frozen peas in the last 2 minutes of cooking.

Potatoes
- Store potatoes in a cool dark location. Do not refrigerate because some of the potato starch will turn to sugar. The potatoes may taste sweeter and they are more likely to darken when cooked.
- If potatoes have turned green, cut away all the green parts. The green is caused by overexposure to light, creating a slightly toxic chemical called solanine. It also makes the potato taste bitter. The rest of the potato is safe to eat.
- There are 3 medium or 2 large potatoes in a pound.
- When baking potatoes, if you like a crisp skin, pierce the skin and bake at 425°F for 45 to 50 minutes or until done. If you like a soft skin, pierce the potato with a fork and wrap in aluminum foil. Bake at 350°F for 60 minutes or until done.
- To prevent a rare foodborne illness from potatoes baked in foil, do not leave them out at room temperature for any significant period of time. Eat them soon after cooking or refrigerate them promptly.

- If you need a baked potato in a hurry, pierce the potato with a fork and microwave for 3 to 5 minutes. Remove and place in a 425°F oven. Bake until done.

Tomatoes and Peaches
- To peel whole tomatoes or peaches, cut an X in the bottom of the fruit. Drop them into a pan of rapidly boiling water for 10 to 30 seconds. Remove with a slotted spoon and hold under cold running water. The skin will slide right off.

MAKE IT LOOK AND SMELL GOOD

Kitchen Aroma
- To create a good home-cooking aroma in your kitchen, simmer a cinnamon stick in a pan of water.

Serving Dishes
- Collect some colorful pottery serving bowls. Even the simplest foods can be dressed up for family and friends by serving them in lovely bowls.
- When serving cheese on a silver or wood tray, protect the finish by lining it with lettuce greens.

Garnishes
- Dress up your dishes with an attractive garnish:
- Sprig of a fresh herb
- Chopped parsley
- Finely chopped green onions
- Seasoned bread crumbs
- Crumbled bacon bits
- Nuts
- Lemon wedge
- Slice of fresh fruit or vegetable
- Sprinkle of powdered sugar
- Freshly grated cheese

Reference: *Food Lover's Tiptionary,* by Sharon Tyler Herbst (New York: Hearst Book, 1994). This book is filled with interesting food information.

Food Safety Tips

Safe handling, cooking, and serving of food is necessary to prevent bacteria and other microorganisms from multiplying and causing food poisoning. The following food-handling tips will help you lower the risk of potential food contamination.

Most importantly, safe food handling begins with frequent and careful hand washing. Wash hands by lathering with soap and warm water after using the restroom, blowing your nose, handling garbage, changing baby diapers, and touching or cleaning up after pets, before handling food, and between handling raw and cooked foods. Don't forget to clean under your nails. Be sure that small children wash their hands also.

AT THE GROCERY STORE

• Check expiration dates on foods and do not buy foods that are past that date.
• Do not buy or use canned goods that are swollen, dented, or otherwise damaged.
• Place raw meat and poultry packages into plastic bags to prevent leakage onto other groceries.
• If food will be held in a warm car for longer that 30 minutes, put perishable foods in a cooler to keep them cold.
• Do not buy frozen foods that have thawed.

STORING FOOD

• Keep perishable foods in a refrigerator kept at 35 to 40°F or in a freezer at 0°F or below.
• Place uncooked meat, fish, and poultry into separate plastic bags and place in the refrigerator so juices cannot drip onto or come in contact with other foods.
• Thaw meat in the refrigerator, not on the counter.
• Food stored in the freezer needs to be wrapped in freezer bags or freezer paper.
• Defrosted foods should be cooked soon after the defrosting is complete. Food may be refrozen only if it still has ice crystals.
• Refrigerate leftovers immediately in covered containers. For more rapid cooling, use small, shallow containers. Foods placed in the refrigerator in large containers may stay warm in the center of the pan for a dangerously long time.
• Arrange food in the refrigerator so the cool air can circulate around the food containers.
• Remove stuffing from poultry or meats and refrigerate in separate containers.
• Throw out refrigerated leftovers after four or five days.

• Do not eat moldy food. You can save hard cheese and firm fruits and vegetables by cutting the mold out. Remove a large area around the mold. All other moldy food should be discarded.

• Do not taste or eat food with an unusual odor or if it looks strange.

PREPARING FOOD

• Keep everything that touches food clean—hands, utensils, bowls, countertops, dishcloths, etc.

• Use separate plates, cutting boards, knives, and utensils for raw and cooked meat, poultry, and fish. It's best to use one cutting board for meat and a separate one for fruits and vegetables.

• Keep juices from raw meat, poultry, and fish from coming into contact with all other foods.

• Cook meat, poultry, and fish thoroughly. Red meat is well done at 160°F. Poultry should be cooked to 180°F or until it is no longer pink and the juices run clear. Fish should be cooked until it changes color and flakes with a fork.

• Cook hamburgers and any ground meats until brown throughout and juices run clear. Use a thermometer and check to make sure the middle reaches 160°F.

• Cook stuffing separately from poultry. The cavity of a turkey or chicken may not get hot enough to thoroughly cook the ingredients in the stuffing. The raw juices from the poultry that are released during the cooking process into the stuffing may not be thoroughly cooked.

• If you are using pork sausage or other ground raw meats in a stuffing or dressing, be sure they are thoroughly cooked before mixing with the other ingredients. This has two purposes. The time and temperature needed to cook the raw meat in the stuffing may not be long enough to kill harmful bacteria, especially if the stuffing is in a rolled meat. The other reason is to remove the excess fat from the product.

• Never eat undercooked or raw eggs or foods that may contain undercooked or raw eggs, such as some Caesar salad dressings or desserts that contain raw eggs.

• Never taste any mixture that has raw meat, poultry, shellfish, or egg in order to adjust the seasoning.

• Do not eat steak tartare (raw hamburger), raw oysters, or ceviche (raw fish "cooked" in lime juice).

• When marinating meat, seafood, or poultry, keep it refrigerated. Do not use a marinade that has been in contact with raw meat as a sauce for the cooked food without first bringing the marinade to a boil for at least 1 minute.

• Thoroughly wash all fruits and vegetables with clean running water. Use a brush if necessary. Take special care to wash all produce that will be eaten raw. Be especially careful to wash greens such as spinach and lettuce.

• Use oven mitts to remove hot items from the oven. This prevents nasty burns from the oven rack or the heating elements on electric ovens. Never use a wet mitt. The heat from pans or the stove can cause the water to steam and burn your hands.

SERVING FOOD

- Do not leave cooked meats or other perishable foods out for longer than 2 hours. Bacteria that can cause food poisoning grow quickly at room temperature.
- At a buffet table, make sure the hot food is hot and the cold food is cold.
- Use a clean plate for cooked meat. Don't use the same plate the raw meat was on. Utensils and knives should be washed in between contact with raw and cooked foods.
- Keep food at safe temperatures. Keep cold foods cold (at or below 40°F) and hot foods hot (at or above 140°F).
- When in doubt, throw it out.

CLEANING

- For easy cleanup, keep a toothbrush by the sink to use on graters, choppers, beaters, coffee grinders, and other small utensils.
- Wash counters and utensils with warm soapy water after working with raw meat, poultry, or eggs.
- Use the dishwasher to wash dishes whenever possible. The water temperature is higher and there is bleach in the dishwasher powder.
- Sanitize cutting surfaces and countertops by washing with a solution of 2 teaspoons of household bleach in 1 quart of water. It is convenient to keep this solution in a spray bottle for easier cleaning. Rinse thoroughly with water. There are other commercial preparations available if you do not want to make your own cleaning solution.

- When cleaning raw meat, poultry, seafood, and eggs from cooking and countertop surfaces, use paper towels instead of sponges or dishcloths. Discard the paper towel after use. This prevents contaminating your sponges and dishcloths with bacteria and it keeps them fresher.
- Every night pour a small amount of bleach in the kitchen drain, especially if you have a garbage disposal, to eliminate odors and sanitize the drain. Avoid using the garbage disposal for grease, oil, and peels and trimmings from bananas, onions, bell peppers, and garlic. This will eliminate lingering odors and prevent drain blockage.
- Take out the kitchen garbage on a regular basis.
- Change the dishcloth and dishtowel daily. Wash dishcloths and dishtowels with a small amount of bleach.
- Place kitchen brushes and sponges in the dishwasher daily. Allow them to dry thoroughly.

Adapted from *The Cancer Survival Cookbook*, by Donna Weihofen and Christina Marino (John Wiley & Sons, 1998).

Chapter 1
Appetizers

Artichoke Stuffed with Crab

Beer Cheese Spread

Blue Cheese Spread with Brandied Cherries

Broccoli and White Bean Canapés

Chili Cheese Dip

Chili Pepper and Tomato Salsa

Chipped Beef on Toast

Cocktail Meatballs

Crab and Swiss Melt

Cranberry Chutney

Garlic Cheddar Cheese Spread

Mini Ham and Cheese Frittatas

Mushroom and Bacon Melt

Mushroom, Walnut, and Olive Spread

Olive Nut Cheese Ball

Pepperoni Pie

Pistachio Nut and Olive Tapenade

Refrigerator Pickles

Reuben Dip

Sassy Guacamole

Sausage-Stuffed Mushrooms

Savory Spinach Spread

Smoked Salmon Bruschetta

Spinach Squares

Tostado Spread

Veggie Cream Cheese Ball

Artichoke Stuffed with Crab

This recipe can be made fast and easy with canned artichoke bottoms. They are ready to be stuffed with this creamy crab and brandy mixture. They can be made ahead and refrigerated until ready to bake.

Serves 6

12 canned artichoke bottoms (two 14-ounce cans), drained
1 tablespoon butter or margarine
2 tablespoons finely chopped green onions
1 tablespoon flour
1/2 cup fat-free half-and-half
1 tablespoon brandy
6 ounces canned crabmeat, drained
1/8 teaspoon white pepper
Salt and freshly ground pepper to taste
2 tablespoons grated Parmesan cheese
Dash paprika

Note: Evaporated fat-free milk can be substituted for the fat-free half-and-half.

1. Preheat oven to 350°F. Grease a 9" x 13" baking pan. Arrange artichoke bottoms in pan. In a small saucepan, melt butter. Add green onions and cook over medium heat until soft. Add flour and cook for 3 minutes, stirring constantly. Add half-and-half and bring to a boil, stirring constantly until mixture thickens. Add brandy, crab, and white pepper. Season with salt and pepper. Stir in Parmesan cheese.

2. Spoon mixture into the artichoke bottoms. Sprinkle with paprika. Bake for 10 to 15 minutes or until heated through. Serve on a cocktail plate with a fork.

Nutritional information per serving:

Calories	110
Fat, gm.	3
Protein, gm.	8
Carbohydrate, gm.	13
Cholesterol, mg.	30
Fiber	high

Beer Cheese Spread

An old Wisconsin favorite. Spread it on crackers or bread sticks.

Serves 8

$^1/_2$ cup light beer
I cup shredded reduced-fat Cheddar cheese
2 ounces blue cheese
I tablespoon butter or margarine
$^1/_3$ cup finely chopped onion
$^1/_4$ teaspoon garlic powder
$^1/_2$ teaspoon Worcestershire sauce
Dash hot pepper sauce to taste

In a small saucepan, heat beer; let cool to room temperature. In a food processor, combine Cheddar cheese, blue cheese, butter, onion, garlic powder, and Worcestershire sauce. Process until smooth. Add just enough beer to thin mixture to a spreading consistency. Add hot pepper sauce to taste.

Nutritional information per serving:

Calories	60
Fat, gm.	4
Protein, gm.	5
Carbohydrate, gm.	I
Cholesterol, mg.	10
Fiber	0

Blue Cheese Spread with Brandied Cherries

The blend of blue cheese with the tart, brandy-flavored cherries makes for a fabulous appetizer.

Serves 12

4 ounces fat-free cream cheese
2 ounces blue cheese
1 tablespoon finely chopped onion
8 ounces canned sweet cherries in syrup
1/4 cup orange juice
1 tablespoon cornstarch
1 tablespoon brandy, optional

In a food processor, combine cream cheese, blue cheese, and onion. Process until smooth. Spread on an 8-inch serving plate and set aside. In a small saucepan, combine undrained cherries, orange juice, and cornstarch. Bring to a boil and cook for 1 minute or until thickened. Chill in refrigerator for 10 minutes. Stir in brandy if desired. Place in food processor and blend until cherries are finely chopped. To serve, spoon cherry mixture over the cheese. Serve with crackers.

Nutritional information per serving without crackers:

Calories	40
Fat, gm.	1
Protein, gm.	2
Carbohydrate, gm.	5
Cholesterol, mg.	5
Fiber	low

Broccoli and White Bean Canapés

This is healthy, low in calories, and tasty too!

Serves 16

2 cups broccoli florets
15 ounces canned great northern beans, drained and rinsed
2 tablespoons fresh lemon juice
1 teaspoon minced garlic
1 tablespoon olive oil
1 tablespoon mixed herbs*
Salt and freshly ground pepper to taste
Toasted French baguette slices
1 teaspoon lemon zest

*Any combination of herbs of your choice can be used. One commercial brand is Lawry's Pinch of Herbs.

In a medium saucepan, steam broccoli until very tender. Drain and transfer to a food processor. Add beans, lemon juice, garlic, olive oil, and herbs. Process until smooth. (If using a small food processor, blend in small batches.) Add salt and pepper to taste. Spread broccoli mixture on top of toasted French baguette slices. Garnish with lemon zest.

Nutritional information per serving without baguette slice:

Calories	35
Fat, gm.	1
Protein, gm.	2
Carbohydrate, gm.	5
Cholesterol, mg.	0
Fiber	medium

Chili Cheese Dip

This is an appetizer that kids love. It is so good,
and good for you, that it can be served on pita bread for supper.

Serves 20

1 pound extra-lean ground beef
1 medium onion, finely chopped
15 ounces canned hot chili with beans
15 ounces chunky tomato sauce
1 pound fat-free processed American cheese
Hot pepper sauce to taste

Note: This recipe should be made with processed cheese because it melts better than regular cheese. A Mexican pepper-flavored, processed cheese would work well also.

In a large nonstick skillet, brown beef. Cook until completely done. Add onion and cook until translucent. Add chili with beans, tomato sauce, and cheese. Cook over medium heat, stirring constantly, until cheese has melted and mixture is heated through. Add hot pepper sauce to taste. Serve with corn chips.

Nutritional information per serving without chips:

Calories	115
Fat, gm.	4
Protein, gm.	16
Carbohydrate, gm.	4
Cholesterol, mg.	35
Fiber	medium

Chili Pepper and Tomato Salsa

Twenty years ago, this appetizer was served at our gourmet group dinner. We all thought it was so unusual and we raved about its unique flavor. There are now hundreds of commercial salsas available, but homemade is still the best.

Serves 6

4 ounces canned green chili peppers, drained
1/2 cup chopped ripe olives
1/2 cup chopped green onions
3 large tomatoes, seeded and chopped
2 tablespoons extra-virgin olive oil
2 tablespoons balsamic vinegar
1/4 cup chopped fresh cilantro
Salt and freshly ground pepper to taste
Dash Tabasco sauce, optional

Note: Fresh or canned jalapeño peppers can be used in place of the mild green chilies. Use the amount that suits your taste but watch out for the heat!

In a medium bowl, combine all ingredients. Cover and refrigerate for several hours. Drain. Serve with corn chips.

Nutritional information per serving without chips:

Calories	80
Fat, gm.	6
Protein, gm.	1
Carbohydrate, gm.	5
Cholesterol, mg.	0
Fiber	low

Chipped Beef on Toast

This tasty appetizer is served warm. The beauty of this recipe is that it is low in calories and fat and yet it seems so creamy. It can be made ahead of time and heated in the oven when ready to serve.

Serves 8

¹/₂ tablespoon butter or margarine
1 small onion, finely chopped
¹/₄ medium green pepper, finely chopped
8 ounces fat-free or low-fat cream cheese
¹/₂ cup fat-free sour cream
¹/₄ teaspoon white pepper
¹/₂ teaspoon dill weed
Dash red pepper flakes, optional
3 ounces dried beef
¹/₄ cup chopped pecans
4 bread slices, toasted

Note: Chopped olives are a good addition to this recipe.

1. Preheat oven to 300°F. In a small nonstick skillet, heat butter. Add onion and green pepper. Cook over medium heat until onions are translucent. Add cream cheese and stir over low heat until it softens. Remove from heat. Add sour cream, white pepper, dill weed, and red pepper flakes. Tear dried beef into small pieces and add to cream cheese mixture. Spoon mixture into an 8-inch pie pan. Top with nuts. Heat in oven for 10 minutes or just until heated through.

2. Serve with toasted bread cut into quarters or with crackers.

Nutritional information per serving without toast or crackers:

Calories	60
Fat, gm.	1
Protein, gm.	8
Carbohydrate, gm.	5
Cholesterol, mg.	15
Fiber	low

Cocktail Meatballs

Baking the meatballs will save a lot of time and they can be kept warm in one of the zesty sauces. They can even be made ahead and rewarmed when you need them.

Serves 12

1 pound extra-lean ground beef
1 cup crushed corn flakes (2 cups corn flakes)
$1/2$ cup evaporated fat-free milk
$1/2$ cup finely chopped onion
 cup barbecue sauce
1 teaspoon Worcestershire sauce
1 teaspoon salt
$1/2$ teaspoon freshly ground pepper
Dash Tabasco sauce, optional

Sweet-and-Sour Sauce:

1 cup ketchup
2 tablespoons cider vinegar
$1/4$ cup brown sugar
2 tablespoons soy sauce

Maple Syrup–Cranberry Sauce:

16 ounces canned whole cranberry
 sauce
1 cup chili sauce
$1/4$ cup maple syrup
1 tablespoon fresh lemon juice

Brandied Peach Sauce:

12 ounces peach preserves
$1/2$ cup brown sugar
1 teaspoon cornstarch
$1/2$ cup peach, apricot,
 or regular brandy
$1/4$ teaspoon nutmeg

1. Preheat oven to 400°F. Butter two 9" x 13" pans. In a medium bowl, combine ground beef with all remaining (nonsauce) ingredients. Stir to mix. With the help of a melon baller, shape mixture into small $3/4$ -inch balls. Place meatballs in baking pans. Bake uncovered for 15 to 20 minutes or until brown on the outside and completely done on the inside.

2. While meatballs are baking, choose the sauce recipe you would like to use. Combine sauce ingredients in small saucepan. Cook over low heat, stirring constantly, until mixture is heated through. When meatballs are done, gently combine with sauce and keep warm until ready to serve. Serve with toothpicks.

Nutritional information per serving with the sweet-and-sour sauce:

Calories	145
Fat, gm.	5
Protein, gm.	12
Carbohydrate, gm.	13
Cholesterol, mg.	30
Fiber	low

Crab and Swiss Melt

This is elegant as an appetizer or serve it in a larger portion for a sandwich meal.
Keep the ingredients on hand and you can put it together very quickly for unexpected guests.

Serves 6

6 ounces canned crabmeat, drained
1 1/2 cups grated Swiss cheese
1/2 cup low-fat or fat-free mayonnaise
2 tablespoons finely chopped green onions
1 teaspoon fresh lemon juice
1/4 teaspoon salt
1/4 teaspoon curry powder
Dash Tabasco sauce, optional
3 English muffins, cut in halves

Note: The flavor will vary depending on the curry powder you choose. The recipe is also good without the crab.

Preheat oven broiler. In a small bowl, mix crab, cheese, mayonnaise, onions, lemon juice, salt, curry powder, and Tabasco. Stir to mix well. Divide mixture among 6 English muffin halves. Spread mixture evenly on muffins and place on baking sheet. Broil until cheese melts and is lightly browned. Watch carefully to prevent burning. Cut each English muffin into small bite-size pieces to serve as an appetizer.

Nutritional information per serving:

Calories	230
Fat, gm.	10
Protein, gm.	16
Carbohydrate, gm.	19
Cholesterol, mg.	50
Fiber	very low

Cranberry Chutney

This makes a wonderfully distinctive appetizer. Serve the colorful tangy chutney on top of fat-free cream cheese or baked Brie cheese. The cranberry chutney is also great served with chicken or pork.

Serves 20

1 medium lemon, seeded and chopped
1 medium orange, seeded and chopped
3 cups fresh or frozen cranberries
2 cups brown sugar
1 cup golden raisins
1/2 cup white vinegar
1/2 teaspoon cinnamon
1/4 teaspoon cloves
1/4 teaspoon nutmeg
1 stick cinnamon
1 tablespoon Marsala wine, optional
8 ounces fat-free cream cheese, optional

1. In a medium saucepan, combine all ingredients except wine and cream cheese. Stir to blend. Cook over medium heat until mixture comes to a boil. Continue to boil gently for 20 minutes. Remove from heat and stir in wine. Refrigerate until ready to serve.

2. Spoon chutney over fat-free cream cheese or warmed Brie cheese. Serve with crackers.

Nutritional information per serving without Brie or cream cheese:

Calories	90
Fat, gm.	0
Protein, gm.	0
Carbohydrate, gm.	23
Cholesterol, mg.	0
Fiber	medium

Garlic Cheddar Cheese Spread

The flavorful sharp Cheddar is extended with fat-free cream cheese to cut the total fat and calories. Use it as a dip for veggies or spread it on crackers.

Serves 25

1 teaspoon butter or margarine
2 cloves garlic, minced
16 ounces sharp Cheddar cheese spread
8 ounces fat-free cream cheese
1/3 cup fat-free half-and-half

Note: Evaporated fat-free milk can be substituted for the fat-free half-and-half.

In a small skillet, melt butter. Add garlic and cook for 1 minute. In a food processor, combine garlic, Cheddar cheese, cream cheese, and half-and-half. Process until smooth. Add extra half-and-half or milk, if needed, to make the desired consistency.

Nutritional information per serving:

Calories	80
Fat, gm.	6
Protein, gm.	6
Carbohydrate, gm.	1
Cholesterol, mg.	20
Fiber	0

Mini Ham and Cheese Frittatas

These are tasty and easy-to-make appetizers that are sure to please.
The mixture can be made ahead and refrigerated until ready to bake.

Serves 18

$1/2$ cup finely chopped onion
2 ounces ham, finely c hopped
2 tablespoons finely chopped fresh parsley
$1/2$ cup shredded Cheddar cheese
$1/8$ teaspoon ground thyme
$1/8$ teaspoon freshly ground black pepper
$1/8$ teaspoon salt
2 large eggs, lightly beaten

Preheat oven to 350°F. Coat mini-muffin pan with cooking spray. In a medium bowl, combine all ingredients. Stir to mix well. Spoon mixture into 18 cups of muffin pan. Bake for 20 minutes or until frittatas are set in the middle. Remove from pan and cool a few minutes before serving.

Nutritional information per serving:

Calories	25
Fat, gm.	1.8
Protein, gm.	2.0
Carbohydrate, gm.	0.6
Cholesterol, mg.	25
Fiber	low

Mushroom and Bacon Melt

I have served these for years. They are good with a glass of wine before dinner.

Serves 12

3 slices of bacon
1 small onion, finely chopped
8 ounces fat-free or low-fat cream cheese, room temperature
1 egg, lightly beaten
1/4 cup grated Parmesan cheese
1/4 teaspoon garlic powder
1/8 teaspoon white pepper
4 ounces canned mushrooms, drained and chopped
50 Triscuit crackers

Note: This can be made ahead and refrigerated until ready to serve.

1. In a small skillet, fry bacon until crisp. Remove bacon and crumble. Set aside. Discard all but 1 tablespoon of bacon fat. Add onions to skillet and cook until translucent. Set aside. In a small bowl, combine cream cheese, egg, Parmesan cheese, garlic powder, and white pepper. Beat with electric mixer or food processor until smooth. Stir in reserved bacon and onions. Add mushrooms and stir until well mixed. Refrigerate until ready to serve.

2. Preheat oven broiler. Spread mixture 1/2 inch thick on Triscuit crackers. Place on a baking sheet. Broil for 2 to 4 minutes or until lightly browned. Watch carefully to prevent burning.

Nutritional information per serving without crackers:

Calories	45
Fat, gm.	2
Protein, gm.	5
Carbohydrate, gm.	2
Cholesterol, mg.	20
Fiber	low

Mushroom, Walnut, and Olive Spread

This is one of those appetizers that is hard to stop eating.

Serves 10

1 medium onion, finely chopped
1 tablespoon olive oil
$^1/_2$ pound fresh mushrooms, finely chopped
2 tablespoons white wine
$^1/_2$ teaspoon Worcestershire sauce
4 ounces fat-free cream cheese
4 ounces low-fat cream cheese
$^1/_2$ cup chopped black or green olives
Dash red pepper flakes
$^1/_2$ cup chopped walnuts, toasted

In a medium skillet, cook onion in oil over moderately high heat until translucent. Add mushrooms and cook until tender. Add wine, Worcestershire sauce, and cream cheese. Stir constantly over medium heat until mixture is completely blended. Remove from heat. Stir in olives and red pepper flakes. Spread on an 8-inch plate. Top with walnuts. Serve warm or at room temperature with firm crackers or a sliced baguette.

Nutritional information per serving without bread:

Calories	90
Fat, gm.	5
Protein, gm.	4
Carbohydrate, gm.	8
Cholesterol, mg.	10
Fiber	low

Olive Nut Cheese Ball

Cheese balls lost their appeal because they were usually high in calories and fat.
This low-fat recipe tastes great. Serve it on crackers for an appetizer or on a bagel for lunch.

Serves 20

8 ounces fat-free or low-fat cream cheese, room temperature
2 cups shredded reduced-fat Cheddar cheese
1/4 cup fat-free or low-fat mayonnaise
1/2 teaspoon Worcestershire sauce
1/4 teaspoon garlic powder
1/4 teaspoon white pepper
1 tablespoon green olive juice
1/3 cup chopped green olives
1/3 cup chopped black olives
Dash Tabasco sauce or to taste, optional
1/2 cup finely chopped pecans

1. In a food processor, combine cream cheese, Cheddar cheese, mayonnaise, Worcestershire sauce, garlic powder, white pepper, and olive juice. Mix until smooth. Add green olives and black olives. Process briefly just until mixed. Stir in Tabasco sauce to taste. Spoon mixture on plate and form into a ball. Refrigerate until firm.

2. Sprinkle with nuts. Press lightly to make nuts adhere to the ball. Place cheese ball on a serving plate surrounded by crackers.

Nutritional information per serving without crackers:

Calories	45
Fat, gm.	2
Protein, gm.	4
Carbohydrate, gm.	2
Cholesterol, mg.	2
Fiber	low

Pepperoni Pie

This is an appetizer that kids love.

Serves 12

8 ounces fat-free or low-fat cream cheese, room temperature
1 cup canned extra-thick spaghetti sauce
1/2 cup sliced black olives
1/2 cup finely chopped green onions
2 cups shredded mozzarella cheese
2 ounces turkey pepperoni slices

Note: For a lower-fat version of this recipe, substitute thin slices of Canadian bacon in place of the pepperoni.

Preheat oven to 325°F. Spread cream cheese in bottom of a 9-inch glass or ceramic pie pan. Spread with spaghetti sauce. Top with olives and onions. Sprinkle with cheese. Arrange pepperoni on top. Bake for 10 minutes or just until heated through. Serve with crackers.

Nutritional information per serving without crackers:

Calories	120
Fat, gm.	7
Protein, gm.	9
Carbohydrate, gm.	6
Cholesterol, mg.	15
Fiber	low

Pistachio Nut and Olive Tapenade

This has a fabulous flavor. Serve it as an appetizer with sliced toasted French bread or on the side with chicken.

Serves 4

$1/4$ cup chopped pistachio nuts
$1/2$ cup chopped black olives
$1/2$ cup diced roasted red peppers
$1/2$ medium Granny Smith apple, finely diced
2 tablespoons finely chopped fresh parsley
$1/4$ cup finely chopped onion
1 tablespoon extra-virgin olive oil
1 tablespoon balsamic vinegar
2 tablespoons roasted garlic, optional
Freshly ground pepper to taste

In a small bowl, combine all ingredients. (Ingredients may be chopped in a small food processor.) Refrigerate any leftovers.

Nutritional information per serving:

Calories	90
Fat, gm.	6
Protein, gm.	1
Carbohydrate, gm.	8
Cholesterol, mg.	0
Fiber	medium

Refrigerator Pickles

This is a super-simple way to prepare homemade pickles.

Serves 20

2 1/2 pounds cucumbers (about 4 medium)
2 tablespoons salt
1 medium green bell pepper, sliced
1 medium onion, sliced
1 1/2 cups sugar
1 cup cider vinegar
1 teaspoon celery seed
1 teaspoon mustard seed

Note: If you prefer, in place of a plastic bag, choose a bowl or jar that allows the vinegar-sugar solution to cover the cucumbers.

1. Slice unpeeled cucumbers into 1-inch cubes. Place in large bowl and sprinkle with salt. Mix gently and let stand for 1 hour. Meanwhile combine green pepper, onion, sugar, vinegar, celery seed, and mustard seed in a small saucepan. Bring to a boil and stir until sugar is dissolved. Remove from heat and cool to room temperature.

2. Rinse cucumbers with cold water and drain. Place cucumbers in a gallon-size resealable plastic bag. Pour vinegar solution over cucumbers. Refrigerate. Turn occasionally, keeping cucumbers in the vinegar solution. Keeps for weeks in the refrigerator.

Nutritional information per serving:

Calories	40
Fat, gm.	0
Protein, gm.	0
Carbohydrate, gm.	10
Cholesterol, mg.	0
Fiber	low

Reuben Dip

This is an appetizer that is very popular at large parties. It is usually the first dish to be empty.

Serves 20

$^1/_2$ tablespoon canola oil
1 medium onion, finely chopped
1 cup fat-free sour cream
1 cup low-fat mayonnaise
16 ounces sauerkraut, drained
$^1/_3$ pound chipped beef, diced
1 cup shredded Swiss cheese
2 tablespoons creamy horseradish
1 tablespoon caraway seeds, optional

Preheat oven to 325°F. Grease a 7" x 11" baking dish. In a small skillet, heat oil. Add onion and cook over medium heat until translucent. In a large mixing bowl, combine sour cream and mayonnaise. Add onion and all remaining ingredients. Stir until well mixed. Spoon into prepared baking pan. Bake until heated through. Serve with small rye crackers.

Nutritional information per serving without crackers:

Calories	70
Fat, gm.	3
Protein, gm.	5
Carbohydrate, gm.	7
Cholesterol, mg.	15
Fiber	low

Sassy Guacamole

This is best made and served the same day. Avocados are a rich source of monounsaturated fat.

Serves 8

3 large ripe avocados
½ small onion, finely chopped
2 tablespoons fresh lemon juice
½ teaspoon salt
¼ teaspoon chili powder
¼ teaspoon oregano
¼ teaspoon garlic powder
2 small Italian tomatoes, seeded and finely chopped
Tabasco sauce to taste

Note: If you prefer a smoother texture, combine all ingredients except tomatoes in a food processor. Process until smooth. Add water to make a thinner consistency if desired. Stir in tomatoes.

Halve avocados and remove the pits. Remove the skin. Place in medium bowl and add onion, lemon juice, salt, chili powder, oregano, and garlic powder. Mash thoroughly with a hand potato masher and stir to blend the spices. Stir in tomatoes. Add Tabasco to taste. Serve with corn chips.

Nutritional information per serving without chips:

Calories	100
Fat, gm.	8
Protein, gm.	1
Carbohydrate, gm.	6
Cholesterol, mg.	0
Fiber	high

Sausage-Stuffed Mushrooms

These will be the hit of the party.

Serves 20

4 pounds fresh whole mushrooms
16 ounces low-fat Italian sausage
16 ounces low-fat turkey sausage
1/4 cup seasoned bread crumbs
2 large eggs, lightly beaten
1 teaspoon fennel seeds
1/2 teaspoon Italian seasoning
Dash Tabasco sauce to taste

Note: These may be made ahead and reheated with a small amount of broth in a slow cooker or over low heat in a saucepan on the stove.

Preheat oven to 400°F. Place 2 cooking racks on top of a large baking sheet with sides. Wash mushrooms and remove base stem. Discard stems and set caps aside. In a large bowl, combine all remaining ingredients. Mix well with a wooden spoon. Fill each mushroom cap with sausage mixture. Press in firmly. Place filled mushrooms on racks. Bake for 15 to 20 minutes or until sausage is completely done and mushrooms are tender. Remove from oven and serve warm.

Nutritional information per serving:

Calories	160
Fat, gm.	11
Protein, gm.	9
Carbohydrate, gm.	6
Cholesterol, mg.	45
Fiber	medium

Savory Spinach Spread

A flavorful and rich-tasting spread that is low in calories and low in fat.
Serve on fresh bread, pita bread, or crackers.

Serves 8

1 ¹/₂ cups fat-free sour cream
1 ¹/₂ ounces dry onion soup mix
¹/₂ cup fat-free or low-fat mayonnaise
¹/₂ cup chopped green onions
10 ounces frozen chopped spinach, squeezed dry

Notes: Tofu can be substituted for the sour cream in this recipe. Use a reduced-fat, firm tofu. It is a great way to enjoy extra soy.

For a wonderful appetizer, spread the spinach mixture on Triscuit crackers and top with shredded cheese of your choice. Place under the broiler until cheese is melted.

In a food processor, combine sour cream, soup mix, and mayonnaise. Process until smooth. Stir in onions and spinach. Refrigerate until ready to serve.

Nutritional information per serving:

Calories	55
Fat, gm.	0
Protein, gm.	3
Carbohydrate, gm.	11
Cholesterol, mg.	0
Fiber	medium

Smoked Salmon Bruschetta

You can't feel guilty enjoying this great-tasting appetizer!

Serves 20

8 ounces baguette bread
Olive oil spray
$1/2$ cup shredded mozzarella cheese
$1/4$ cup fat-free sour cream
$1/4$ cup low-fat mayonnaise
$1/8$ teaspoon white pepper
$1/8$ teaspoon dill weed
$1/8$ teaspoon ground thyme
$1/2$ cup finely chopped green onions
2 tablespoons capers, drained
3 ounces smoked salmon, crumbled
2 tablespoons grated Parmesan cheese

Preheat broiler. Cut bread into 20 thin slices. Place on baking sheet and lightly spray both sides of bread slices with olive oil spray. Place under broiler and toast on both sides. Remove from oven and set aside. In a medium bowl, combine mozzarella cheese, sour cream, mayonnaise, pepper, dill weed, thyme, onions, and capers. Stir to mix well. Stir in salmon. Spread a layer of the mixture on one side of the toasted bread slices. Spread completely to cover the edges. (This will prevent the edges of the bread from burning.) Sprinkle with Parmesan cheese. Place on baking sheet and broil until heated through and slightly brown on top.

Nutritional information per serving:

Calories	50
Fat, gm.	1
Protein, gm.	3
Carbohydrate, gm.	7
Cholesterol, mg.	5
Fiber	low

Spinach Squares

These are tasty and easy to eat as finger-food appetizers.
Don't tell anyone that they are healthy too!

Serves 30

$1/2$ tablespoon butter or margarine
1 medium onion, finely chopped
3 eggs
1 cup evaporated fat-free milk
1 cup flour
1 teaspoon salt
$1/2$ teaspoon paprika
$1/2$ teaspoon white pepper
$1/2$ teaspoon baking powder
10 ounces frozen chopped spinach, squeezed dry
1 cup shredded Cheddar cheese, divided

1. Preheat oven to 350°F. Heavily butter a 9" x 9" nonstick baking pan. In a small skillet, melt butter. Add onion and cook over medium heat until translucent. Set aside. In a medium bowl, combine eggs, milk, flour, salt, paprika, white pepper, and baking powder. Beat until well mixed. Stir in onion, spinach, and ¾ cup of the cheese. Pour mixture into baking pan. Top with remaining cheese. Bake for 30 to 40 minutes or until it is lightly browned and set in the middle. Let stand at room temperature for 20 minutes before cutting.

2. Serve warm or at room temperature. Cut into 30 small squares to serve as appetizers.

Nutritional information per serving:

Calories	50
Fat, gm.	2
Protein, gm.	3
Carbohydrate, gm.	5
Cholesterol, mg.	25
Fiber	low

Tostado Spread

This recipe was adapted from a popular high-calorie version but it tastes just as good. In fact, it is wonderful! At a recent cocktail party, it was the favorite appetizer. It can be made ahead of time and just heated when ready to serve.

Serves 8

8 ounces fat-free or low-fat cream cheese, room temperature
8 ounces canned chili without beans
2 green onions, finely chopped
2 ounces canned jalapeño peppers, drained and chopped
¾ cup shredded reduced-fat Cheddar cheese

Note: The milder canned green chilies can be substituted for the canned jalapeño peppers.

Preheat oven to 350°F. Spread cream cheese in bottom of a 9-inch pie plate. Pour chili on top. Sprinkle with green onions and peppers. Sprinkle cheese on top. Bake for 15 minutes or just until heated through and cheese is melted. Serve with corn chips.

Nutritional information per serving without chips:

Calories	90
Fat, gm.	2
Protein, gm.	9
Carbohydrate, gm.	8
Cholesterol, mg.	10
Fiber	low

Veggie Cream Cheese Ball

This is a very old recipe. It was served at my friend's wedding shower and she has been married for 30 years.

Serves 24

16 ounces low-fat cream cheese, room temperature
8 ounces crushed pineapple, drained
¹/₃ cup finely chopped green bell pepper
¹/₄ cup finely chopped onion
1 teaspoon salt
2 cups chopped pecans, divided

In a large bowl, combine cream cheese, pineapple, green pepper, onion, salt, and 1 cup pecans. Stir to mix well. Form into ball shape. Press remaining pecans around the ball. Cover with plastic wrap and refrigerate until ready to serve. Serve with crackers.

Nutritional information per serving without crackers:

Calories	80
Fat, gm.	6
Protein, gm.	2
Carbohydrate, gm.	4
Cholesterol, mg.	10
Fiber	low

Chapter Two
Salads

Amaretto-Marinated Fruit Bowl

Baby Spinach with Dates, Apples, and Caramelized Walnuts

Calico Beans

Corn and Bean Salad with Lime Dressing

Country Coleslaw

Couscous Salad with Dried Mixed Fruit

Creamy Coleslaw

Cucumber and Onion Salad

Curried Wild Rice Salad

Fresh Fruit Salad with Cinnamon Orange Dressing

Green Bean and Feta Cheese Salad

Mixed Greens and Apples with Honey Mustard Dressing

Pasta Salad

Raspberry Spinach Salad

Red Potato and Bacon Salad

Scandinavian Cucumbers

Shrimp and Pasta Salad

Strawberry Kiwi Salad with Honey Raspberry Dressing

Sweet-and-Sour Spinach Salad

Three-Bean Salad

Tomato and Red Onion Salad

Tuna and Green Bean Salad

Amaretto-Marinated Fruit Bowl

The amaretto and honey add elegance to a simple fresh fruit salad.

Serves 6

1 pint strawberries, hulled and quartered
1 cup seedless grapes, cut into halves
1 cup melon balls
2 medium kiwi, peeled and sliced
2 medium apples, cored and diced

Marinade:

1/4 cup amaretto (almond-flavored liqueur)
3 tablespoons honey
1 tablespoon fresh lime juice
1 tablespoon sugar, optional

Note: Use any combination of fresh fruit.

In a large bowl, combine the fresh fruit. In a cup, combine amaretto, honey, and lime juice. Pour over fruit and gently stir to mix. Taste fruit and if it needs more sweetening, sprinkle with sugar and mix. It is best if it marinates for several hours before serving. Serve in small individual bowls or parfait glasses.

Nutritional information per serving:

Calories	125
Fat, gm.	0
Protein, gm.	1
Carbohydrate, gm.	30
Cholesterol, mg.	0
Fiber	high

Baby Spinach with Dates, Apples, and Caramelized Walnuts

An impressive colorful salad.

Serves 6

¹/₂ cup balsamic vinegar
12 ounces (12 cups) fresh baby spinach, washed and dried
3 large red apples, cored and diced
¹/₂ cup diced pitted dates
¹/₂ cup walnut oil or olive oil
¹/₄ cup white wine vinegar
Salt and freshly ground pepper to taste
¹/₂ cup shredded sharp Cheddar cheese

Note: Other dried fruits such as cranberries, cherries, or apricots may be substituted for the dates.

Caramelized Walnuts:

¹/₃ cup sugar
1 tablespoon balsamic vinegar
1 cup walnuts

1. To prepare caramelized walnuts, preheat oven to 325°F. Line a rimmed baking sheet with foil. Spray foil with nonstick spray. Combine sugar and 1 tablespoon balsamic vinegar in a small saucepan. Stir over medium heat until mixture comes to a rolling boil and sugar dissolves. Add nuts and toss to coat. Transfer to baking sheet. Bake for 10 minutes or until nuts are deep brown. Stir occasionally. Watch carefully to prevent burning. Cool completely on baking sheet. Break nuts apart and store in airtight container at room temperature.

2. For the salad, pour ¹/₂ cup balsamic vinegar into a small saucepan. Bring to a boil and continue to boil until reduced by half. Pour into a small pitcher and set aside. Place spinach, apples, and dates in large salad bowl. Combine walnut oil, white wine vinegar, salt, and pepper in a small jar. Shake to mix and pour over salad. Divide onto individual salad plates. Top with cheese. Drizzle salad and edges of the plate with reduced balsamic vinegar.

Nutritional information per serving:

Calories	350
Fat, gm.	20
Protein, gm.	5
Carbohydrate, gm.	36
Cholesterol, mg.	10
Fiber	very high

Calico Beans

This dish is attractive with a light, refreshing flavor.
It can be served as a side salad or a main course salad.

Serves 8

1 cup cooked rice
15 ounces canned kidney beans, drained
15 ounces black beans, rinsed and drained
11 ounces canned corn, drained
1/2 cup finely chopped green onions
1/4 cup red wine vinegar
1/4 cup olive oil
2 tablespoons chopped fresh basil
Salt to taste
Freshly ground pepper to taste

In a large bowl, combine all ingredients. Stir to mix well. Chill until ready to serve.

Nutritional information per serving:

Calories	190
Fat, gm.	5
Protein, gm.	7
Carbohydrate, gm.	29
Cholesterol, mg.	0
Fiber	very high

Corn and Bean Salad with Lime Dressing

This salad is absolutely beautiful. It is so colorful and full of flavor. It is a perfect salad to serve with grilled chicken or meat. It can also be served as an entrée luncheon salad. Leftovers keep well for days.

Serves 10

2 tablespoons extra-virgin olive oil
$^1/_2$ cup fresh lime juice
$^1/_4$ teaspoon freshly ground pepper
1 teaspoon cumin
2 large cloves garlic, minced
11 ounces canned corn, drained
15 ounces canned kidney beans, drained and rinsed
15 ounces canned black beans, drained and rinsed
15 ounces canned navy beans, drained and rinsed
$^1/_2$ cup chopped red onion
1 medium red bell pepper, diced
1 medium green bell pepper, diced
$^1/_4$ cup chopped fresh cilantro
2 tablespoons chopped fresh parsley
2 tablespoons minced scallions
Salt and freshly ground pepper to taste

Note: For more flavor, add 1 or 2 more teaspoons of cumin. If you prefer a milder flavor, use basil in place of cumin.

In a small jar, combine olive oil, lime juice, pepper, cumin, and garlic. Shake to mix and set aside. In a large bowl, combine all remaining ingredients. Add dressing and stir to mix. Let stand for at least 1 hour to allow flavors to blend. Cover and refrigerate until ready to serve. Adjust seasonings with salt and pepper.

Nutritional information per serving:

Calories	180
Fat, gm.	3
Protein, gm.	8
Carbohydrate, gm.	30
Cholesterol, mg.	0
Fiber	very high

Country Coleslaw

This coleslaw has a tangy vinegar, oil, and sugar dressing.

Serves 8

8 cups finely shredded cabbage
1 cup shredded carrots
1 small onion, finely chopped

Dressing:
1/3 cup cider vinegar
2 tablespoons light olive oil
1/2 cup sugar
1/2 teaspoon salt
1/2 teaspoon celery seed
1/2 teaspoon dry mustard

Note: This salad will keep several weeks in the refrigerator, getting better with age.

In a large bowl, combine cabbage, carrots, and onion. In a small saucepan, combine vinegar, oil, sugar, salt, celery seed, and dry mustard. Bring to a boil, stirring constantly. Boil for 1 minute. Pour boiling mixture over cabbage mixture. Toss to mix well.

Nutritional information per serving:

Calories	110
Fat, gm.	3
Protein, gm.	1
Carbohydrate, gm.	20
Cholesterol, mg.	0
Fiber	low

Couscous Salad with Dried Mixed Fruit

This is a nice side dish, and a great main dish with some shrimp or chicken added.
The recipe makes a large amount but it keeps well in the refrigerator.

Serves 12

2 cups water or chicken broth
1 1/2 cups uncooked couscous
1 cup diced dried fruit
1/2 cup finely chopped green onions
1 teaspoon curry powder
1/4 cup finely chopped fresh basil
1 cup frozen green peas
15 ounces canned chickpeas (garbanzo beans), drained

Dressing:
1/4 cup fresh lemon juice
1/4 cup orange juice
1/4 cup olive oil
1 teaspoon lemon zest
2 cloves garlic, minced
Salt and freshly ground pepper to taste

In a medium saucepan, bring water or broth to a boil. Add couscous, dried fruit, green onions, curry powder, and basil. Stir to mix. Remove from heat and cover pan. Let stand for 10 minutes. Uncover pan and add peas and garbanzo beans. In a small jar, combine all dressing ingredients. Cover and shake to mix. Pour over couscous mixture. Stir to mix. Cover and chill.

Nutritional information per serving:

Calories	190
Fat, gm.	5
Protein, gm.	6
Carbohydrate, gm.	31
Cholesterol, mg.	0
Fiber	very high

Creamy Coleslaw

This salad has a mayonnaise and sour cream dressing, but it is fat-free and tasty too!

Serves 8

6 cups shredded cabbage
1 cup shredded carrots

Dressing:
$^1/_2$ cup fat-free or low-fat mayonnaise
$^1/_2$ cup fat-free sour cream
3 tablespoons sugar
3 tablespoons cider vinegar
1 tablespoon Dijon mustard
$^1/_4$ teaspoon salt
Freshly ground pepper to taste

In a large bowl, combine cabbage and carrots. In a small bowl, combine mayonnaise, sour cream, sugar, vinegar, mustard, and salt. Taste dressing and add additional sugar or vinegar to suit your taste. Mix dressing with cabbage and carrots. Cover and refrigerate until ready to serve. Add pepper to taste.

Nutritional information per serving:

Calories	55
Fat, gm.	0
Protein, gm.	1
Carbohydrate, gm.	13
Cholesterol, mg.	0
Fiber	medium

Cucumber and Onion Salad

Just simple.

Serves 6

¹/₂ cup cider vinegar
¹/₃ cup sugar
¹/₄ cup water
1 tablespoon light olive oil
¹/₂ teaspoon salt
¹/₄ teaspoon white pepper
4 medium cucumbers, thinly sliced
1 medium onion, thinly sliced

In a small saucepan, combine vinegar, sugar, water, oil, salt, and white pepper. Heat until sugar dissolves. Cool. Pour into a large resealable plastic bag. Add cucumbers and onion. Mix gently. Refrigerate for several hours or overnight. Remove cucumbers and onion slices from marinade before serving.

Nutritional information per serving:

Calories	50
Fat, gm.	1
Protein, gm.	1
Carbohydrate, gm.	10
Cholesterol, mg.	0
Fiber	medium

Curried Wild Rice Salad

This salad has a unique blend of flavors and textures. The dressing is wonderful.

Serves 6

1 ½ cups cooked wild rice
1 ½ cups cooked white rice
1 stalk celery, diced
2 green onions, diced
1 cup seedless grapes, cut into halves
1 medium apple, cored and diced
¼ cup golden raisins
8 ounces canned pineapple chunks
½ cup chopped pecans, optional

Dressing:

½ cup low-fat mayonnaise
1 tablespoon pineapple juice
2 tablespoons orange marmalade
¼ teaspoon sweet curry powder
⅛ teaspoon salt

Note: Use freshly cooked rice that has been cooled to room temperature for this recipe. Do not use rice that has been made ahead of time and refrigerated. Cold rice gets hard and will not absorb the flavorful dressing.

Cool rice to room temperature. In a large bowl, combine wild rice, white rice, celery, onions, grapes, apples, and raisins. Drain pineapple and reserve juice. Add pineapple to bowl. Stir gently. In a small bowl combine all dressing ingredients. Stir to mix. Add to rice and fruit. Mix gently. Cover and refrigerate until ready to serve. Top with pecans if desired.

Nutritional information per serving:

Calories	240
Fat, gm.	2
Protein, gm.	4
Carbohydrate, gm.	52
Cholesterol, mg.	0
Fiber	high

Fresh Fruit Salad with Cinnamon Orange Dressing

The dressing is special. Serve it with any combination of fresh fruits.

Serves 6

1/3 cup low-fat mayonnaise
2/3 cup fat-free sour cream
8 ounces crushed pineapple, drained
1 tablespoon orange juice or orange liqueur
2 teaspoons orange zest
1 teaspoon vanilla extract
1/2 teaspoon cinnamon
1 teaspoon poppy seeds
6 cups fresh fruit of your choice

In a small bowl, combine mayonnaise, sour cream, pineapple, orange juice, orange zest, vanilla, cinnamon, and poppy seeds. Mix well. Cover and refrigerate. When ready to serve, mix dressing with any combination of fresh fruits.

Nutritional information per serving:

Calories	150
Fat, gm.	1
Protein, gm.	2
Carbohydrate, gm.	34
Cholesterol, mg.	0
Fiber	high

Green Bean and Feta Cheese Salad

This salad is beautiful, elegant, and easy. My friend Liz created it.

Serves 6

1 ½ pounds fresh green beans
1 medium red onion, thinly sliced
1 medium tomato, seeded and chopped
1 medium cucumber, peeled, seeded, and chopped
1 cup crumbled low-fat seasoned feta cheese

Note: There are a variety of seasoned feta cheeses available. This recipe is excellent with the Mediterranean flavor, which is a blend of basil and sun-dried tomatoes.

Dressing:

3 tablespoons white wine vinegar
3 tablespoons extra-virgin olive oil
1 clove garlic, minced
¼ teaspoon salt
¼ teaspoon freshly ground pepper
⅓ cup chopped fresh mint

In a medium saucepan, cook beans in boiling water until crisp-tender. Chill under cold running water. Drain well. In a large bowl, combine beans, onion, tomato, cucumber, and feta cheese. In a small jar, combine vinegar, olive oil, garlic, salt, pepper, and mint. Shake well. When ready to serve, add to bean mixture and gently stir until well blended.

Nutritional information per serving:

Calories	120
Fat, gm.	8
Protein, gm.	4
Carbohydrate, gm.	8
Cholesterol, mg.	15
Fiber	high

Mixed Greens and Apples with Honey Mustard Dressing

This is a very tasty, low-fat dressing that complements a green salad.

Serves 10

8 cups mixed greens
3 medium red apples, cored and diced

Dressing:

1 cup fat-free plain yogurt
1/3 cup honey
1/3 cup low-fat mayonnaise
1/4 cup Dijon mustard
2 tablespoons yellow mustard
2 tablespoons apple cider vinegar

Note: Any variety of fruit can be combined with the greens.

Combine greens and apples in a large salad bowl. In a small bowl or pint-size jar, combine all dressing ingredients. Mix well. Pour desired amount of dressing over greens and toss to mix.

Nutritional information per serving:

Calories	100
Fat, gm.	1
Protein, gm.	3
Carbohydrate, gm.	21
Cholesterol, mg.	0
Fiber	medium

Pasta Salad

*This is an attractive, colorful pasta salad. It is very easy to toss together,
and other ingredients can be added to make it a hearty entrée salad.*

Serves 8

12 ounces bow tie or other shaped pasta
2 large fresh tomatoes, seeded and chopped
1 small cucumber, peeled, seeded, and chopped
1 small red onion, finely sliced
$1/2$ cup sliced black olives
4 ounces reduced-fat Swiss cheese, cubed
$1/2$ cup fat-free Italian Parmesan salad dressing

Note: Crumbled feta cheese or another cheese of your choice
can be substituted for the Swiss cheese. For a main dish salad,
add pepperoni, reduced-fat sausage, or other cooked poultry or
meat. If the salad is prepared a day in advance, you may want to
add a small amount of additional dressing before serving.

Cook pasta in a large cooking pot in boiling water until al dente.
Pour into colander and chill under cold running water. Drain
well. Set aside. In a large bowl combine tomatoes, cucumber,
onion, olives, and cheese. Add pasta. Add dressing and stir until
blended. Store in the refrigerator until ready to serve.

Nutritional information per serving:

Calories	210
Fat, gm.	2
Protein, gm.	10
Carbohydrate, gm.	38
Cholesterol, mg.	10
Fiber	medium

Raspberry Spinach Salad

This is a beautiful special occasion salad.

Serves 6

6 cups fresh spinach, washed and dried
2 cups fresh or frozen loose-pack raspberries

Dressing:

1/4 cup raspberry jam
1/4 cup raspberry-flavored wine vinegar
2 tablespoons honey
2 tablespoons extra-virgin olive oil
Dash salt
1/2 cup chopped macadamia nuts or almonds

In a large salad bowl, combine spinach and raspberries. In a small jar, combine jam, vinegar, honey, oil, and salt. Cover and shake until well mixed. When ready to serve, pour dressing over spinach and fruit. Toss to mix. Divide onto 6 salad plates. Sprinkle each serving with nuts.

Nutritional information per serving:

Calories	150
Fat, gm.	7
Protein, gm.	2
Carbohydrate, gm.	20
Cholesterol, mg.	0
Fiber	high

Red Potato and Bacon Salad

This is an interesting, mildly flavored, warm potato salad.

Serves 6

6 medium red potatoes
4 slices bacon
1 small onion, finely chopped
1 stalk celery, diced
1/2 medium green bell pepper, chopped

Dressing:

1/4 cup red wine vinegar
2 tablespoons extra-virgin olive oil
1/4 cup sugar
Salt and freshly ground pepper to taste
2 hard-cooked eggs, optional

1. In a large saucepan, boil potatoes in salted water just until tender. Drain. Dice potatoes and place in large bowl. While potatoes are cooking, fry bacon in medium skillet. Remove bacon; crumble and set aside. Pour off bacon fat and return 2 tablespoons back to the skillet. Add onion and celery to skillet and cook until onion is translucent. Add green pepper and cook for 2 minutes or until just tender-crisp. Spoon into bowl with potatoes.

2. In a small jar, mix vinegar, olive oil, and sugar. Add dressing to bowl. Toss gently. Add salt and pepper to taste. Garnish with slices of hard-cooked eggs if desired.

Nutritional information per serving:

Calories	170
Fat, gm.	6
Protein, gm.	3
Carbohydrate, gm.	25
Cholesterol, mg.	5
Fiber	medium

Scandinavian Cucumbers

This is a way to dress up cucumbers.
They are good enough to take to your next potluck supper.

Serves 6

$1/2$ cup fat-free sour cream
1 tablespoon sugar
2 tablespoons tarragon vinegar
2 tablespoons chopped fresh parsley
$1/4$ teaspoon dill weed
$1/4$ teaspoon salt
Dash white pepper
1 small onion, thinly sliced
3 medium cucumbers, sliced

Note: In place of tarragon vinegar, cider vinegar and $1/8$ teaspoon dried tarragon work fine.

In a small bowl, combine sour cream, sugar, vinegar, parsley, dill weed, salt, and pepper. Stir to mix well. In a medium bowl, combine onion and cucumbers. Add dressing and gently stir to blend. Cover and refrigerate until ready to serve.

Nutritional information per serving:

Calories	50
Fat, gm.	0
Protein, gm.	2
Carbohydrate, gm.	11
Cholesterol, mg.	5
Fiber	medium

Shrimp and Pasta Salad

This is a great low-fat, healthy, and attractive luncheon salad. The old recipes used regular mayonnaise, which added hundreds of calories. The low-fat mayonnaise works well if creatively seasoned.

Serves 6

6 ounces rotini or pasta shells
$1/2$ cup chopped green onions
$1/2$ cup chopped celery
$1/2$ medium red bell pepper, diced
1 cup frozen peas
1 pound cooked and peeled shrimp

Note: Crab or surimi can be substituted for the shrimp.

Dressing:

$1/2$ cup low-fat mayonnaise
$1/4$ cup fat-free sour cream
1 tablespoon fresh lemon juice
2 teaspoons sugar
$1/8$ teaspoon dill weed
$1/8$ teaspoon tarragon
Salt and freshly ground pepper to taste

Alternate dressing:

$2/3$ cup low-fat or fat-free mayonnaise
2 tablespoons fat-free French dressing
2 teaspoons fresh lemon juice
Salt and freshly ground pepper to taste

In a large saucepan, cook rotini pasta in boiling salted water just until al dente. Pour into colander. Chill under cold running water and drain well. In a large bowl, combine pasta, onions, celery, pepper, peas, and shrimp. In a small bowl, combine all of the dressing ingredients from your chosen dressing, except salt and pepper. Mix dressing with shrimp and pasta. Add salt and pepper to taste.

Nutritional information per serving with first dressing listed:

Calories	230
Fat, gm.	2
Protein, gm.	21
Carbohydrate, gm.	32
Cholesterol, mg.	115
Fiber	high

Strawberry Kiwi Salad with Honey Raspberry Dressing

What could be more attractive and refreshing than this colorful light salad?

Serves 6

6 cups red leaf lettuce
1 quart fresh strawberries, hulled and quartered
4 medium kiwi, peeled and sliced

Note: This recipe is also great prepared with other fresh fruits such as blueberries, raspberries, or apples.

Dressing:
1/4 cup honey
1/4 cup raspberry-flavored wine vinegar
2 tablespoons vegetable oil
1/8 teaspoon dill weed

Wash, drain, and tear lettuce leaves. In a large salad bowl, combine lettuce, strawberries, and kiwi. In a small jar, combine honey, vinegar, oil, and dill weed. Cover and shake well. When ready to serve, pour dressing over the salad. Mix gently.

Nutritional information per serving:

Calories	165
Fat, gm.	5
Protein, gm.	2
Carbohydrate, gm.	28
Cholesterol, mg.	0
Fiber	high

Sweet-and-Sour Spinach Salad

This special dressing has a wonderful flavor that you won't find in a bottle.

Serves 6

6 cups torn spinach, room temperature
1 medium red onion, thinly sliced
1 cup mandarin oranges, drained
6 slices bacon, fried and crumbled

Note: Romaine or leaf lettuce can be substituted for the spinach.

Dressing:
$^1/_3$ cup sugar
2 tablespoons honey
$^1/_4$ cup fresh lemon juice
2 tablespoons cider vinegar
$^1/_2$ teaspoon paprika
$^1/_8$ teaspoon salt
2 tablespoons olive oil

In a large salad bowl, combine spinach, onion, oranges, and bacon. In a small saucepan combine sugar, honey, lemon juice, vinegar, paprika, and salt. Bring to a boil and cook for 1 to 2 minutes. Remove from heat. Add olive oil. Mix well and pour over salad. Toss to coat.

Nutritional information per serving:

Calories	180
Fat, gm.	7
Protein, gm.	4
Carbohydrate, gm.	25
Cholesterol, mg.	5
Fiber	medium

Three-Bean Salad

This is an easy salad to put together and it keeps for days in the refrigerator.

Serves 10

15 ounces canned green beans, drained
15 ounces canned yellow beans, drained
15 ounces canned kidney beans, drained
1 medium red onion, chopped
1 medium green bell pepper, diced

Note: Other combinations of beans can be used. Add additional seasonings of your choice such as fresh mint, dill weed, Italian seasoning, or oregano.

Dressing:

$1/3$ cup extra-virgin olive oil
$2/3$ cup white vinegar
$3/4$ cup sugar
$1/2$ teaspoon salt
$1/4$ teaspoon freshly ground pepper

In a large bowl, combine the beans, onion, and green pepper. In a pint jar, combine dressing ingredients. Shake well and pour over beans. Stir to mix. Cover and refrigerate until ready to serve.

Nutritional information per serving:

Calories	180
Fat, gm.	7
Protein, gm.	3
Carbohydrate, gm.	27
Cholesterol, mg.	0
Fiber	medium

Tomato and Red Onion Salad

A way to dress up fresh tomatoes.

Serves 6

6 medium tomatoes, cut into wedges
$^{1}/_{4}$ cup chopped fresh mint
2 medium red onions, thinly sliced
2 tablespoons extra-virgin olive oil
2 tablespoons white wine vinegar
1 clove garlic, crushed
1 tablespoon sugar
$^{1}/_{2}$ teaspoon salt

Note: Any fresh herb of your choice can be substituted for the mint.

Place tomatoes, mint, and onions in a large resealable plastic bag. In a cup, combine oil, vinegar, garlic, sugar, and salt. Mix and pour over tomatoes. Reseal bag and gently toss to coat. Marinate for several hours before serving. Turn occasionally. Arrange in serving bowl when ready to serve.

Nutritional information per serving:

Calories	85
Fat, gm.	4
Protein, gm.	1
Carbohydrate, gm.	12
Cholesterol, mg.	0
Fiber	medium

Tuna and Green Bean Salad

This is a new twist for an old salad.

Serves 4

2 cups fresh green beans, cut into 1-inch pieces
$1/4$ cup fat-free or low-fat mayonnaise
2 stalks celery, finely chopped
$1/4$ cup finely chopped green onions
1 teaspoon fresh lemon juice
1 teaspoon soy sauce
$1/8$ teaspoon white pepper
$1/4$ teaspoon curry powder
6 ounces canned tuna in water
4 lettuce leaves
1 cup chow mein noodles

In a small saucepan, cook green beans until tender. Chill under cold water and drain well. Set aside. In a medium bowl, combine mayonnaise, celery, onions, lemon juice, soy sauce, white pepper, and curry powder. Mix well. Add tuna and green beans. Mix gently. Refrigerate until ready to serve. Arrange lettuce leaves on 4 serving plates. Spoon tuna mixture on top. Sprinkle with chow mein noodles.

Nutritional information per serving:

Calories	155
Fat, gm.	4
Protein, gm.	14
Carbohydrate, gm.	16
Cholesterol, mg.	15
Fiber	medium

Chapter Three
Soups and Stews

American Onion Soup

This is an easy-to-make and lighter version of the traditional French onion soup.

Serves 6

2 tablespoons butter or margarine
3 jumbo onions, thinly sliced
1 clove garlic, minced
3 tablespoons flour
6 cups low-fat chicken broth, divided
$1/8$ teaspoon thyme
$1/8$ teaspoon white pepper
$1/4$ cup dry sherry wine
Salt and freshly ground pepper to taste

Note: If desired, spoon soup into individual ovenproof bowls. Top with a piece of French bread and sprinkle with freshly grated Parmesan cheese. Place under the broiler until cheese melts.

In a soup pot, melt butter. Add onions and cook, stirring occasionally, over medium heat until golden brown. Add garlic and cook for 1 minute. In a shaker, mix flour and $3/4$ cup of the chicken broth. Add to pan along with the remaining chicken broth. Add thyme and white pepper. Bring to a boil, reduce heat, and simmer for 1 hour or until onions are very tender. Add sherry and adjust seasoning with salt and pepper.

Nutritional information per serving without bread and cheese topping:

Calories	75
Fat, gm.	4
Protein, gm.	3
Carbohydrate, gm.	6
Cholesterol, mg.	10
Fiber	low

Beef Barley Soup

The aroma of this soup will fill your kitchen with memories of family suppers on cold winter days.

Serves 12

3 pounds lean beef roast
$\frac{1}{2}$ teaspoon salt
$\frac{1}{2}$ teaspoon freshly ground pepper
1 tablespoon vegetable oil
2 medium onions, chopped
2 stalks celery, chopped
49 ounces canned low-fat beef broth
2 quarts water
4 beef bouillon cubes
$\frac{1}{2}$ cup chopped fresh parsley
1 bay leaf
$\frac{1}{2}$ teaspoon thyme
1 teaspoon Italian seasoning
4 medium potatoes, peeled and cubed
$\frac{1}{2}$ cup barley
3 cups shredded cabbage
20 ounces frozen mixed vegetables

Note: Choose any fresh or frozen vegetables of your choice. The recipe can be cut in half if you prefer a smaller quantity.

1. Trim any visible fat from meat and cut into 1-inch cubes. Sprinkle with salt and pepper. In a large soup pot, heat oil over medium heat. Add meat and brown on all sides. Add onions and celery. Cook until onions are translucent. Add beef broth and enough water to cover meat. Add bouillon, parsley, bay leaf, thyme, and Italian seasoning. Boil gently for 1$\frac{1}{2}$ hours or until meat is tender.

2. Add potatoes and barley. Cook for 30 minutes or until potatoes are tender. Check occasionally and add additional water if soup gets too thick. Add cabbage and mixed vegetables. Cook for 20 minutes or until vegetables are tender. Adjust seasoning with extra salt and pepper if desired. Remove bay leaf before serving.

Nutritional information per serving:

Calories	260
Fat, gm.	7
Protein, gm.	29
Carbohydrate, gm.	20
Cholesterol, mg.	65
Fiber	high

Chicken Gumbo

A gumbo is a thick soup or stew that is often served over rice.
It can be thickened with filé powder or flour if desired.

Serves 6

1 tablespoon cooking oil
2 pounds boned and skinned chicken breasts, cut into 1-inch cubes
1/2 pound reduced-fat kielbasa, cut into 1-inch cubes
1 medium onion, chopped
15 ounces stewed tomatoes
2 cups fat-free chicken broth
1 bay leaf
1 pound frozen mixed vegetables
Salt and freshly ground pepper to taste
2 tablespoons flour, optional

1. In a soup pot, heat oil. Add chicken and kielbasa. Fry over medium-hot heat until brown. Add onion and cook until translucent. Add tomatoes, chicken broth, and bay leaf. Bring to a boil. Reduce heat and simmer for 20 to 30 minutes.

2. Add vegetables; cover and cook until tender. Add water if it gets too thick. Add salt and pepper to taste. Remove bay leaf. If a thicker gumbo is desired, mix flour in 1/2 cup water. Stir into gumbo and bring to a boil, stirring constantly.

Nutritional information per serving:

Calories	310
Fat, gm.	9
Protein, gm.	40
Carbohydrate, gm.	17
Cholesterol, mg.	100
Fiber	high

Chili

Chili is so easy to make and it tastes so good.

Serves 6

1 pound extra-lean ground beef
¹/₂ teaspoon salt
¹/₂ teaspoon freshly ground pepper
1 large onion, chopped
30 ounces canned kidney beans, undrained
46 ounces tomato juice or V8 vegetable juice
30 ounces Italian-style stewed or diced tomatoes
1 tablespoon chili powder
¹/₂ teaspoon cumin

Note: In place of kidney beans, seasoned chili beans will add extra flavor.

In a large heavy nonstick pan, brown beef over medium heat. Sprinkle with salt and pepper. Add onion and cook until translucent. Drain off any meat fat. Add kidney beans, vegetable juice, tomatoes, chili powder, and cumin. Bring to a boil, reduce heat, and simmer for 1 hour or until chili reaches the desired consistency. Adjust seasoning with extra salt, pepper, or chili powder.

Nutritional information per serving:

Calories	395
Fat, gm.	11
Protein, gm.	32
Carbohydrate, gm.	42
Cholesterol, mg.	60
Fiber	very high

Corn Chowder

Corn chowder can be mild and soothing or heat it up with added chili peppers.

Serves 6

2 tablespoons butter or margarine
1 small onion, finely chopped
2 tablespoons flour
2 cups fat-free milk
3 cups canned or frozen corn
1 cup fat-free half-and-half
$1/8$ teaspoon nutmeg
$1/2$ cup finely chopped roasted chilies, optional
Salt and freshly ground pepper to taste

Note: Choose mild or hot chili peppers to suit your taste.

In a large saucepan, melt butter. Add onion and cook over medium heat until translucent. Add flour, stirring constantly for 2 minutes. Add milk and bring to a boil, stirring constantly until mixture thickens. Add corn. Pour mixture into a food processor and process until partially smooth. Pour mixture back into the saucepan. Add half-and-half, nutmeg, and chilies if desired. Add additional milk if soup is too thick. Heat through. Add salt and pepper to taste.

Nutritional information per serving:

Calories	260
Fat, gm.	5
Protein, gm.	10
Carbohydrate, gm.	44
Cholesterol, mg.	15
Fiber	high

Garden Vegetable Soup

This is a very attractive, hearty soup. Add the vegetables of your choice.

Serves 6

1 tablespoon vegetable oil
1 large onion, chopped
2 large carrots, peeled and diced
2 cloves garlic, minced
1/2 teaspoon basil
49 ounces low-fat chicken broth
2 large potatoes, peeled and diced
15 ounces canned seasoned white beans, undrained
1 cup green beans, cut into 1-inch pieces
1 small fresh zucchini, sliced
2 large fresh tomatoes, peeled, seeded, and diced
1 cup pasta shells
Salt and freshly ground pepper to taste
1 cup grated Parmesan cheese, optional

Note: Canned or frozen vegetables can be substituted for the fresh vegetables. Any mixture of vegetables can be used.

1. In a large soup pot, heat vegetable oil. Cook onion and carrots over medium heat until onion is translucent. Add garlic and cook for 1 minute. Add basil, chicken broth, and potatoes. Bring to a boil, reduce heat, and simmer for 30 minutes or until potatoes are tender.

2. Add white beans, green beans, zucchini, tomatoes, and pasta shells. Cook for 10 to 15 minutes or until pasta is tender. Add extra broth if soup is too thick. Adjust seasoning with salt and pepper. Serve soup topped with grated cheese if desired.

Nutritional information per serving:

Calories	190
Fat, gm.	4
Protein, gm.	8
Carbohydrate, gm.	30
Cholesterol, mg.	0
Fiber	high

Hamburger Soup

Just simple and good!

Serves 6

1 tablespoon vegetable oil
1 pound extra-lean ground beef
1/2 teaspoon salt
1/4 teaspoon freshly ground pepper
1 medium onion, finely chopped
2 stalks celery, finely chopped
2 large carrots, peeled and finely chopped
2 cloves garlic, minced
1/2 pound fresh mushrooms, sliced
3 tablespoons flour
49 ounces low-fat beef broth, divided
1/2 teaspoon thyme
1/2 teaspoon marjoram
1/4 cup dry red wine, optional

In a heavy soup pot, heat oil over medium heat. Add meat to pan; sprinkle with salt and pepper. Cook until meat is brown. Add onion and cook until translucent. Drain off any excess fat. Add celery, carrots, garlic, and mushrooms. Cook until mushrooms are tender. In a shaker, mix flour and 1 cup of broth and add to pan. Add remaining beef broth, thyme, and marjoram. Bring to a boil while stirring. Reduce heat and simmer for 30 minutes or until vegetables are tender and flavors have blended. When ready to serve, add wine if desired.

Nutritional information per serving:

Calories	275
Fat, gm.	15
Protein, gm.	25
Carbohydrate, gm.	10
Cholesterol, mg.	50
Fiber	low

Hearty Minestrone Soup

This is a great flavorful vegetarian soup.

Serves 6

2 tablespoons olive oil
2 medium onions, chopped
2 stalks celery, diced
1 medium green bell pepper, diced
2 medium zucchini, sliced
3 cloves garlic, minced
1 teaspoon cumin
1 tablespoon chili powder
1 teaspoon oregano
1/2 teaspoon freshly ground black pepper
4 large tomatoes, peeled, seeded, and diced
30 ounces vegetable broth
15 ounces canned kidney beans, undrained
15 ounces canned white beans, undrained
1 cup corn, canned, frozen, or fresh
1 small jalapeño pepper, finely chopped
Salt to taste

Note: Canned tomatoes (30 ounces diced) may be used in place of fresh tomatoes.

1. In a large heavy soup pot, heat olive oil. Add onions and cook over medium heat until translucent. Add celery, green pepper, zucchini, and garlic. Cook until tender. Add cumin, chili powder, oregano, and black pepper while vegetables are cooking. Add tomatoes, broth, kidney beans, white beans, corn, and jalapeño pepper. Cook for 15 to 30 minutes or until heated through and flavors have blended.

2. If soup is too thick, add additional broth. Adjust seasoning with salt and extra chili powder if desired.

Nutritional information per serving:

Calories	270
Fat, gm.	6
Protein, gm.	12
Carbohydrate, gm.	42
Cholesterol, mg.	0
Fiber	high

Old-Fashioned Chicken Soup

This cookbook would not be complete without a real chicken soup.
It brings back so many good memories.

Serves 10

1 whole chicken or 3 pounds chicken pieces
6 chicken bouillon cubes
1 bay leaf
1/2 teaspoon thyme
4 medium potatoes, peeled and diced
2 cups chopped cabbage
1 tablespoon Worcestershire sauce
1 tablespoon soy sauce
1/2 teaspoon poultry seasoning, optional
1 tablespoon vegetable oil
1 large onion, chopped
2 stalks celery, chopped
2 cups peeled and chopped carrots
Salt and freshly ground pepper to taste

Note: Noodles may be added if desired.

1. Place chicken in a large soup pot. Add enough water to cover chicken. Add bouillon, bay leaf, and thyme. Bring to a boil. Reduce heat, cover, and simmer for 1 hour.

2. Remove chicken and place in a bowl to cool slightly. Remove meat from bones and set aside. Discard skin and bones. Add potatoes, cabbage, Worcestershire sauce, soy sauce, and poultry seasoning to soup pot. Bring to a boil. Reduce heat and boil gently for 30 to 45 minutes or until potatoes are tender. Check occasionally and add additional water if soup is too thick.

3. In a medium skillet, heat vegetable oil. Cook onion over medium heat until translucent. Add celery and carrots. Cook until celery is tender. Add cooked vegetables to soup pot.

4. Return meat to soup pot. Adjust seasoning with salt and pepper to taste. Discard bay leaf. For extra flavor, add additional chicken bouillon.

Nutritional information per serving:

Calories	265
Fat, gm.	9
Protein, gm.	26
Carbohydrate, gm.	20
Cholesterol, mg.	75
Fiber	high

Potato Soup

If you want an easy, great-tasting soup recipe, this is the one.

Serves 4

8 slices bacon
2 medium onions, diced
2 stalks celery, diced
3 large carrots, peeled and diced
4 large potatoes, peeled and diced (about 6 cups)
$1/2$ teaspoon marjoram
$1/2$ teaspoon thyme
$1/2$ teaspoon white pepper
1 bay leaf
49 ounces fat-free chicken broth
Salt and freshly ground pepper to taste
$1/4$ cup chopped fresh parsley

Note: For a thicker soup, remove 1 to 2 cups of the soup and place in blender. Process until smooth and return mixture to soup pan.

1. In a large soup pan, fry bacon until crisp. Remove and crumble. Add onions, celery, and carrots to bacon fat. Cook over medium heat until onions are translucent. Pour off any remaining fat and discard. Add potatoes, marjoram, thyme, white pepper, bay leaf, broth, and bacon. Bring to a boil. Reduce heat and simmer uncovered for 1 hour or until potatoes are very tender.

2. Adjust seasoning with salt and freshly ground pepper. When ready to serve, stir in parsley and discard bay leaf.

Nutritional information per serving:

Calories	180
Fat, gm.	6
Protein, gm.	10
Carbohydrate, gm.	22
Cholesterol, mg.	10
Fiber	high

Seafood Chowder

Anyone who likes seafood will love this soup.

Serves 4

8 slices of bacon
1 medium onion, chopped
4 stalks celery, finely chopped
4 large carrots, peeled and finely chopped
4 medium potatoes, peeled and chopped
3 cups low-fat chicken broth
1/4 teaspoon dill weed
8 ounces cod or haddock, cut into 1-inch chunks
5 tablespoons flour
2 cups fat-free milk, divided
Salt and freshly ground pepper to taste

Note: Use any mild-flavored fish or seafood of your choice.

1. In a large heavy pan, fry bacon until crisp. Remove from pan, crumble, and set aside. Add onion to pan. Cook until translucent. Add celery and carrots; cook until soft. Drain off excess bacon fat. Add potatoes, chicken broth, and dill weed. Cook for 30 minutes or until vegetables are tender.

2. Add fish and cook for 3 to 5 minutes or until fish is cooked through. In a shaker combine flour and 1 cup milk. Add slowly to the hot soup. Bring to a boil, stirring gently until soup thickens slightly. Add bacon. Adjust seasoning with salt and pepper. Add remaining milk to thin to desired consistency.

Nutritional information per serving:

Calories	310
Fat, gm.	7
Protein, gm.	24
Carbohydrate, gm.	38
Cholesterol, mg.	35
Fiber	high

Shrimp and Black Bean Chili

Shrimp adds a new twist to this hearty chili.

Serves 8

1 tablespoon vegetable oil
1 medium onion, chopped
¹/₂ small red bell pepper, chopped
¹/₂ small yellow bell pepper, chopped
30 ounces canned diced Italian seasoned tomatoes
30 ounces canned black beans, drained and rinsed
2 cups low-fat chicken broth
¹/₂ teaspoon cumin
2 teaspoons chili powder
¹/₂ teaspoon basil
2 pounds cleaned, cooked shrimp
Salt and freshly ground pepper to taste

Note: Canned crushed or stewed tomatoes can be used in place of the diced tomatoes if you prefer not to have pieces of tomato in the soup.

In a soup pan, heat oil. Add onion and cook over medium heat until translucent. Add red and yellow peppers. Cook for 2 minutes. Add all remaining ingredients except shrimp. Bring to a boil, reduce heat, and simmer for 20 to 30 minutes or until soup has reached desired consistency. Add additional water or broth to thin if desired. Add shrimp and cook until heated through. Add salt and pepper to taste.

Nutritional information per serving:

Calories	250
Fat, gm.	4
Protein, gm.	30
Carbohydrate, gm.	24
Cholesterol, mg.	170
Fiber	very high

Split Pea Soup

What a great meal to make ahead!
Make an extra-large batch and freeze leftovers in small containers.

Serves 8

3 cups dry green split peas
1 tablespoon vegetable oil
1 large onion, chopped
3 stalks celery, chopped
2 large carrots, peeled and chopped
1 clove shallot, minced
2 cloves garlic, minced
2 large potatoes, peeled and diced
4 chicken bouillon cubes
1/2 teaspoon thyme
1 bay leaf
1 pound lean ham, diced
Salt and freshly ground pepper to taste

Note: For a very smooth consistency, process soup in a food processor or blender.

1. Wash peas in a colander. Place peas in a large cooking pot and cover with water. Bring to a boil. Remove from heat and let sit for 1 to 2 hours. Drain off water. Add fresh water and bring to a boil again. Reduce heat and simmer for 1 to 2 hours until peas are tender and mushy. Add extra water if needed. (Do not add any salt, salty foods, or high-acid foods before the peas are soft. Salt and acid ingredients will prevent the peas from becoming soft.)

2. While peas are cooking, heat oil in medium skillet. Add onion and cook until translucent. Add celery and carrots. Cook until soft. Add shallot and garlic. Cook for 1 minute. Remove from heat.

3. When peas are soft, add cooked vegetables, potatoes, bouillon, thyme, bay leaf, and ham. Cook until potatoes are tender and soup has reached desired consistency. If soup is too thick, thin with water or chicken stock. Adjust seasoning with extra chicken bouillon, salt, and pepper to taste. Discard bay leaf.

Nutritional information per serving:

Calories	370
Fat, gm.	5
Protein, gm.	30
Carbohydrate, gm.	52
Cholesterol, mg.	25
Fiber	very high

Wild Rice and Mushroom Soup

This elegant soup is so filling that you can serve it as a main course. I first tried it when my brother gave me wild rice for Christmas. He had collected the rice by hand, with the help of a Native American guide, in the wetlands of northern Wisconsin. Wild rice is not a true rice but the seed of a tall aquatic grass.

Serves 6

1 tablespoon butter or margarine
1 medium onion, chopped
$1/2$ pound fresh mushrooms, sliced
$1/2$ cup finely shredded carrots
2 tablespoons flour
4 cups low-fat chicken broth, divided
$1/2$ cup fat-free half-and-half
$2^1/2$ cups cooked wild rice*
$1/4$ teaspoon white pepper
$1/4$ cup dry sherry wine
Salt and freshly ground pepper to taste

*Two-thirds cup of raw wild rice will make $2^1/2$ cups of cooked wild rice.

In a large heavy soup pan, melt butter. Add onion and cook over medium heat until translucent. Add mushrooms and carrots. Cook until soft. In a shaker, mix flour with 1 cup of the chicken broth. Add mixture to the pan. Add the remaining chicken broth and cook, stirring constantly, until mixture comes to a boil and thickens. Stir in half-and-half, rice, and white pepper. Simmer for 30 minutes or until soup reaches desired consistency. When ready to serve, add sherry and heat through. Add salt and freshly ground pepper to taste.

Nutritional information per serving:

Calories	135
Fat, gm.	2
Protein, gm.	6
Carbohydrate, gm.	23
Cholesterol, mg.	10
Fiber	medium

Zucchini Soup

A perfect summer soup when you have lots of fresh zucchini.

Serves 4

1 tablespoon butter or margarine
1 medium onion, chopped
2 pounds (4 cups) zucchini, peeled, seeds removed, and sliced
2 medium potatoes, peeled and diced
4 cups fat-free chicken broth
1/4 teaspoon white pepper
1/2 cup shredded carrots
1/2 cup white wine
Salt and freshly ground pepper to taste

1. In a large saucepan, melt butter. Add onion and cook over medium heat until translucent. Add zucchini, potatoes, chicken broth, and white pepper. Boil gently for 30 minutes or until vegetables are tender.

2. Remove 2 cups of the soup and place in blender or food processor. Blend until smooth. Return to pan. Add carrots and cook for 10 minutes or until carrots are tender. Add wine and keep warm until ready to serve. Add additional broth if soup is too thick. Season with salt and pepper.

Nutritional information per serving:

Calories	120
Fat, gm.	3
Protein, gm.	6
Carbohydrate, gm.	17
Cholesterol, mg.	10
Fiber	high

Chapter Four
Meatless Meals

Baked Orange French Toast

Broccoli Cheese Quiche

Cheesy Potato Pie

Corn Pudding

Golden Garden Vegetable Casserole

Light Fettuccine Alfredo

Mediterranean Couscous Salad

Mexican Macaroni Salad

Mushroom Nut Loaf

Pasta with Garlic Tomato Sauce

Potato and Pepper Frittata

Spinach Cheese Pie

Spinach Manicotti

Stuffed Bell Peppers

Sun-Dried Tomatoes and Mushrooms with Linguine

Swiss Corn Bake

Taco Cheese Pie

Vegetarian Chili

Veggie Cheese Pie

Wild Rice and Mushroom Casserole

Zucchini Casserole

Baked Orange French Toast

This is a popular recipe served to guests at bed-and-breakfasts.

Serves 6

1 loaf unsliced French bread
4 eggs
2/3 cup orange juice
1/3 cup fat-free milk
1/4 cup sugar
1/4 teaspoon nutmeg
1/2 teaspoon vanilla extract
1/4 cup butter or margarine, melted

1. Cut 1-inch slices of French bread. Arrange as many slices as will fit in a 9" x 13" baking pan. In a medium bowl, combine all remaining ingredients except butter. Mix with wire whip until well blended. Pour mixture over the bread. Cover pan and refrigerate for several hours or overnight.

2. When ready to bake, preheat oven to 400°F. Pour butter onto a cookie sheet that has a 1-inch side or use a 10" x 15" baking pan. Remove bread from refrigerator and arrange slices on the cookie sheet, leaving a small amount of space between pieces. Bake for 10 minutes. Turn slices over and bake for another 10 to 15 minutes or until lightly browned.

3. Serve with Caramel Cinnamon Sauce (page 254).

Nutritional information per serving:

Calories	355
Fat, gm.	12
Protein, gm.	11
Carbohydrate, gm.	51
Cholesterol, mg.	140
Fiber	low

Broccoli Cheese Quiche

This quiche is low-fat and healthy. It is a great meatless meal, but if you prefer, ham or bacon can be added.

Serves 8

2 cups chopped fresh or frozen broccoli
1 cup fat-free ricotta cheese
1 cup evaporated fat-free milk
3 eggs
1/2 teaspoon salt
1/4 teaspoon white pepper
1/4 teaspoon nutmeg
2 ounces fat-free processed Swiss cheese
4 ounces Swiss cheese, grated
1/2 cup finely chopped green onions
9-inch unbaked pie crust
3 tablespoons grated fat-free Parmesan cheese

Preheat oven to 400°F. In a medium saucepan, cook broccoli in boiling water for 2 to 3 minutes or just until broccoli is tender-crisp. In a colander, chill under cold running water. Drain well and set aside. In a food processor, combine ricotta cheese, milk, eggs, salt, white pepper, and nutmeg. Blend until smooth. Add Swiss cheese and blend. Stir in broccoli and green onions. Pour into unbaked pie crust. Top with grated Parmesan cheese. Bake for 15 minutes. Reduce heat to 350°F and continue baking for 40 minutes or until golden brown on top and a knife inserted in the center comes out clean.

Note: It is important to have the broccoli cut into small bite-size pieces. Cut the stem pieces smaller than the flower pieces for more even cooking. A combination of fat-free and regular cheese is used in this recipe to reduce the fat, yet provide great flavor. Other cheeses of your choice can be used. Canned or sautéed mushrooms are a good addition to this quiche.

Nutritional information per serving:

Calories	245
Fat, gm.	13
Protein, gm.	16
Carbohydrate, gm.	16
Cholesterol, mg.	90
Fiber	medium

Cheesy Potato Pie

If you like potatoes, this may become a favorite meatless meal.
It can also be served as a side dish with a meat or poultry entrée.

Serves 4

1 tablespoon butter or margarine
1 medium onion, finely chopped
3 large potatoes
$\frac{1}{2}$ teaspoon salt
$\frac{1}{4}$ teaspoon white pepper
1 cup grated Swiss cheese
1 cup fat-free milk
2 eggs
1 teaspoon Dijon mustard
$\frac{1}{4}$ teaspoon salt
2 tablespoons chopped fresh parsley
Dash Tabasco sauce

Note: Potatoes have to be finely grated or they will not be completely tender when the pie is done. Potatoes can be grated with a hand grater but it is so much easier in a food processor.

Preheat oven to 375°F. Heavily butter a deep 9-inch pie pan. In a small skillet, melt butter. Add onion and cook over medium heat until translucent. Remove from heat. Peel and quarter potatoes. Place potatoes in food processor in batches. Process until finely grated. In a medium bowl, combine potatoes, onion, salt, and pepper. Stir to mix. Spoon into pie pan and press potatoes over bottom and sides of the pan to form a shell. Sprinkle cheese over potatoes. In a medium bowl, beat together milk, eggs, mustard, salt, parsley, and Tabasco. Pour into shell. Bake for 40 to 45 minutes or until set and golden brown.

Nutritional information per serving:

Calories	240
Fat, gm.	13
Protein, gm.	14
Carbohydrate, gm.	17
Cholesterol, mg.	125
Fiber	low

Corn Pudding

This can be served as a side dish or in larger portions as a meatless meal. Kids love it too.

Serves 4

¼ cup chopped onion

1 cup fat-free milk

2 eggs

1 tablespoon flour

½ teaspoon salt

¼ teaspoon white pepper

15 ounces canned corn

Preheat oven to 325°F. Butter an 8" x 8" baking pan. In a food processor or blender, combine onion, milk, eggs, flour, salt, and white pepper. Blend until smooth. Add corn and blend briefly. Some corn should remain intact. Pour into baking pan. Bake for 30 to 40 minutes or until knife inserted in the center comes out clean.

Nutritional information per serving:

Calories	185
Fat, gm.	3
Protein, gm.	8
Carbohydrate, gm.	32
Cholesterol, mg.	90
Fiber	high

Golden Garden Vegetable Casserole

This is a create-your-own type casserole. Use any fresh or frozen vegetables of your choice.

Serves 6

5 cups mixed fresh or frozen vegetables
1 cup shredded reduced-fat Cheddar cheese
1 cup shredded reduced-fat mozzarella cheese
4 eggs
1 cup fat-free milk
1 teaspoon Italian seasoning
$1/4$ cup chopped fresh parsley
$1/2$ teaspoon salt
$1/4$ teaspoon freshly ground pepper
$1/4$ tablespoon paprika

Note: Top with extra shredded cheese if desired.

Preheat oven to 350°F. Grease a 2-quart casserole dish. In a large saucepan, blanch the vegetables in boiling water for 2 to 3 minutes. Drain well. In a large bowl, combine vegetables, Cheddar cheese, and mozzarella cheese. In a small bowl, combine eggs, milk, Italian seasoning, parsley, salt, and pepper. Beat well. Pour into bowl with vegetables. Stir until mixed. Pour into casserole. Sprinkle with paprika. Bake for 45 minutes or until knife inserted in the middle comes out clean.

Nutritional information per serving:

Calories	215
Fat, gm.	8
Protein, gm.	17
Carbohydrate, gm.	18
Cholesterol, mg.	135
Fiber	high

Light Fettuccine Alfredo

*The old-time recipes for fettuccine Alfredo are loaded with calories and fat.
This is a great low-fat adaptation. It can be served as a side dish or as an entrée.*

Serves 4

1 tablespoon butter or margarine
2 cloves garlic, minced
1 tablespoon flour
1 1/4 cups fat-free half-and-half
2 tablespoons low-fat cream cheese
3/4 cup grated fresh Parmesan cheese
2 tablespoons chopped fresh parsley
1/4 teaspoon white pepper
Salt to taste
8 ounces fettuccine
Freshly ground pepper to taste

Note: If this is the main entrée for 4, you may want to double the recipe.

1. In a medium skillet, melt butter. Add garlic and cook for 1 minute. Add flour and cook, stirring constantly, for 2 minutes. Add half-and-half and cook, stirring constantly, until mixture thickens. Stir in cream cheese and Parmesan cheese. Add parsley and season with white pepper and salt. Reduce heat to warm.

2. In a large saucepan, cook fettuccine in boiling water until al dente. Drain well. Stir fettuccine into cheese mixture. Serve with freshly ground pepper to taste. Offer additional grated Parmesan cheese if desired.

Nutritional information per serving:

Calories	365
Fat, gm.	9
Protein, gm.	16
Carbohydrate, gm.	55
Cholesterol, mg.	25
Fiber	low

Mediterranean Couscous Salad

*This is so attractive and very tasty. It may be served
as an entrée or as a side dish. It is lovely on a buffet table.*

Serves 4

1 large tomato, seeded and chopped
1/2 cup chopped scallions
1/4 cup chopped fresh mint
15 ounces canned kidney beans, drained
2 cups cooked couscous
4 ounces low-fat Swiss cheese, cubed
1/4 cup chopped walnuts

Dressing:

2 tablespoons fresh lemon juice
2 tablespoons extra-virgin olive oil
1/4 teaspoon salt
1/4 teaspoon freshly ground pepper
Dash hot pepper sauce

In a large bowl, combine tomatoes, scallions, mint, kidney beans, couscous, cheese, and walnuts. In a small jar, combine lemon juice, olive oil, salt, pepper, and hot pepper sauce. Shake until well mixed. Pour over couscous mixture. Stir gently to blend. Refrigerate until ready to serve.

Nutritional information per serving:

Calories	325
Fat, gm.	10
Protein, gm.	18
Carbohydrate, gm.	41
Cholesterol, mg.	10
Fiber	high

Mexican Macaroni Salad

Some like it hot!

Serves 6

8 ounces elbow macaroni
15 ounces canned hot chili beans, drained
4 ounces reduced-fat mozzarella cheese, diced

Dressing:

¾ cup fat-free or low-fat mayonnaise
¼ cup finely chopped onion
1 teaspoon chili powder
⅛ teaspoon garlic powder
Dash hot pepper sauce
Salt and freshly ground pepper to taste

Note: For a milder dish, substitute kidney beans for the hot chili beans.

In a large saucepan, cook macaroni in boiling salted water just until tender. (Do not overcook.) Drain. Rinse immediately under cold running water. Drain well. In a large bowl, combine macaroni, chili beans, and cheese. In a small bowl, combine mayonnaise, onion, chili powder, garlic powder, and hot pepper sauce. Combine with macaroni and beans. Gently mix well. Adjust seasoning with salt, pepper, and extra hot pepper sauce if desired. Refrigerate until ready to serve.

Nutritional information per serving:

Calories	265
Fat, gm.	4
Protein, gm.	13
Carbohydrate, gm.	44
Cholesterol, mg.	10
Fiber	high

Mushroom Nut Loaf

This is an unusual but very tasty recipe that comes from a friend in California who is a vegetarian. I served this in small portions as an appetizer at a large family gathering and I know it passed with flying colorswhen even my dad liked it.

Serves 8

3 eggs, lightly beaten
$^3/_4$ cup chopped walnuts
2 cups grated Cheddar cheese
$1^1/_2$ cups ($^1/_4$ pound) finely chopped fresh mushrooms
$^1/_2$ cup finely chopped onion
$^1/_2$ teaspoon garlic powder
1 tablespoon soy sauce
2 cups cooked rice

Preheat oven to 350°F. Butter a 9" x 9" baking pan or casserole dish. In a large bowl, combine all ingredients. Pour into pan. Bake for 45 minutes or until set in the middle.

Notes:

• This can be served as an entrée or it can be cut into small squares to serve as an appetizer.
• For a larger quantity, double the recipe and use a 9" x 13" pan.
• For a Garden Loaf, use this recipe but substitute $2^1/_2$ cups of finely chopped vegetables for the mushrooms and add 1 teaspoon of basil.
• As an entrée, this dish is good served with Sherry Mushroom Sauce (page 263).

Nutritional information per serving without sauce:

Calories	220
Fat, gm.	12
Protein, gm.	11
Carbohydrate, gm.	17
Cholesterol, mg.	100
Fiber	high

Pasta with Garlic Tomato Sauce

This is as simple as combining seasoned canned tomatoes with the pasta of your choice. The textured soy protein flakes can be omitted, but it looks and tastes like there is meat in the sauce when it is added. The soy also adds protein to the sauce.

Serves 6

1 tablespoon olive oil
1 medium onion, finely chopped
1/2 red bell pepper, diced
2 cloves garlic, minced
30 ounces canned garlic-seasoned crushed tomatoes
15 ounces tomato sauce
1 teaspoon Italian seasoning
1 teaspoon sugar
1/8 teaspoon red pepper flakes, optional
1/3 cup textured soy protein flakes
1/4 cup Burgundy or red wine
1/2 cup grated Parmesan cheese
Salt and freshly ground pepper to taste

Note: Other seasoned crushed tomatoes may be used if desired.

In a large skillet heat olive oil. Add onion and cook over medium heat until translucent. Add red pepper and garlic and cook until soft. Add tomatoes, tomato sauce, Italian seasoning, sugar, red pepper flakes, and soy protein. Bring to a boil. Reduce heat, and simmer for 30 minutes or until sauce reaches desired consistency and flavors have blended. Add water if sauce becomes too thick. When ready to serve, add wine and heat through. Add salt and pepper. Serve over cooked pasta. Top individual servings with grated cheese.

Nutritional information per serving without pasta:

Calories	130
Fat, gm.	5
Protein, gm.	8
Carbohydrate, gm.	14
Cholesterol, mg.	5
Fiber	high

Potato and Pepper Frittata

This lovely meatless meal is good for breakfast, lunch, or supper. It is easier to make than an omelet but it looks as though you went to a lot of work. Add any other vegetables of your choice.

Serves 3

2 large potatoes (about 1 pound), peeled and quartered
1 tablespoon butter or margarine
1/2 medium red bell pepper, diced
1/2 medium green bell pepper, diced
1/4 cup chopped green onions
6 eggs
2 tablespoons water
1/2 teaspoon salt
1/4 teaspoon freshly ground pepper
1/2 cup shredded reduced-fat Cheddar cheese

Note: For 1 or 2 servings, cut the recipe in half and use a 7-inch nonstick skillet.

1. In a small saucepan, cook potatoes in 2 inches of water for about 30 minutes, or until fork-tender. Remove from heat, drain, and set aside. When cool, dice potatoes.

2. Preheat broiler. Melt butter in a 10-inch nonstick, ovenproof skillet. Add potatoes and brown lightly. Add peppers and onions and cook until tender-crisp. In a small bowl, beat eggs, water, salt, and pepper. Pour egg mixture into skillet. Cook over medium heat. With a wide spatula, lift cooked portions of egg and allow uncooked egg mixture to flow under cooked portion. Continue cooking until almost set. Sprinkle with cheese. Place pan under the broiler and cook until the cheese melts and the top puffs up slightly and browns. Cut into wedges and serve.

Nutritional information per serving:

Calories	280
Fat, gm.	13
Protein, gm.	18
Carbohydrate, gm.	23
Cholesterol, mg.	375
Fiber	medium

Spinach Cheese Pie

This is an extremely attractive dish and the bonus is that it is low in calories and fat too.
There is no high-fat crust and the combination of regular and fat-free cheese is the secret.

Serves 8

6 eggs
1 1/2 cups fat-free milk
1 1/2 cups grated Swiss cheese, divided
2 ounces fat-free processed Swiss cheese, cut into small pieces
2 slices bread, torn in small pieces
1/3 cup finely chopped onion
1 teaspoon salt
1/2 teaspoon white pepper
1/8 teaspoon nutmeg
10 ounces frozen chopped spinach, thawed and squeezed dry
1/2 cup fat-free sour cream, optional

....

Note: The calories and fat are low but the flavor is great because of the combination of regular Swiss cheese with fat-free processed Swiss cheese. Use all regular cheese if you prefer.

Preheat oven to 350°F. Butter a 9-inch pie pan. In a large bowl, beat eggs until light. Add milk, 1 cup grated Swiss cheese, processed Swiss cheese, bread, onion, salt, white pepper, nutmeg, and spinach. Spoon into pie pan. Top with remaining 1/2 cup Swiss cheese. Bake for 45 to 50 minutes or until it is golden brown and knife inserted in the center comes out clean. Let stand for 5 minutes before cutting. Garnish each serving with a dollop of sour cream if desired.

Nutritional information per serving:

Calories	190
Fat, gm.	9
Protein, gm.	16
Carbohydrate, gm.	11
Cholesterol, mg.	160
Fiber	low

Spinach Manicotti

Choose this recipe when you have some time to play in the kitchen. It is not hard but it takes several pans and some time to assemble. The white sauce with a hint of nutmeg is a fantastic flavor combination with the spinach and pasta.

Serves 6
Sauce:

4 tablespoons butter or margarine

$^1/_4$ cup flour

$^1/_4$ teaspoon basil

$^1/_4$ teaspoon nutmeg

12 ounces evaporated fat-free milk

$^1/_4$ cup fat-free milk

14 ounces fat-free chicken broth

Salt and freshly ground pepper to taste

Note: If you prefer a tomato sauce with manicotti, use the recipe for Garlic Tomato Sauce (page 79).

Filling:

10 ounces frozen spinach, thawed and squeezed dry

2 cups fat-free ricotta cheese

4 ounces canned sliced mushrooms, drained

$^1/_4$ cup chopped green onions

$^1/_4$ teaspoon freshly ground pepper

$^1/_4$ teaspoon salt

8 ounces manicotti (12 individual pieces), cooked and drained

1 cup shredded reduced-fat Cheddar cheese

1. Preheat oven to 325°F. Grease a 9" x 13" baking pan. In a medium saucepan, melt butter. Add flour and cook, stirring constantly over medium heat, for 3 minutes. Add basil, nutmeg, evaporated milk, milk, and broth. Cook, stirring constantly, until mixture boils and thickens. Adjust seasonings with salt and pepper. Pour half of the sauce into the baking pan and set the remainder aside.

2. In a bowl, combine spinach, ricotta cheese, mushrooms, onions, pepper, and salt. Divide mixture into 12 portions. Stuff the cooked shells with spinach mixture. Lay shells over sauce in the pan. Cover with remaining sauce. Sprinkle with Cheddar cheese. Loosely cover with foil and bake for 15 to 20 minutes or until heated through. (Increase baking time if the recipe has been made ahead and refrigerated.)

Nutritional information per serving:

Calories	390
Fat, gm.	10
Protein, gm.	29
Carbohydrate, gm.	46
Cholesterol, mg.	40
Fiber	high

Stuffed Bell Peppers

These are very attractive and the Italian-seasoned stuffing is great.
They can be served as a main meatless entrée or cut in half for an impressive vegetable side dish.

Serves 4

$1/2$ cup long-grain r ice
4 large red or green bell peppers
$1/2$ teaspoon salt
$1/2$ teaspoon freshly ground pepper, divided
$1/2$ tablespoon vegetable oil
$1/2$ cup finely chopped onion
8 ounces tomato sauce
$1/3$ cup water
2 teaspoons Italian seasoning
11 ounces canned corn, drained
$1^{1}/2$ cups shredded reduced-fat Cheddar cheese, divided

Note: This serves 4 as an entrée or 8 as a side dish. For a side dish, use a 9" x 13" pan, cut peppers in half lengthwise, and stuff.

1. Cook rice in 1 cup water for 20 minutes or until water is absorbed. Set aside. Preheat oven to 350°F. Grease a 9" x 9" baking pan. Cut tops off peppers and clean out inside seeds and membranes. Sprinkle inside with salt and $1/4$ teaspoon pepper.

2. In a small nonstick skillet, heat oil. Add onion and cook over medium heat until translucent. Add tomato sauce, water, Italian seasoning, and $1/4$ teaspoon pepper. Simmer for 10 minutes. Stir in corn, rice, and 1 cup of cheese. Stuff peppers and place in baking pan. Sprinkle with remaining cheese. Bake for 40 to 50 minutes or until peppers are tender-crisp.

Nutritional information per serving:

Calories	320
Fat, gm.	6
Protein, gm.	16
Carbohydrate, gm.	50
Cholesterol, mg.	10
Fiber	high

Sun-Dried Tomatoes and Mushrooms with Linguine

A tasty light dish with the appearance of richness but very low in fat.

Serves 4

8 sun-dried tomato halves
12 ounces linguine
1 tablespoon olive oil
¾ pound fresh mushrooms
¼ teaspoon rosemary, crushed
¼ teaspoon Italian seasoning or oregano
2 cloves garlic, minced
15 ounces low-fat chicken broth, divided
2 tablespoons cornstarch
Salt and freshly ground pepper to taste
⅓ cup freshly grated Parmesan cheese
¼ cup chopped fresh parsley

1. Place sun-dried tomatoes in a small bowl of boiling water. Set aside. Cook linguine in a large saucepan of boiling water until just tender. Drain and set aside. In a large skillet, heat oil over medium heat. Add mushrooms, rosemary, and Italian seasoning. Cook until mushrooms are tender. Add garlic and cook for 1 minute. In a small custard cup, mix ¼ cup of the broth with cornstarch. Add to the skillet with remaining broth. Bring to a boil, stirring constantly until mixture thickens to desired consistency. Add extra broth if mixture is too thick.

2. Remove tomatoes from water and dice. Add to broth. Add linguine and heat through. Add salt and freshly ground pepper to taste. Top with freshly grated Parmesan cheese when ready to serve. Garnish with fresh parsley.

Nutritional information per serving:

Calories	575
Fat, gm.	9
Protein, gm.	23
Carbohydrate, gm.	100
Cholesterol, mg.	5
Fiber	very high

Swiss Corn Bake

This makes a tasty meatless meal, or served in smaller amounts, it is an interesting side dish.

**Serves 8 as a side dish
or 4 as a meatless entrée**

1 tablespoon butter or margarine
1 small onion, finely chopped
1/2 medium red bell pepper, finely chopped
16 ounces frozen corn, thawed
1 cup evaporated fat-free milk
1 egg, lightly beaten
1/4 teaspoon white pepper
1/2 teaspoon salt
1 1/2 cups grated reduced-fat Swiss cheese, divided
2 tablespoons seasoned bread crumbs

Preheat oven to 325°F. Butter a 1 1/2-quart casserole. In a small skillet, melt butter. Add onion and cook over medium heat until translucent. Add bell pepper and cook until tender. In a large bowl, combine onion-pepper mixture, corn, milk, egg, white pepper, salt, and 1 cup of the cheese. Stir until well mixed. Pour into casserole. Top with bread crumbs and remaining Swiss cheese. Bake for 60 minutes or until a knife inserted in the center comes out clean.

Nutritional information per serving:

Calories	300
Fat, gm.	7
Protein, gm.	22
Carbohydrate, gm.	37
Cholesterol, mg.	70
Fiber	high

Taco Cheese Pie

This can be a great meatless meal or cut it into small pieces for an appetizer.
To dress up this spicy pie, serve it with sliced avocados, salsa, and a dollop of fat-free sour cream.

Serves 6

2 cups grated reduced-fat Monterey jack cheese, divided
9-inch unbaked pie crust
1 tablespoon butter or margarine
1 medium onion, finely chopped
1/2 medium red bell pepper, diced
1/2 medium green bell pepper, diced
3 tablespoons taco seasoning mix
2 eggs
1/4 cup flour
1 cup fat-free milk
1 cup salsa or picante sauce

Note: Use any cheese of your choice. A pizza cheese mixture works well.

1. Preheat oven to 375°F. If using a glass or nonstick pan, preheat oven to 350°F. Sprinkle 1/2 cup cheese in bottom of pie crust. Set aside. In a small skillet, melt butter. Add onion and peppers. Cook over medium heat until tender. Add taco seasoning and cook 1 more minute. Remove from heat.

2. In a medium bowl, beat eggs, flour, and milk together. Add onion-pepper mixture and 1 cup of cheese. Stir until well mixed. Pour into pie shell. Top with remaining 1/2 cup of cheese. Bake for 45 to 55 minutes or until pie is firm and knife inserted in the middle comes out clean. Allow to set at room temperature for 10 minutes before cutting. Serve with salsa or picante sauce on the side.

Nutritional information per serving:

Calories	300
Fat, gm.	16
Protein, gm.	15
Carbohydrate, gm.	24
Cholesterol, mg.	75
Fiber	low

Vegetarian Chili

Developed by my friend and colleague Ann Martin, this meatless chili recipe that tastes as good as regular chili thanks to the bulgur. Bulgur is made from branless wheat kernels that are partially cooked and then cracked. When the bulgur is cooked in this chili, it has the appearance, texture, and taste of ground beef.

Serves 8

1 tablespoon olive oil
1 medium onion, chopped
1 medium green bell pepper, diced
1 stalk celery, diced
2 cloves garlic, minced
2 large carrots, peeled and chopped
30 ounces canned kidney beans, undrained
30 ounces canned crushed tomatoes, undrained
15 ounces canned Italian seasoned diced tomatoes
8 ounces green chilies, chopped
3/4 cup bulgur wheat
1 tablespoon chili powder
1/2 teaspoon cumin
Dash Tabasco sauce, optional
Salt and freshly ground pepper to taste
1 cup shredded reduced-fat Cheddar cheese

In a large heavy saucepan or deep skillet, heat oil. Add onion and cook until translucent. Add bell pepper, celery, and garlic and cook until tender. Add carrots, kidney beans, tomatoes, chilies, bulgur, chili powder, and cumin. Bring to a boil. Reduce heat and boil gently for 30 to 40 minutes or until bulgur is tender and chili is reduced to the desired consistency. Stir occasionally. Add Tabasco, salt, and pepper to taste. Top each serving with shredded cheese.

Nutritional information per serving:

Calories	245
Fat, gm.	4
Protein, gm.	13
Carbohydrate, gm.	39
Cholesterol, mg.	5
Fiber	very high

Veggie Cheese Pie

This is a very beautiful dish. It may be served as an entrée or as a vegetable side dish.
Leftovers warm up beautifully in the microwave.

Serves 6

4 slices whole-wheat bread, cubed
2 cups frozen mixed vegetables
1 1/2 cups shredded reduced-fat Cheddar cheese, divided
1 1/2 cups fat-free milk
2 eggs, lightly beaten
1/2 teaspoon dry mustard
1/2 teaspoon white pepper
1/2 teaspoon salt

Note: Choose the vegetables and the variety of cheese to suit your taste.

Preheat oven to 350°F. Butter a deep 9-inch pie pan. Arrange bread cubes in pie pan. Cook vegetables in boiling water for 2 minutes or just until tender-crisp. Drain well. Place vegetables over bread. Sprinkle with 1 cup cheese. In a small bowl, combine milk, eggs, dry mustard, white pepper, and salt. Pour into pan. Sprinkle with remaining 1/2 cup cheese. Bake for 45 to 50 minutes or until knife inserted in the middle comes out clean. Let stand for 10 minutes before serving.

Nutritional information per serving:

Calories	215
Fat, gm.	7
Protein, gm.	15
Carbohydrate, gm.	23
Cholesterol, mg.	75
Fiber	high

Wild Rice and Mushroom Casserole

This looks elegant and complicated but it is fast and easy. The flavor is wonderful!

Serves 4

1 tablespoon butter or margarine
1/2 medium onion, chopped
1/2 pound fresh mushrooms, sliced
1 tablespoon flour
3/4 cup fat-free milk
1/4 teaspoon Italian seasoning
1/8 teaspoon nutmeg
1/2 teaspoon salt
1/8 teaspoon white pepper
2 cups cooked wild rice*
1/3 cup chopped pecans, optional

Note: Other spices or herbs of your choice can be substituted for the Italian seasoning. A wild rice and brown rice blend can be substituted for all wild rice.

*Cook 2/3 cup of wild rice in 3 cups of water with a chicken bouillon cube to make 2 cups cooked rice. When rice is done, drain well.

Preheat oven to 350°F. Butter a 1 1/2-quart casserole. In a medium skillet, melt butter. Cook onion over medium heat until translucent. Add mushrooms and cook until tender. In a shaker, mix flour and milk until smooth. Add to the pan. Bring to a boil stirring constantly until mixture thickens. Add Italian seasoning, nutmeg, salt, and white pepper. Stir to blend. Spoon rice into casserole. Pour sauce over the top. Mix gently. Top with nuts if desired. Bake for 20 to 25 minutes or until heated through.

Nutritional information per serving:

Calories	150
Fat, gm.	3
Protein, gm.	6
Carbohydrate, gm.	24
Cholesterol, mg.	5
Fiber	high

Zucchini Casserole

This can be served as a meatless entrée or a vegetable side dish.

Serves 8

2 tablespoons butter or margarine
6 cups sliced zucchini
1 cup shredded carrots
$^1/_2$ cup chopped onion
$^1/_4$ teaspoon salt
$^1/_4$ teaspoon freshly ground pepper
$2^1/_2$ cups herb-seasoned stuffing cubes, divided
1 can (10$^3/_4$ ounces) cream of mushroom soup
$^1/_2$ cup fat-free sour cream
Butter spray

Preheat oven to 350°F. Butter a 1$^1/_2$-quart casserole. In a large skillet, melt butter. Add zucchini, carrots, and onion. Cook until vegetables are tender-crisp. Remove from heat. Add salt, pepper, 1$^1/_2$ cups of the stuffing cubes, soup, and sour cream. Stir to mix well. Spoon into casserole. Top with remaining stuffing cubes. Spray with butter spray. Bake for 30 to 40 minutes or until heated through.

Nutritional information per serving:

Calories	190
Fat, gm.	5
Protein, gm.	7
Carbohydrate, gm.	35
Cholesterol, mg.	10
Fiber	medium

Chapter Five
Casseroles and Pasta

Baked Chicken and Rice

Beef Goulash

Beef, Spinach, and Noodle Casserole

Broccoli and Ham Strata

Chicken and Artichoke Casserole

Chicken Cashew Casserole

Chicken Cordon Bleu Casserole

Chicken Pie

Chow Mein Casserole

Hamburger and Macaroni Casserole

Kielbasa, Cabbage, and Potatoes

Layered Dinner

Linguine Carbonara

Moroccan Chicken and Vegetables with Couscous

No Peek Beef Stew

Potato Vegetable Bake

Shepherd's Pie

Sicilian Supper

Spaghetti Pie

Tuna Noodle Casserole

Turkey Tetrazzini

Baked Chicken and Rice

*This is one of the easiest casseroles you will ever prepare. It can be put together in 3 minutes.
It doesn't take any mixing bowls and it bakes without any attention. Kids love it.*

Serves 4

1 can (10³/4 ounces) cream of chicken soup
1 cup water
³/4 cup uncooked rice
1/2 teaspoon paprika, divided
1/4 teaspoon white pepper
4 boned and skinned chicken breast halves
1/4 teaspoon salt
1/4 teaspoon freshly ground pepper

Preheat oven to 375°F. In an 8" x 8" baking pan, mix soup, water, rice, 1/4 teaspoon paprika, and white pepper. Sprinkle chicken with salt, pepper, and 1/4 teaspoon paprika. Place on top of rice mixture. Cover tightly with aluminum foil. Bake for 45 to 60 minutes or until rice is tender and chicken is completely done.

Nutritional information per serving:

Calories	250
Fat, gm.	4
Protein, gm.	24
Carbohydrate, gm.	30
Cholesterol, mg.	50
Fiber	low

Beef Goulash

Didn't every grandma or mother make some form of goulash?
This one will bring back memories of family suppers together.

Serves 6

1 tablespoon vegetable oil
2 pounds beef top round, cubed
1/2 teaspoon salt
1/2 teaspoon freshly ground pepper
1 large onion, chopped
3 cloves garlic, minced
2 1/2 cups fat-free beef broth, divided
1 tablespoon paprika
4 large carrots, peeled and sliced
4 medium potatoes, peeled and diced
1/4 cup tomato paste
3 tablespoons flour
1 1/2 cups frozen peas
1 cup fat-free sour cream

1. Preheat oven to 325°F. In a large ovenproof pan, heat vegetable oil. Cook beef over medium-hot heat until brown on all sides. Sprinkle with salt and pepper. Reduce heat to medium and add onion. Cook until onion is translucent. Add garlic and cook for 1 minute. Add 2 cups of beef broth, paprika, carrots, potatoes, and tomato paste. Cover and bake in oven for 2 hours or until meat is tender. Check occasionally and add water if it gets too dry.

2. Remove from oven and place pan on the stove. If the gravy needs to be thickened, mix flour in 1/2 cup of beef broth in a shaker. Pour into pan, stirring constantly, until mixture comes to a boil and reaches desired consistency. When ready to serve, stir in peas and sour cream. Heat through but do not boil. Serve on cooked noodles.

Nutritional information per serving without noodles:

Calories	430
Fat, gm.	16
Protein, gm.	41
Carbohydrate, gm.	31
Cholesterol, mg.	100
Fiber	high

Beef, Spinach, and Noodle Casserole

It takes a little time to put this casserole together but it is worth the extra effort. It is colorful, attractive, and very good. This recipe was adapted from a rich and decadent old recipe. It still tastes rich but it really isn't.

Serves 8

8 ounces noodles
1 pound extra-lean ground beef
1 medium onion, finely chopped
23 ounces tomato sauce*
1/2 teaspoon basil
1/2 teaspoon oregano
1/2 teaspoon sugar
1/4 teaspoon garlic powder
1/2 teaspoon salt
1/4 teaspoon freshly ground pepper
1 cup fat-free sour cream
8 ounces fat-free or low-fat cream cheese, room temperature
1/2 cup fat-free milk
10 ounces frozen spinach, thawed and squeezed dry
1 cup shredded reduced-fat Cheddar cheese

*Use one 15-ounce can and one 8-ounce can of sauce.

1. Preheat oven to 350°F. Grease a 9" x 13" baking pan. In a large saucepan cook noodles in boiling water until al dente. Drain and set aside. In a large skillet cook beef until brown and completely done. Add onion and cook until translucent. Drain off any fat. Stir in tomato sauce, basil, oregano, sugar, garlic powder, salt, and pepper. Bring to a boil; reduce heat and simmer for 10 minutes. In a small bowl combine sour cream, cream cheese, and milk. Beat until smooth with an electric mixer. Set aside.

2. To assemble casserole layer half the noodles, half the meat, half the cream cheese mixture, and all the spinach. Top with remaining noodles and meat. Cover and bake for 30 minutes. Remove from oven and spread with the remaining cream cheese mixture. Top with Cheddar cheese. Bake uncovered for 10 minutes or until cheese has melted.

Nutritional information per serving:

Calories	355
Fat, gm.	12
Protein, gm.	26
Carbohydrate, gm.	36
Cholesterol, mg.	80
Fiber	medium

Broccoli and Ham Strata

This recipe has special meaning because I prepared it for my daughter's christening brunch 25 years ago.

Serves 8

10 ounces frozen chopped broccoli

10 slices bread

2 cups shredded reduced-fat Cheddar cheese

1 pound lean ham, diced

6 eggs

3½ cups fat-free milk

¼ cup minced onion

½ teaspoon salt

½ teaspoon freshly ground pepper

½ teaspoon dry mustard

¼ teaspoon nutmeg

1 teaspoon steak sauce

Note: Strata recipes work best when the bread is partially dry. If using fresh bread, lightly toast it in the oven.

1. Butter a 9" x 13" baking pan. In a small saucepan, cook broccoli in boiling water for 2 minutes. Drain well and set aside. Using a cookie cutter or a glass, cut bread slices into circles. Set these aside. Cut the remaining scraps of bread into cubes and place in the baking pan. Sprinkle cheese over bread. Layer broccoli over cheese. Layer ham over broccoli. Arrange round pieces of bread on top. In a medium bowl, combine all remaining ingredients. Beat until well mixed. Pour over the bread. Cover pan and refrigerate for several hours or overnight.

2. When ready to bake, preheat oven to 325°F. Bake, uncovered, for 55 to 65 minutes or until knife inserted in the middle comes out clean. Let set for 10 to 15 minutes before cutting.

Nutritional information per serving:

Calories	290
Fat, gm.	9
Protein, gm.	29
Carbohydrate, gm.	24
Cholesterol, mg.	170
Fiber	medium

Chicken and Artichoke Casserole

Make this ahead and refrigerate it for a day or more before serving.
It is a wonderful, tasty casserole.

Serves 8

1 tablespoon canola oil
4 boned and skinned chicken breast halves, cubed
1 large red bell pepper, thinly sliced
1/2 cup chopped green onions
2 cups peeled and julienne-sliced carrots
5 tablespoons butter or margarine
1/3 cup flour
1/2 teaspoon salt
1/4 teaspoon white pepper
14 ounces fat-free chicken broth
12 ounces evaporated fat-free milk
1/4 cup dry sherry
6 slices bacon, cooked and crumbled, divided
1 cup shredded mozzarella cheese
14 ounces artichoke hearts, drained and quartered
1 1/2 cups frozen peas
4 cups cooked noodles
1/4 cup bread crumbs

Preheat oven to 350°F. Butter a 9" x 13" baking dish. In a large nonstick skillet, heat oil. Add chicken cubes and cook over medium-hot heat until lightly browned. Add red pepper, onions, and carrots. Add 1/4 cup water, cover, and cook until tender. Remove from heat and set aside. In a large heavy saucepan, melt butter. Add flour and cook over medium heat for 2 minutes, stirring constantly. Whisk in salt, pepper, chicken broth, and milk. Bring to a boil, stirring constantly until sauce boils and thickens. Stir in sherry, half of crumbled bacon, mozzarella cheese, artichoke hearts, peas, cooked noodles, and reserved chicken-vegetable mixture. Spoon into baking pan. Cover with foil and bake for 30 minutes. Uncover, sprinkle with remaining diced bacon and bread crumbs. Bake an additional 20 minutes.

Nutritional information per serving:

Calories	405
Fat, gm.	17
Protein, gm.	25
Carbohydrate, gm.	38
Cholesterol, mg.	80
Fiber	very high

Chicken Cashew Casserole

This is an old-time crunchy casserole with lots of flavor.
It was a standard at big family potlucks.

Serves 6

1 tablespoon butter or margarine
4 boned and skinned chicken breast halves
1 medium onion, finely chopped
1 stalk celery, finely chopped
1/2 pound mushrooms, sliced
1/2 cup low-fat chicken broth
1 can (10¾ ounces) reduced-fat cream of mushroom soup
1 cup frozen green peas
1/4 teaspoon white pepper
1/4 teaspoon salt
3 cups chow mein noodles, divided
1/3 cup chopped cashews

Preheat oven to 350°F. Butter a 1½-quart casserole. In a large nonstick skillet, melt butter. Cut chicken into bite-size pieces and cook over medium heat until brown and thoroughly cooked. Add onion and cook until translucent. Add celery and mushrooms and cook until tender. Add chicken broth and stir to deglaze the pan. Add soup, peas, white pepper, salt, and 2 cups of the chow mein noodles. Spoon into casserole. Top with 1 cup chow mein noodles and cashews. Bake for 30 minutes.

Note: This casserole is also very good made with regular egg noodles in place of the chow mein noodles. Substitute 3 cups of cooked noodles for the 2 cups of chow mein noodles that are blended with the chicken and vegetable mixture. Top the casserole with 1 cup of chow mein noodles and 1/3 cup of chopped cashews. If you are counting on leftovers, this one warms up better.

Nutritional information per serving:

Calories	330
Fat, gm.	14
Protein, gm.	20
Carbohydrate, gm.	31
Cholesterol, mg.	40
Fiber	high

Chicken Cordon Bleu Casserole

This recipe has been a favorite for years.

Serves 4

2 tablespoons butter or margarine

4 boned and skinned chicken breast halves

2 cups seasoned bread stuffing cubes

4 ounces lean ham slices

1 cup shredded reduced-fat Cheddar cheese

1 can (10¾ ounces) low-fat cream of mushroom soup

Note: Swiss cheese or other cheese of your choice can be substituted for the Cheddar cheese.

Preheat oven to 325°F. Butter a 7" x 11" or a 9" x 9" baking pan. Melt butter in a medium skillet. Add chicken and quickly fry over medium-hot heat until brown on all sides. Remove chicken from pan and set aside on a plate. (Chicken does not need to be completely cooked at this point.) Add stuffing cubes to the skillet. Stir to absorb any remaining butter and juice. Place ¾ of stuffing cubes in bottom of baking pan. Layer chicken, ham, and then cheese over stuffing. Top with soup. Sprinkle with remaining stuffing mixture. Bake for 60 minutes.

Nutritional information per serving:

Calories	375
Fat, gm.	16
Protein, gm.	37
Carbohydrate, gm.	21
Cholesterol, mg.	90
Fiber	low

Chicken Pie

This is a very old recipe. Some say it was even used by Martha Washington. If you would like the flavor of an old-time chicken pie but don't want to work as hard as Martha Washington, substitute refrigerated biscuits for the homemade biscuits.

Serves 6

2 tablespoons butter or margarine
4 boned and skinned chicken breast halves, diced
1 medium onion, chopped
1/2 pound fresh mushrooms, sliced
1/3 cup flour
4 cups low-fat chicken broth, divided
1/2 teaspoon basil
1 pound frozen mixed vegetables
Salt and freshly ground pepper to taste

Topping:

Buttermilk Baking Powder Biscuits (recipe on page 235) or use commercial canned biscuits

1. Preheat oven to 425°F. Grease a 9" x 13" baking pan. In a large nonstick skillet, melt butter. Add chicken and fry over medium heat until brown and thoroughly cooked. Add onion and mushrooms and cook until tender. Mix flour and 1 cup of broth in a shaker until smooth. Add this mixture and remaining chicken broth to pan. Cook, stirring constantly, until mixture thickens. Add basil and mixed vegetables. Reduce heat and cook for 5 to 8 minutes or until vegetables are tender-crisp. Add additional broth if mixture is too thick. Add salt and pepper to taste. Pour into baking pan.

2. *Topping:* Prepare Buttermilk Baking Powder Biscuits. Place biscuits on top of casserole. Bake for 10 to 15 minutes or until biscuits are golden brown.

Nutritional information per serving without biscuits:

Calories	195
Fat, gm.	5
Protein, gm.	19
Carbohydrate, gm.	18
Cholesterol, mg.	45
Fiber	high

Chow Mein Casserole

This is the classic church potluck casserole.

Serves 6

1 pound extra-lean ground beef
1 medium onion, finely chopped
2 stalks celery, diced
1 can (10¾ ounces) reduced-fat cream of mushroom soup
2 tablespoons soy sauce
1¼ cups low-fat chicken broth
¾ cup white rice
1 cup frozen green peas
1 cup chow mein noodles

Preheat oven to 350°F. Grease a 2-quart casserole. In a medium skillet, brown meat over medium heat. Add onion and celery and cook until tender. Drain any fat. Stir in soup, soy sauce, chicken broth, and rice. Bring to a boil. Spoon into casserole. Cover casserole. Bake for 40 to 45 minutes or until the rice is tender. Remove from oven. Add peas and stir to mix. Sprinkle with noodles. Return to oven and bake uncovered for 10 more minutes.

Nutritional information per serving:

Calories	360
Fat, gm.	13
Protein, gm.	27
Carbohydrate, gm.	33
Cholesterol, mg.	60
Fiber	low

Hamburger and Macaroni Casserole

When you are hungry for an old-fashioned casserole, try this one.

Serves 6

1 1/2 pounds extra-lean ground beef
1 medium onion, finely chopped
1 cup diced celery
1/2 medium green bell pepper, diced
15 ounces canned tomatoes
30 ounces tomato sauce
1 teaspoon salt
1/4 teaspoon celery salt, optional
1/8 teaspoon freshly ground black pepper
1 teaspoon Worcestershire sauce
2 cups cooked macaroni
4 ounces canned mushrooms, optional

Preheat oven to 350°F. In a large nonstick skillet, brown meat over medium heat. Add onion, celery, and bell pepper. Cook until tender. Drain any fat. Add all remaining ingredients. Spoon into 1 1/2-quart casserole. Bake for 30 to 40 minutes.

Nutritional information per serving:

Calories	410
Fat, gm.	16
Protein, gm.	38
Carbohydrate, gm.	29
Cholesterol, mg.	90
Fiber	high

Kielbasa, Cabbage, and Potatoes

This is a good Sunday night dinner.

Serves 6

1 tablespoon vegetable oil
1 pound reduced-fat kielbasa, cut into 1-inch-thick slices
1 large onion, chopped
3 large carrots, peeled and chopped
1 clove garlic, minced
6 cups coarsely chopped cabbage
2 pounds red potatoes, sliced
1 cup fat-free chicken broth
$^{1}/_{2}$ teaspoon caraway seeds, optional
Salt and freshly ground pepper to taste

In a large nonstick skillet, heat oil. Cook kielbasa until brown. Add onion and carrots and cook until onion is translucent. Add garlic and cook for 1 minute. Drain and discard fat. Add cabbage, sliced potatoes, broth, and caraway seeds. Bring to a boil; reduce heat, and cover pan. Simmer for 30 to 40 minutes or until potatoes and cabbage are tender. Check occasionally and add additional broth if needed. Season with salt and pepper to taste.

Nutritional information per serving:

Calories	330
Fat, gm.	16
Protein, gm.	16
Carbohydrate, gm.	30
Cholesterol, mg.	50
Fiber	high

Layered Dinner

This was adapted from an old church cookbook.

Serves 6

1 pound extra-lean ground beef
1 medium onion, chopped
1 teaspoon salt, divided
1/2 teaspoon freshly ground pepper, divided
6 medium potatoes, peeled and thinly sliced
1 1/2 cups peeled and sliced carrots
2 stalks celery, diced
15 ounces seasoned canned tomatoes
1/3 cup chicken broth
1 cup frozen peas

Note: This casserole can be baked the day before serving if desired. Refrigerate it overnight; then warm it in a 300°F oven.

1. Preheat oven to 325°F. Grease a 9" x 13" baking pan. In a medium nonstick skillet, brown beef. Add onion and cook until translucent. Drain off any meat fat. Sprinkle with salt and pepper. Set aside. Arrange potato slices in baking pan. Sprinkle with salt and pepper. Spoon ground beef and onions over potatoes. Layer carrots, celery, and tomatoes on top. Add chicken broth. Cover and bake for 60 to 70 minutes or until vegetables are tender.

2. Remove cover and top with peas. Gently stir peas into the tomato layer. Return to the oven and bake for an additional 5 minutes.

Nutritional information per serving:

Calories	325
Fat, gm.	10
Protein, gm.	27
Carbohydrate, gm.	32
Cholesterol, mg.	60
Fiber	high

Linguine Carbonara

One of my favorite restaurants serves a very rich linguine carbonara.
This is a low-fat adaptation and it tastes just as good.

Serves 4

4 slices bacon, chopped
2 cloves garlic, minced
$1/2$ pound fresh mushrooms, sliced
$1/2$ cup pitted green olives, sliced
$1/2$ cup white wine
$1/4$ teaspoon thyme
$1/4$ teaspoon oregano
1 pound frozen mixed vegetables
1 cup fat-free half-and-half
2 teaspoons cornstarch
$1/2$ cup grated Parmesan cheese
8 ounces linguine
Salt and freshly ground pepper to taste

Note: Choose the frozen or fresh vegetables you like best.

1. In a large skillet, fry bacon until crisp. Discard bacon fat, reserving 1 tablespoon in the pan. Add garlic and mushrooms. Cook until mushrooms are tender. Add olives, wine, thyme, oregano, and vegetables. Cover and cook until vegetables are tender. Combine half-and-half with cornstarch. Add to skillet and cook, stirring constantly, until mixture comes to a boil and thickens. Add cheese. Hold over low heat.

2. In a large saucepan cook linguine in boiling water until al dente. Drain well. Add cooked linguine to vegetables in the skillet. Toss to mix. Add salt and pepper to taste. Top each serving with extra Parmesan cheese if desired.

Nutritional information per serving:

Calories	450
Fat, gm.	9
Protein, gm.	20
Carbohydrate, gm.	72
Cholesterol, mg.	15
Fiber	high

Moroccan Chicken and Vegetables with Couscous

Chicken with white beans, tomatoes, and dried apricots are combined with a wonderful blend of aromatic spices.

Serves 6

1 tablespoon olive oil
4 boned and skinned chicken breasts, diced
$^1/_2$ teaspoon salt
$^1/_2$ teaspoon freshly ground pepper
1 large onion, diced
2 cloves garlic, minced
1-inch piece fresh gingerroot, peeled and minced
1 cup peeled and diced carrots
2 cups diced zucchini
1 medium red bell pepper, thinly sliced
15 ounces canned seasoned diced tomatoes
15 ounces canned chickpeas (garbanzo beans)
$^1/_2$ cup quartered dried apricot halves
$^1/_2$ teaspoon cumin
$^1/_2$ teaspoon coriander
$^1/_2$ teaspoon turmeric
1 tablespoon lemon zest
$^1/_2$ cup chicken broth, optional
3 cups cooked couscous

In a large skillet, heat oil. Add chicken and cook over medium-high heat until browned. Sprinkle with salt and pepper. Add onion and cook until translucent. Add garlic and ginger and cook for 1 minute. Add carrots, zucchini, red pepper, tomatoes, chickpeas, apricot halves, cumin, coriander, turmeric, and lemon zest. Cover and cook for 10 to 15 minutes or until vegetables are tender, stirring occasionally. Add chicken broth if desired. Adjust seasoning with salt and pepper to taste. To serve, spoon couscous into individual bowls. Spoon chicken and vegetable stew over couscous.

Nutritional information per serving:

Calories	370
Fat, gm.	4
Protein, gm.	35
Carbohydrate, gm.	49
Cholesterol, mg.	65
Fiber	very high

No Peek Beef Stew

This is a perfect recipe when you want a meal that everyone will love.
Double the recipe for a big family gathering.

Serves 8

1 tablespoon cooking oil
2 pounds beef top round, cut into cubes
1 large onion, diced
1 teaspoon salt
1/2 teaspoon freshly ground pepper
6 medium carrots, peeled and diced
6 medium potatoes, peeled and diced
2 stalks celery, diced
15 ounces stewed tomatoes
1 can (10¾ ounces) beef consommé or broth
1 teaspoon sugar
1/4 cup tapioca
1/2 cup Burgundy

Preheat oven to 275°F. In a large heavy Dutch oven, heat oil. Add meat and brown over medium heat. Add onion and cook until translucent. Sprinkle with salt and pepper. Add carrots, potatoes, celery, tomatoes, broth, sugar, and tapioca. Bring to a boil and cook for 10 minutes, stirring occasionally. Remove from heat. Add Burgundy. Cover tightly and bake for 4 hours or until meat is very tender. Add additional broth if it gets too dry or a thinner gravy is desired.

Note: The stew needs to be brought to a boil before placing in low-temperature oven in order to bring the mixture to a safe temperature quickly. The stew may also be cooked in a slow cooker in place of the oven.

Nutritional information per serving:

Calories	365
Fat, gm.	12
Protein, gm.	39
Carbohydrate, gm.	26
Cholesterol, mg.	90
Fiber	high

Potato Vegetable Bake

This is a nice blend of vegetables and potatoes that is mildly seasoned. Kids will like it.

Serves 8

1 tablespoon olive oil
1 medium onion, finely chopped
4 cups (14 ounces) frozen mixed vegetables, cut into bite-size pieces
2 tablespoons water
8 eggs
12 ounces evaporated fat-free milk
1/2 cup fat-free milk
2 teaspoons salt
1 teaspoon freshly ground pepper
1 teaspoon dry mustard
1 tablespoon Italian seasoning
1/2 teaspoon cumin
24 ounces frozen Southern-style hash brown potatoes
1 1/2 cups shredded low-fat Cheddar cheese, divided
1 cup salsa, optional

Note: Southern-style hash brown potatoes are cut into small cubes.

Preheat oven to 350°F. Butter a 9" x 13" baking pan. In a medium skillet, heat oil. Add onion and cook until lightly brown. Add vegetables and water. Cover and cook just until tender-crisp. Remove from heat and set aside. In a large bowl, combine eggs, evaporated milk, milk, salt, pepper, dry mustard, Italian seasoning, and cumin. Beat well. Stir in reserved vegetables, hash brown potatoes, and 1/2 of cheese. Spoon into baking pan. Cover pan with foil and bake for 45 minutes. Uncover pan and sprinkle with remaining cheese. Return to oven and bake for another 20 minutes or until center is set. Let stand for 10 minutes before serving. Serve with salsa on the side if desired.

Nutritional information per serving:

Calories	325
Fat, gm.	10
Protein, gm.	19
Carbohydrate, gm.	39
Cholesterol, mg.	200
Fiber	medium

Shepherd's Pie

*For those meat and mashed potato lovers. Add the vegetables
of your choice for a colorful and healthy old-fashioned dinner.*

Serves 4

1 pound extra-lean ground beef
1 medium onion, finely chopped
1/2 teaspoon salt
1/4 teaspoon freshly ground pepper
2 tablespoons cornstarch
1 1/2 cups low-fat beef broth
1 cup frozen green beans
1 cup peeled and sliced carrots
1 cup frozen green peas
2 cups mashed potato flakes
Butter spray
1/4 teaspoon paprika

Note: In place of the 2 cups of mashed potato flakes, prepare
either fresh or instant mashed potatoes to serve 4.

1. In a large nonstick skillet, brown ground beef. Add onion and cook until translucent. Drain any fat. Add salt and pepper. Mix cornstarch in beef broth. Add to skillet and bring to a boil, stirring constantly until mixture thickens slightly. Add frozen beans and carrots. Cover pan and cook for 10 to 20 minutes or until vegetables are tender. Add additional beef broth or water if sauce gets too thick. Stir in peas. Pour mixture into a 7" x 11" baking dish or a 2-quart casserole.

2. Preheat oven to 350°F. Prepare mashed potatoes, using 2 cups flakes, according to package directions. Spread mashed potatoes on top of casserole. Spray lightly with butter spray and sprinkle with paprika. Bake for 10 minutes or until potatoes are lightly brown and casserole is heated through.

Nutritional information per serving:

Calories	445
Fat, gm.	16
Protein, gm.	39
Carbohydrate, gm.	37
Cholesterol, mg.	90
Fiber	high

Sicilian Supper

This is one of the most attractive casseroles I have served and it tastes fantastic. This was adapted from my mother-in-law's recipe that had over 600 calories and 38 grams of fat per serving.

Serves 6

8 ounces (about 4 cups) uncooked egg noodles
1 pound extra-lean ground beef
$1/2$ teaspoon salt
$1/2$ teaspoon freshly ground pepper
1 medium onion, finely chopped
$1/2$ medium red bell pepper, chopped
15 ounces tomato sauce
$1/2$ teaspoon oregano
8 ounces fat-free or low-fat cream cheese, room temperature
1 cup fat-free milk
$1/2$ cup grated Parmesan cheese
$1/4$ teaspoon garlic powder
$1/4$ teaspoon white pepper

1. Preheat oven to 325°F. Grease a 9" x 13" baking pan. Cook noodles in boiling water just until barely tender. Drain and set aside. In a medium skillet, brown beef. Sprinkle with salt and pepper. Add onion and red pepper. Cook until onion is translucent. Drain any fat. Stir in tomato sauce and oregano. Simmer for 5 to 10 minutes.

2. Meanwhile, in a large bowl beat cream cheese, adding milk gradually to keep mixture smooth. Add Parmesan cheese, garlic powder, and white pepper. Mix until smooth. Stir in cooked noodles.

3. Alternate rows of meat sauce and noodles in the baking pan. It works best to start with a row of noodles on each end of the dish and one row in the middle. Spoon sauce in 2 rows between the noodles. Cover loosely with aluminum foil. Bake for 20 minutes or just until heated through.

Nutritional information per serving:

Calories	415
Fat, gm.	16
Protein, gm.	30
Carbohydrate, gm.	38
Cholesterol, mg.	100
Fiber	low

Spaghetti Pie

This is a great family supper you can prepare ahead of time.

Serves 6

6 ounces spaghetti
1 tablespoon butter or margarine
$1/3$ cup grated Parmesan cheese
2 eggs, lightly beaten
1 pound extra-lean ground beef
1 small onion, finely chopped
$1/2$ medium green bell pepper, finely chopped
8 ounces canned tomatoes
6 ounces tomato paste
1 teaspoon sugar
1 teaspoon oregano or Italian seasoning
$1/2$ teaspoon garlic powder
1 cup fat-free ricotta cheese
$1/2$ cup shredded reduced-fat mozzarella cheese

Note: This can be prepared ahead of time and covered and refrigerated until ready to bake. If it is chilled, increase baking time to 45 to 60 minutes or until heated through.

1. Preheat oven to 350°F. Butter a deep 10-inch pie pan. Cook spaghetti in rapidly boiling water until just tender. Drain well. Stir in butter, Parmesan cheese, and eggs. Press spaghetti mixture into pie pan to form a crust. Set aside. In a medium nonstick skillet, brown ground beef over medium heat. Add onion and bell pepper. Cook until onion is translucent. Drain off any meat fat. Add canned tomatoes, tomato paste, sugar, oregano, and garlic powder. Heat through.

2. Spread ricotta cheese over spaghetti crust. Fill pie with tomato mixture. Bake uncovered for 20 minutes. Sprinkle with mozzarella cheese. Bake an additional 5 minutes or until the cheese melts.

Nutritional information per serving:

Calories	445
Fat, gm.	17
Protein, gm.	40
Carbohydrate, gm.	33
Cholesterol, mg.	140
Fiber	medium

Tuna Noodle Casserole

This is definitely a childhood memory.

Serves 6

8 ounces (5 cups) medium egg noodles
1 can (10³/₄ ounces) cream of mushroom soup
³/₄ cup fat-free milk
¹/₄ teaspoon salt
¹/₄ teaspoon freshly ground pepper
2 stalks celery, finely chopped, optional
6 ounces canned tuna, drained
1 ¹/₂ cups frozen peas
3 ounces fat-free potato chips, crushed

Note: Use the celery if you like a little texture.

Preheat oven to 350°F. Butter a 2-quart casserole. In a large saucepan, cook noodles in boiling salted water until al dente. Drain well. In a large bowl combine soup, milk, salt, and pepper. Stir to mix. Add celery, tuna, peas, and noodles. Spoon into casserole. Top with potato chips. Bake for 30 to 35 minutes or until heated through.

Nutritional information per serving:

Calories	275
Fat, gm.	3
Protein, gm.	17
Carbohydrate, gm.	45
Cholesterol, mg.	50
Fiber	medium

Turkey Tetrazzini

My recipe card for this is yellow and curled.
It is marked with "Ray loves this!" It definitely is a family favorite.

Serves 6

8 ounces spaghetti
1 tablespoon butter or margarine
1 medium onion, finely chopped
1/2 pound fresh mushrooms, sliced
1/2 medium red bell pepper, finely chopped
1/2 medium green bell pepper, finely chopped
1/4 cup flour
15 ounces low-fat chicken broth
12 ounces evaporated fat-free milk
3 ounces fat-free or low-fat cream cheese
1/4 cup grated Parmesan cheese, divided
1/4 cup dry sherry wine
1/4 teaspoon white pepper
1/2 teaspoon salt
1 pound baked skinless turkey breast, cut into 1/2-inch cubes
1/4 cup fat-free milk, optional

1. Preheat oven to 325°F. Grease a 2-quart baking pan. In a large saucepan cook spaghetti in lightly salted boiling water until just tender. Drain well and set aside. In a medium skillet, heat butter over medium heat. Cook onion until translucent. Add mushrooms and peppers. Cook until tender.

2. In a shaker, mix flour with broth until smooth. Add broth and evaporated milk to the pan. Cook over medium heat, stirring constantly, until mixture thickens. Stir in cream cheese, 2 tablespoons Parmesan cheese, sherry, white pepper, salt, and turkey. If mixture is too thick, add milk to thin. Stir in spaghetti. Spoon mixture into baking dish. Top with 2 tablespoons Parmesan cheese. Bake for 20 to 30 minutes or until heated through.

Nutritional information per serving:

Calories	360
Fat, gm.	5
Protein, gm.	32
Carbohydrate, gm.	47
Cholesterol, mg.	45
Fiber	medium

Chapter Six
Meats

Always Good Meat Loaf

Bavarian Pork and Cabbage

Beef and Broccoli Stir-Fry

Beef Brisket in Beer

Beef Burgundy

Beef Fondue with Cabernet Sauvignon

Beef Stroganoff

Bourbon and Sweet Marinated Tenderloin

French Pot Roast

Fruit-Glazed Ham Steak

Fruit-Stuffed Loin of Pork

Ham Steak with Cranberry Sauce

Hungarian Ground Beef and Mushroom Stroganoff

Italian Spaghetti Sauce

Jamaican Pork Tenderloin

Meatballs in Sour Cream Sauce

Pepper Steak

Pizza Burgers

Poor Man's Stroganoff

Porcupine Meatballs

Pork Chops with Brandy Orange Sauce

Red Wine–Marinated Beef Tenderloin

Roast Pork with Red Cabbage and Apples

Rolled Pork Loin with Teriyaki Marinade

Saucy Pork and Apples

Sauerkraut and Pork Roast

Sherried Beef Sirloin Tips

Sicilian Steak

Sloppy Joes

Sunday Pot Roast

Swedish Meatballs

Sweet-and-Sour Ribs

Swiss Steak

Tenderloin and Vegetable Kebabs

Always Good Meat Loaf

This is an old standard recipe that is always good.

Serves 8

1 1/2 pounds extra-lean ground beef
1 cup fat-free milk
2/3 cup cracker crumbs
2 eggs, lightly beaten
1/2 cup onion, finely chopped
1 1/2 teaspoons salt
1/2 teaspoon freshly ground pepper
3/4 teaspoon poultry seasoning or sage

Preheat oven to 350°F. Grease a 5" x 9" loaf pan. In a large bowl, combine ground beef and milk. Add all remaining ingredients. Mix well with a wooden spoon. Spoon into loaf pan. Bake for 1 to 1 1/2 hours or until brown on top and completely done in the middle (165°F). Let stand for 10 to 15 minutes before serving.

Nutritional information per serving:

Calories	260
Fat, gm.	12
Protein, gm.	28
Carbohydrate, gm.	10
Cholesterol, mg.	115
Fiber	very low

Bavarian Pork and Cabbage

This is an old-fashioned, wonderful hearty meal.

Serves 4

1 tablespoon butter or margarine
1 1/4 pounds lean pork loin chops
1/2 teaspoon salt
1/2 teaspoon freshly ground pepper
1 medium onion, finely chopped
1 can (10 3/4 ounces) reduced-fat cream of mushroom soup
1/2 cup fat-free milk
1/2 teaspoon caraway seeds
1 pound cabbage, cut into wedges
2 cups peeled and chopped carrots

1. In a large skillet, melt butter. Remove any visible fat from pork chops. Sprinkle with salt and pepper. Place pork in skillet and cook over medium heat until brown on both sides. Add onion and cook until translucent. Add soup, milk, and caraway seeds. Cover and simmer over low heat for 20 minutes.

2. Add vegetables, cover, and cook for 35 to 45 minutes or until cabbage and carrots are tender. Stir occasionally. Uncover and cook to desired consistency.

Nutritional information per serving:

Calories	395
Fat, gm.	16
Protein, gm.	45
Carbohydrate, gm.	18
Cholesterol, mg.	140
Fiber	medium

Beef and Broccoli Stir-Fry

My daughters put this colorful and flavorful combination together.

Serves 4

1 pound lean beef
1 1/2 cups low-fat chicken broth
3 tablespoons soy sauce
2 cloves garlic, minced
1 tablespoon Worcestershire sauce
1/4 teaspoon freshly ground pepper
1/8 teaspoon red pepper flakes, optional
1/2 teaspoon ginger
1 tablespoon vegetable oil
1/2 pound fresh mushrooms
4 cups broccoli florets
1/2 medium red bell pepper, thinly sliced
2 tablespoons cornstarch
2 tablespoons dry sherry wine

1. Slice beef into 1/4-inch slices. Place meat in a large resealable plastic bag. Add chicken broth, soy sauce, garlic, Worcestershire sauce, ground pepper, red pepper, and ginger. Mix well and refrigerate for several hours.

2. When ready to serve, remove meat from marinade and reserve marinade. Dry off meat with a paper towel. In a large, nonstick skillet, heat oil. Add meat and fry until brown. Push meat to the side and add mushrooms, broccoli, and red pepper. Stir until mushrooms are tender. In a small bowl combine reserved marinade, cornstarch, and sherry. Stir into skillet and cook until mixture thickens. Add extra broth if it gets too thick. Cover pan and cook just until broccoli is tender-crisp. Serve over rice.

Nutritional information per serving without rice:

Calories	285
Fat, gm.	10
Protein, gm.	32
Carbohydrate, gm.	17
Cholesterol, mg.	65
Fiber	very high

Beef Brisket in Beer

This is one of my mother-in-law's recipes. I didn't have to modify it except to cut down on the size of the meat portion. Her family was accustomed to eating large amounts of meat in the days when protein was king.

Serves 8

2 1/2 pounds lean beef brisket
12 ounces light beer
1/2 cup ketchup
1 medium onion, chopped
1/2 teaspoon garlic powder
1/2 teaspoon salt
1/4 teaspoon freshly ground pepper
1/4 teaspoon thyme
1/4 teaspoon tarragon
1/4 teaspoon marjoram
1 bay leaf

Preheat oven to 300°F. Trim any visible fat from meat. Place meat in heavy Dutch oven. In a small bowl, combine all remaining ingredients. Mix and pour over meat. Cover pan. Bake for 3 to 5 hours or until meat is very tender. Turn meat occasionally and add water if it gets too dry. Remove bay leaf before serving.

Note: This may also be cooked for a longer period of time in a slow cooker.

Nutritional information per serving:

Calories	350
Fat, gm.	19
Protein, gm.	40
Carbohydrate, gm.	5
Cholesterol, mg.	120
Fiber	0

Beef Burgundy

This recipe spells comfort. The aroma and flavor can never be replaced by packaged mixes or fast foods.

Serves 6

1 1/2 pounds beef top round
1/3 cup flour
1 1/2 teaspoons salt
1/2 teaspoon freshly ground pepper
2 tablespoons vegetable oil, divided
2 cups chopped onions
1/4 pound fresh mushrooms, sliced
1 1/2 cups peeled and chopped carrots
15 ounces low-fat beef broth
1/2 teaspoon thyme
8 ounces tomato sauce
1 cup Burgundy
2 tablespoons flour, optional
1 cup cherry tomatoes, optional

1. Preheat oven to 300°F. Trim any visible fat from meat and cut into 1-inch cubes. In a plastic bag, mix flour, salt, and pepper. Add meat and toss until meat is well coated. Heat 1 tablespoon oil in large nonstick skillet or Dutch oven and add meat. Cook over medium heat until brown on all sides.

2. In a separate medium skillet, heat 1 tablespoon oil. Add onions and cook over medium heat until translucent. Add mushrooms and carrots and cook until mushrooms are soft. Remove from heat and set aside. When meat is brown in the Dutch oven, add beef broth. Stir to deglaze (loosen the brown flour in the bottom of the pan). Add thyme, tomato sauce, and Burgundy. Add vegetables to the pan. Cover tightly and bake for 2 to 3 hours or until meat is tender. Check occasionally and add extra broth or water if it gets too dry.

3. Remove from oven. If juice is too thin, combine 2 tablespoons of flour with 1/2 cup water in a shaker. Add to pan and cook on top of the stove, stirring constantly, until mixture boils and thickens to the desired consistency. Add tomatoes 2 minutes before serving. Serve with cooked noodles.

Nutritional information per serving without noodles:

Calories	355
Fat, gm.	15
Protein, gm.	40
Carbohydrate, gm.	15
Cholesterol, mg.	90
Fiber	medium

Beef Fondue with Cabernet Sauvignon

This is a favorite recipe in my son-in-law's family.
I love it because it is a fondue without fat and it is fabulously tasty.

Serves 4

2 cups Cabernet Sauvignon
1 can (10¾ ounces) beef consommé
1 small onion, chopped
Pinch thyme
Pinch marjoram
Pinch garlic powder
1 pound beef tenderloin, cubed

In an electric fondue pot, combine Cabernet, beef consommé, onion, thyme, marjoram, and garlic powder. Bring to boiling point and reduce heat to simmering. Using fondue forks, place cubes of meat in pot. Cook each piece the way you like it. Serve with a variety of dipping sauces.

Nutritional information per serving:

Calories	300
Fat, gm.	19
Protein, gm.	32
Carbohydrate, gm.	1
Cholesterol, mg.	90
Fiber	0

Beef Stroganoff

This is an old standard recipe. It is lower in fat than the older version but it still has the great flavor.

Serves 4

1 pound top round steak
¼ cup flour
½ teaspoon salt
½ teaspoon freshly ground pepper
1 tablespoon cooking oil
1 medium onion, chopped
1 pound mushrooms, sliced
2 cloves garlic, minced
15 ounces low-fat beef broth
¼ cup port or Burgundy wine
1 cup fat-free sour cream
Freshly ground pepper to taste

1. Cut meat into thin strips. Combine meat, flour, salt, and pepper in a plastic bag. Set aside. In a large skillet, heat oil. Add onion and cook over medium heat until translucent. Remove from pan. Add flour-coated meat and cook over medium-hot heat until brown. Add mushrooms and garlic. Cook until mushrooms are tender. Return onion to the pan and add beef broth. Cover and simmer over low heat for 2 hours or until meat is tender. Check occasionally and add additional broth if necessary.

2. If broth is too thin, remove cover toward the end of the cooking period and cook until desired consistency. When ready to serve, add wine and stir in sour cream. Heat through but do not boil. Serve over noodles. Add pepper to taste.

Nutritional information per serving without noodles:

Calories	350
Fat, gm.	14
Protein, gm.	33
Carbohydrate, gm.	23
Cholesterol, mg.	75
Fiber	low

Bourbon and Sweet Marinated Tenderloin

*This is fabulous. The meat is so flavorful and tender, and the mustard sauce gives an added flavor dimension.
My index card with this recipe is stained almost beyond recognition because it has been used so often.*

Serves 6

2 1/2 pounds pork tenderloin
1/4 cup soy sauce
2 tablespoons brown sugar
1/2 teaspoon ginger
2 tablespoons vegetable oil
1/4 cup bourbon

Sauce:

1/2 cup low-fat or fat-free mayonnaise
1/2 cup fat-free sour cream
1/4 cup Dijon mustard
1 tablespoon honey
Salt and freshly ground pepper to taste

1. Trim pork tenderloin, removing any fat and the white membrane. Place in resealable plastic bag. Add soy sauce, brown sugar, ginger, oil, and bourbon. Reseal bag and mix well. Refrigerate for several hours or overnight.

2. Prepare sauce in small bowl. Combine mayonnaise, sour cream, mustard, honey, salt, and pepper. Cover and refrigerate.

3. Heat grill to medium-hot. Remove meat from marinade. Grill meat, basting occasionally with reserved marinade. Grill until brown on the outside and 160°F in the inside. Remove from grill and let sit for 20 minutes before cutting. Serve with mustard sauce on the side.

Nutritional information per serving:

Calories	390
Fat, gm.	11
Protein, gm.	60
Carbohydrate, gm.	13
Cholesterol, mg.	150
Fiber	0

French Pot Roast

This is a real homemade, one-dish meal that can never be replaced by take-out food.
The secret is to allow enough time to cook it until the meat is very tender.

Serves 6

1 tablespoon cooking oil
1 1/2 pounds lean beef roast
1/2 teaspoon salt
1/2 teaspoon freshly ground pepper
2 medium onions, quartered
2 cups low-fat beef broth
3/4 cup red wine
1 large bay leaf
1/2 teaspoon crushed thyme
6 medium potatoes
6 medium carrots, peeled and coarsely chopped
1/4 cup flour
1 cup water
1/4 cup minced fresh parsley

Note: The length of time needed to bake a pot roast will depend on the cut of beef that is used. Plan on 3 to 4 hours at 300°F to have a very tender roast.

1. Preheat oven to 300°F. In a large heavy Dutch oven, heat oil. Brown meat over medium-hot heat on all sides. Sprinkle meat with salt and pepper. Add onions and cook until translucent. Remove from heat. Add beef broth, wine, bay leaf, and thyme. Cover pan and bake for 1 1/2 to 2 1/2 hours or until meat is beginning to become tender. Check occasionally and add extra water or broth if needed.

2. An hour before ready to serve, add potatoes and carrots. Cook for another hour or until meat and vegetables are tender. Arrange meat and vegetables on serving platter. Discard bay leaf. Place pan back on stove over medium heat. In a shaker, mix flour with water. Add to boiling broth, stirring constantly until gravy thickens. Add extra broth or water if gravy becomes too thick. Garnish with fresh parsley.

Nutritional information per serving:

Calories	390
Fat, gm.	13
Protein, gm.	40
Carbohydrate, gm.	28
Cholesterol, mg.	90
Fiber	high

Fruit-Glazed Ham Steak

Choose the canned fruit of your choice to dress up the ham.

Serves 6

8 ounces canned pineapple chunks
11 ounces canned mandarin oranges
1 tablespoon cornstarch
2 tablespoons brown sugar
1 tablespoon cider vinegar
1 teaspoon soy sauce
1/8 teaspoon ginger
1/8 teaspoon nutmeg
2 pounds lean ham slices
1/4 cup maraschino cherries

Preheat oven to 350°F. Grease a 9" x 9" baking dish. Drain pineapple chunks and oranges, reserving juice. Set fruit aside. Add enough water to the juice to make 1 cup of liquid. Add cornstarch and stir until well mixed. In a small saucepan, combine juice and cornstarch mixture, brown sugar, vinegar, soy sauce, ginger, and nutmeg. Bring to a boil, stirring constantly, until mixture thickens. Place ham slices in baking dish. Top with reserved fruit. Pour cooked juice mixture over ham and fruit. Bake uncovered for 20 to 30 minutes or until heated through. Add maraschino cherries as a garnish before serving.

Nutritional information per serving:

Calories	260
Fat, gm.	7
Protein, gm.	30
Carbohydrate, gm.	19
Cholesterol, mg.	70
Fiber	low

Fruit-Stuffed Loin of Pork

This is a beautiful way to prepare a pork roast for a special meal.

Serves 8

4 pounds boned, rolled pork loin
1 cup pitted prunes
1 cup dried apricot halves
3 cloves garlic, thinly sliced
Salt and freshly ground pepper to taste
Butter spray
1 tablespoon thyme
1 cup Madeira wine
1 tablespoon molasses

Note: Order a pork loin with a "pocket."

1. Preheat oven to 350°F. Using the handle of a wooden spoon, push the dried fruits into the pocket in the roast, alternating prunes and apricots. With the tip of a knife, make small, deep slits in the roast, spaced at various points around the entire roast. Push each garlic slice into a slit. Tie roast with twine and rub surface with salt and pepper. Set roast in a shallow baking pan and spray with butter spray. Sprinkle with thyme.

2. Stir Madeira and molasses together in a small bowl and pour ¹/₂ of it over roast. Set the pan on the middle rack of the oven and bake for 1 to 1¹/₂ hours or until thermometer inserted in the center reaches 165°F. Baste occasionally with remaining wine mixture and meat drippings in pan. When roast is done, remove from oven and let stand for 20 minutes before slicing.

Nutritional information per serving:

Calories	350
Fat, gm.	11
Protein, gm.	40
Carbohydrate, gm.	23
Cholesterol, mg.	95
Fiber	medium

Ham Steak with Cranberry Sauce

Cranberries are a perfect complement to ham.

Serves 6

¹/2 cup orange juice
2 tablespoons cornstarch
2 tablespoons brown sugar
1 cup cranberry juice cocktail
1 cup dried cranberries
Dash salt
1 tablespoon butter or margarine
2 pounds lean ham slices

In a small saucepan, combine orange juice and cornstarch. Stir until mixed. Add brown sugar, cranberry juice, dried cranberries, and salt. Place over medium heat and bring to a boil, stirring constantly. Remove from heat and set aside. In a medium skillet, melt butter. Add ham slices and cook over medium-hot heat until brown on both sides. Place on serving platter or individual plates and top with warm cranberry sauce.

Nutritional information per serving:

Calories	310
Fat, gm.	8
Protein, gm.	30
Carbohydrate, gm.	29
Cholesterol, mg.	70
Fiber	low

Hungarian Ground Beef and Mushroom Stroganoff

This is a great fast family meal with lots of flavor.

Serves 4

1 pound extra-lean ground beef
1 medium onion, finely chopped
1/2 teaspoon salt
1/2 teaspoon freshly ground pepper
3/4 pound fresh mushrooms, sliced
2 cloves garlic, minced
1/2 cup low-fat beef broth
8 ounces tomato sauce
1 teaspoon dry mustard
1 teaspoon paprika
1 cup fat-free sour cream

1. In a large skillet, cook meat over medium-hot heat until brown. Reduce heat to medium. Add onion and cook until translucent. Drain off any fat. Add salt, pepper, and mushrooms. Cook until mushrooms are tender. Add garlic and cook for 1 minute. Add broth, tomato sauce, dry mustard, and paprika. Bring to a boil. Reduce heat, and simmer for 10 to 15 minutes or until mixture reaches the desired consistency.

2. Stir in sour cream and cook just until heated through. Do not boil. Add additional broth if mixture is too thick. Serve mixture over cooked noodles.

Nutritional information per serving without noodles:

Calories	365
Fat, gm.	15
Protein, gm.	38
Carbohydrate, gm.	20
Cholesterol, mg.	100
Fiber	medium

Italian Spaghetti Sauce

This is so simple but tastes as good as complicated recipes. Kids can easily make it.

Serves 6

1 ½ pounds extra-lean ground beef
½ teaspoon salt
½ teaspoon freshly ground pepper
1 large onion, finely chopped
2 cloves garlic, minced
½ cup water
30 ounces tomato sauce
15 ounces canned diced or crushed tomatoes
1 ½ teaspoons Italian seasoning
1 teaspoon sugar
Salt and freshly ground pepper to taste

Note: For a smooth sauce, the diced tomatoes can be replaced with tomato sauce.

In a large heavy skillet or saucepan, brown ground beef over medium-hot heat. Cook until brown. Sprinkle with salt and pepper. Add onion and cook until translucent. Add garlic and cook for 1 minute. Drain off any grease. Add water and stir to deglaze the pan (loosen the browned meat at the bottom of the pan). Add tomato sauce, diced tomatoes, and Italian seasoning. Bring to a boil. Reduce heat and boil gently, uncovered, for 30 to 45 minutes or until sauce reaches desired consistency. Add water if sauce gets too thick. Add sugar and adjust seasoning with salt and pepper to taste. Serve on hot spaghetti.

Nutritional information per serving without spaghetti:

Calories	330
Fat, gm.	14
Protein, gm.	36
Carbohydrate, gm.	15
Cholesterol, mg.	90
Fiber	high

Jamaican Pork Tenderloin

Add a little spice to your life!

Serves 4

2 pounds pork tenderloin
$^1/_2$ cup orange juice
$^1/_4$ cup soy sauce
$^1/_4$ cup canola oil
1 small onion, chopped
1 small jalapeño pepper, finely chopped
3 tablespoons fresh thyme or 1 teaspoon dried
$^1/_2$ teaspoon allspice
$^1/_2$ teaspoon cinnamon
$^1/_4$ teaspoon nutmeg
$^1/_4$ teaspoon ginger
$^1/_4$ teaspoon freshly ground pepper

Trim white membrane and any fat from pork tenderloin. Place tenderloin in a large resealable plastic bag. Set aside. In a pint jar, combine all remaining ingredients. Shake to mix well. Pour into bag with meat. Seal bag and refrigerate for several hours or overnight. Turn occasionally. When ready to prepare, heat grill to medium-hot. Spray grates with cooking spray. Remove pork from marinade and place on grill. Discard marinade. Grill meat until brown on all sides and slightly pink in the middle. Let stand for 10 minutes before cutting into slices.

Nutritional information per serving:

Calories	260
Fat, gm.	7
Protein, gm.	48
Carbohydrate, gm.	1
Cholesterol, mg.	150
Fiber	low

Meatballs in Sour Cream Sauce

A great family supper.

Serves 6

1 teaspoon butter or margarine
1 small onion, finely chopped
1 pound extra-lean ground beef
1 egg, lightly beaten
¹/₄ cup fat-free milk
¹/₂ cup seasoned bread crumbs
1 teaspoon salt
¹/₄ teaspoon freshly ground pepper
¹/₈ teaspoon marjoram
¹/₄ cup flour

Sauce:

1 can (10³/₄ ounces) reduced-fat cream of mushroom soup
¹/₄ cup fat-free sour cream

1. Preheat oven to 350°F. Grease a 9" x 9" baking pan or casserole. In a small skillet, melt butter. Cook onion over medium heat until translucent. Remove from heat. In a medium bowl, combine onion, ground beef, egg, milk, bread crumbs, salt, pepper, and marjoram. Mix well with a wooden spoon. Form into small balls. Roll balls in flour. Place in baking pan. Bake for 20 minutes or until brown. Remove from oven and drain off any fat.

2. In a small bowl, combine soup and sour cream. Spoon over meatballs. Bake for another 20 to 30 minutes or until heated through. Serve over noodles or mashed potatoes.

Nutritional information per serving without noodles or potatoes:	
Calories	300
Fat, gm.	13
Protein, gm.	26
Carbohydrate, gm.	19
Cholesterol, mg.	95
Fiber	very low

Pepper Steak

Colorful and flavorful.

Serves 4

1 pound beef round steak
1 tablespoon cooking oil
1 medium onion, thinly sliced
1 stalk celery, sliced
15 ounces low-fat beef broth
1 bay leaf
1/4 teaspoon thyme
1 medium green bell pepper, sliced
1 medium red bell pepper, sliced
2 tablespoons soy sauce
1 tablespoon cornstarch
1/4 cup water
1 cup cherry tomatoes

Cut any visible fat from meat and slice into thin bite-size pieces. In a large nonstick skillet, heat oil. Add beef and fry over medium-hot heat until brown. Add onion and celery and cook until tender. Add beef broth, bay leaf, and thyme. Cover skillet and simmer for 1 to 1 1/2 hours or until meat is tender. Check occasionally and add additional broth if it gets too dry. When meat is tender, add peppers and simmer for 5 minutes or until peppers are tender-crisp. In a cup, blend soy sauce, cornstarch, and water. Stir into skillet and cook, stirring constantly, until mixture boils and thickens. Add extra beef broth if mixture is too thick. Add tomatoes 1 minute before ready to serve. Discard bay leaf. Serve with cooked rice.

Note: After adding peppers, cook just long enough for peppers to become tender. Overcooking will diminish their vibrant colors.

Nutritional information per serving without rice:

Calories	265
Fat, gm.	14
Protein, gm.	27
Carbohydrate, gm.	8
Cholesterol, mg.	90
Fiber	medium

Pizza Burgers

The kids will love this.

Serves 6

1 pound extra-lean ground beef
$^1/_2$ teaspoon salt
$^1/_4$ teaspoon freshly ground pepper
1 small onion, finely chopped
1 clove garlic, minced
8 ounces tomato sauce
$^1/_4$ cup chili sauce or ketchup
1 teaspoon Italian seasoning
$^1/_2$ teaspoon anise seed, optional
$^1/_4$ teaspoon red pepper flakes, optional
$^1/_2$ loaf French bread, cut in half lengthwise
1 cup shredded reduced-fat mozzarella cheese
$^1/_2$ cup grated Parmesan cheese

Note: For more pizza taste, substitute Italian sausage for the ground beef.

1. In a large skillet, brown meat over medium-hot heat. Add salt, pepper, and onion. Reduce heat to medium and cook until onion is translucent. Add garlic and cook for 1 minute. Add tomato sauce, chili sauce, Italian seasoning, anise seed, and red pepper. Simmer for 5 to 10 minutes or until mixture reaches desired consistency.

2. Preheat broiler. Spread mixture on cut side of both halves of French bread. Sprinkle with mozzarella cheese and Parmesan cheese. Place under oven broiler until cheese is melted and golden brown. To serve, cut into slices.

Nutritional information per serving:

Calories	360
Fat, gm.	18
Protein, gm.	25
Carbohydrate, gm.	24
Cholesterol, mg.	60
Fiber	medium

Poor Man's Stroganoff

So easy and so good.

Serves 6

1 ¹/₄ pounds extra-lean ground beef
¹/₂ teaspoon salt
¹/₂ teaspoon freshly ground pepper
1 small onion, finely chopped
1 clove garlic, minced
¹/₂ pound fresh mushrooms, sliced
2 tablespoons flour
¹/₂ cup water or chicken broth
1 can (10³/₄ ounces) cream of chicken soup
1 cup fat-free sour cream

In a large nonstick skillet, brown beef. Sprinkle with salt and pepper. Add onion and cook until tender. Add garlic and mushrooms and cook until mushrooms are tender. Drain any fat. In a shaker, mix flour and water. Pour into skillet. Add soup and bring to a boil, stirring constantly until mixture thickens. Add extra water if gravy is too thick. Simmer for 10 minutes. Stir in sour cream and heat through. Serve with noodles or mashed potatoes.

**Nutritional information per serving
without noodles or potatoes:**

Calories	300
Fat, gm.	14
Protein, gm.	30
Carbohydrate, gm.	13
Cholesterol, mg.	80
Fiber	very low

Porcupine Meatballs

Kids love these and dads do too!

Serves 6

1 pound extra-lean ground beef
1/2 cup uncooked white rice
1 tablespoon minced onion
2 tablespoons chili sauce
1 1/2 teaspoons salt
1/4 teaspoon freshly ground pepper
1 cup tomato juice
30 ounces canned seasoned tomatoes, undrained

Note: Canned tomato soup can be substituted for the canned tomatoes.

Preheat oven to 350°F. In a medium bowl, combine ground beef, rice, onion, chili sauce, salt, and pepper. Mix well with wooden spoon. Shape into 12 balls. Place in 1 1/2-quart casserole. Pour tomato juice and canned seasoned tomatoes over the top. Cover and bake for 1 to 1 1/2 hours or until meatballs are thoroughly cooked. Check after 45 minutes and add water if it is too dry or uncover for a thicker consistency. Serve with rice, noodles, or other pasta.

Nutritional information per serving:

Calories	265
Fat, gm.	10
Protein, gm.	24
Carbohydrate, gm.	20
Cholesterol, mg.	60
Fiber	low

Pork Chops with Brandy Orange Sauce

The orange sauce adds a special zest to the pork.

Serves 4

1 tablespoon butter or margarine
1 pound lean boneless pork loin chops
1/2 teaspoon salt
1/4 teaspoon freshly ground pepper
1 cup orange juice
2 tablespoons cornstarch
1/4 cup cold water
1/4 cup white wine
2 tablespoons brown sugar
1 tablespoon orange zest
1 tablespoon brandy
1 medium orange, thinly sliced

In a large nonstick skillet, melt butter. Sprinkle pork with salt and pepper. Place pork in skillet and cook over medium heat until each piece is brown on both sides. Add orange juice to the skillet and stir to deglaze the pan. In a small glass, mix cornstarch and water. Add to skillet and cook, stirring constantly, until mixture comes to a boil and thickens. Stir in wine, brown sugar, and orange zest. Heat through. Add additional water or wine if sauce gets too thick. When ready to serve, add brandy. Spoon sauce over pork and garnish with thin orange slices.

Nutritional information per serving:

Calories	320
Fat, gm.	12
Protein, gm.	34
Carbohydrate, gm.	19
Cholesterol, mg.	100
Fiber	very low

Red Wine–Marinated Beef Tenderloin

This is a very special recipe that always brings rave reviews. Serve it chilled or at room temperature for a dinner party or for a late dinner after a play or concert with small sandwich rolls.

Serves 12

1/4 cup butter, melted
2 cloves garlic, minced
3 pounds beef tenderloin
1 1/3 cups canola or extra-virgin olive oil
1/2 cup red wine vinegar
2 tablespoons chopped fresh parsley
2 teaspoons tarragon
2 teaspoons dry mustard
2 teaspoons salt
1 teaspoon freshly ground pepper
1 teaspoon sugar
1/2 teaspoon garlic powder
Dash Tabasco sauce
1 pound fresh mushrooms, sliced
2 medium red onions, sliced
1 pint cherry tomatoes

1. Preheat oven to 500°F. Combine butter and garlic and brush over meat. Place in a heavy ovenproof pan. Bake for 15 minutes. Turn oven down to 350°F and bake for 10 more minutes or until internal temperature of meat is 140°F (rare) to 160°F (medium-rare). Remove from oven and allow meat to rest for 20 minutes.

2. Combine oil, vinegar, parsley, tarragon, dry mustard, salt, pepper, sugar, garlic powder, and Tabasco. Cover and shake to mix well. Pour mixture into large resealable plastic bag. Add meat to bag. Seal and refrigerate for at least 6 hours or overnight.

3. Two to 3 hours before serving, remove meat and cut into 1/2-inch-thick slices. Add mushrooms, red onions, and cherry tomatoes and continue to marinate in refrigerator. Remove meat and vegetables from marinade and arrange on serving platter.

Nutritional information per serving without rolls:

Calories	270
Fat, gm.	15
Protein, gm.	28
Carbohydrate, gm.	5
Cholesterol, mg.	100
Fiber	low

Roast Pork with Red Cabbage and Apples

The cabbage and apples combination may sound a little strange but it is an old German recipe. It is combined with brown sugar and vinegar for a light sweet-sour accompaniment to the pork. My guests love it.

Serves 6

1 tablespoon vegetable oil
2¹/₂ pounds extra-lean pork loin roast
1 teaspoon salt
¹/₂ teaspoon freshly ground pepper
1 large onion, chopped
6 cups red cabbage, thinly sliced
3 large Granny Smith apples, peeled, cored, and diced
2 tablespoons brown sugar
2 tablespoons balsamic vinegar
1 cup white wine

Preheat oven to 350°F. In a large, heavy ovenproof pan, heat vegetable oil. Add pork and cook over medium-hot heat until brown on all sides. Sprinkle with salt and pepper. Add onion and cook until translucent. Add cabbage, apples, brown sugar, vinegar, and wine. Bring to a boil, then remove from heat. Cover and bake for 60 to 90 minutes or until meat thermometer inserted in the center of the meat reaches 165°F. Stir occasionally and add additional water or wine if it is too dry.

Nutritional information per serving:

Calories	440
Fat, gm.	15
Protein, gm.	59
Carbohydrate, gm.	16
Cholesterol, mg.	150
Fiber	high

Rolled Pork Loin with Teriyaki Marinade

This is an excellent sweet and spicy marinade for pork or chicken.

Serves 6

$^1/_2$ cup soy sauce
$^3/_4$ cup light corn syrup
$^1/_2$ cup fresh lemon juice
2 teaspoons dry mustard
1 teaspoon ginger
$^1/_4$ teaspoon cloves
3 tablespoons steak sauce
$^1/_4$ cup dry sherry wine
Dash hot sauce to taste
3 pounds lean rolled pork loin

1. In a small saucepan, combine soy sauce, corn syrup, lemon juice, dry mustard, ginger, cloves, and steak sauce. Mix well. Bring to a boil. Reduce heat and boil gently for 5 minutes. Remove from heat and add sherry and hot sauce to taste. Cool. Place marinade in resealable plastic bag with the pork roast. Refrigerate for several hours or overnight. Turn occasionally.

2. Heat grill to medium heat. Remove meat from marinade. Place on grill, cover, and cook until meat reaches 160°F in the center. Baste frequently with marinade. When meat is done, remove from grill and let sit for 15 to 20 minutes before cutting. Place any leftover marinade in small saucepan and bring it to a boil. Serve on the side with the meat.

Nutritional information per serving:

Calories	410
Fat, gm.	8
Protein, gm.	49
Carbohydrate, gm.	36
Cholesterol, mg.	150
Fiber	0

Saucy Pork and Apples

Pork and apples just seem to go together.

Serves 4

2 tablespoons butter or margarine, divided
2 large cooking apples
1 pound lean boneless pork loin or tenderloin
1/2 teaspoon salt
1/2 teaspoon freshly ground pepper
3/4 cup apple juice
1/4 teaspoon allspice
1 tablespoon cornstarch
2 tablespoons water
1/4 cup fat-free half-and-half
Freshly ground pepper to taste

Note: Evaporated fat-free milk can be used in place of fat-free half-and-half.

1. In a large skillet, melt 1 tablespoon butter. Core apples and cut into 1/2-inch slices. Place in pan, cover, and cook over medium heat until tender. Remove apples from skillet and place in 10-inch serving bowl. Keep apples warm.

2. Cut pork into 4 individual serving pieces. Sprinkle with salt and pepper. Add 1 tablespoon butter to skillet and add pork. Cook over medium heat until brown on all sides. Add apple juice and allspice. Stir to deglaze the pan. Mix cornstarch in water. Add to pan and cook, stirring constantly, until sauce comes to a boil and thickens. Add half-and-half and heat through. Add pepper to taste. Arrange pork chops on top of warm apples in serving bowl. Pour sauce on top.

Nutritional information per serving:

Calories	315
Fat, gm.	12
Protein, gm.	33
Carbohydrate, gm.	19
Cholesterol, mg.	100
Fiber	medium

Sauerkraut and Pork Roast

Save this aromatic meal for a cold winter day. It will bring back memories.

Serves 6

$^1/_2$ tablespoon vegetable oil
2 pounds lean pork loin roast
4 large potatoes, peeled and quartered
$^1/_2$ teaspoon salt
$^1/_2$ teaspoon freshly ground pepper
1 teaspoon caraway seeds
2 tablespoons brown sugar
6 cups sauerkraut
1 cup low-fat chicken broth

Preheat oven to 300°F. In a large, heavy Dutch oven, heat oil. Brown meat on all sides. Remove from heat and add potatoes. Sprinkle meat and potatoes with salt and pepper. In a medium bowl, mix caraway seeds, brown sugar, and sauerkraut. Spoon on top. Add broth. Cover and bake for 1$^1/_2$ to 2 hours or until meat and potatoes are tender.

Nutritional information per serving:

Calories	400
Fat, gm.	12
Protein, gm.	50
Carbohydrate, gm.	23
Cholesterol, mg.	110
Fiber	high

Sherried Beef Sirloin Tips

The flavor can't be beat and it is so easy. Put it in the oven and forget it.
Make extra because leftovers warm up beautifully.

Serves 6

2 pounds lean beef sirloin, cut into 1-inch cubes
1 can (10¾ ounces) low-fat cream of mushroom soup
1 package (1⅜ ounces) dry onion soup mix
1 pound fresh mushrooms, thickly sliced
2 cups water
½ cup dry sherry wine
½ cup fat-free sour cream

Preheat oven to 325°F. In a large heavy pan or 1½-quart casserole, combine all ingredients except sour cream. Mix well. Cover tightly and bake for 2 to 3 hours or until meat is tender. Turn oven down to 300°F after the first hour. Check occasionally and add additional water if it becomes too dry. Add sour cream right before serving and heat through. Serve over cooked noodles.

Hint: There is no need to brown the meat for this recipe. Adjust the oven temperature to keep the mixture simmering or boiling very gently.

Nutritional information per serving without noodles:

Calories	285
Fat, gm.	9
Protein, gm.	36
Carbohydrate, gm.	15
Cholesterol, mg.	90
Fiber	low

Sicilian Steak

An Italian restaurant in our city was known for this wonderful flavorful steak. It was our favorite Saturday night outing for years. They are now out of business but the recipe lives on.

Serves 4

1 pound beef top round
¹/₃ cup seasoned bread crumbs
¹/₄ cup grated Parmesan cheese
¹/₂ teaspoon basil
¹/₂ teaspoon garlic powder
¹/₂ teaspoon oregano or Italian seasoning
¹/₄ teaspoon salt
¹/₄ teaspoon freshly ground pepper
2 eggs, lightly beaten
2 tablespoons fresh lemon juice
2 tablespoons olive oil

Pound round steaks until very thin. Set aside. In a large flat bowl, combine bread crumbs, cheese, basil, garlic powder, oregano, salt, and pepper. Mix with a fork. In another flat bowl, combine eggs and lemon juice. Heat oil in large nonstick skillet. Dip steak in eggs and then dip into bread crumb mixture. Place in skillet and cook over medium-hot heat until brown on both sides. Serve with pasta and tomato sauce.

Nutritional information per serving without pasta:

Calories	365
Fat, gm.	19
Protein, gm.	40
Carbohydrate, gm.	8
Cholesterol, mg.	180
Fiber	0

Sloppy Joes

*This is my favorite recipe for a barbecue-type sandwich because it isn't too sweet and it is so easy to make.
If you make a double recipe, it tastes even better warmed up the next day.*

Serves 6

1 pound extra-lean ground beef
1 medium onion, finely chopped
1/2 cup finely chopped celery
1/2 cup ketchup
1 can (10¾ ounces) condensed tomato soup
2 tablespoons barbecue sauce
1 tablespoon Worcestershire sauce
Salt and freshly ground pepper to taste

In a medium nonstick skillet, brown ground beef over medium heat. Add onion and celery. Cook until onion is translucent. Discard any meat fat. Add ketchup, tomato soup, barbecue sauce, and Worcestershire sauce. Bring to a boil. Reduce heat and simmer for 10 to 15 minutes or until it reaches desired consistency. Add small amount of water if it gets too thick. Adjust seasoning with salt and pepper to taste. Serve on buns.

Nutritional information per serving without bun:

Calories	235
Fat, gm.	10
Protein, gm.	13
Carbohydrate, gm.	23
Cholesterol, mg.	60
Fiber	low

Sunday Pot Roast

*This is one of our favorite family meals. When kids come home
from college, they always ask for this pot roast dinner.*

Serves 6

2¹/₂ pounds lean beef chuck or round roast
¹/₂ tablespoon vegetable oil
1 teaspoon salt
¹/₂ teaspoon freshly ground pepper
2 medium onions, cut into quarters
1 can (10³/₄ ounces) reduced-fat cream of mushroom soup
1 cup water
6 medium potatoes, peeled and quartered
6 large carrots, peeled and chopped
¹/₄ cup flour
1 cup water

1. Preheat oven to 300°F. Trim any visible fat from the beef roast. In a heavy Dutch oven, heat oil. Add beef and brown on both sides. Sprinkle with salt and pepper. Add onions and cook for 5 minutes. Top with soup and water. Cover and bake for 2 to 3 hours or until meat is very tender. Check occasionally and add water if it is getting too dry.

2. During the last 45 minutes of baking, add potatoes and carrots. Cover and return to the oven to bake until vegetables are tender. Place meat and vegetables in serving bowl. Make gravy with remaining sauce. In a shaker, mix flour and water together and add to pan. Bring to a boil, stirring constantly. Add additional flour and water or plain water to make the gravy the desired consistency.

Nutritional information per serving:

Calories	400
Fat, gm.	12
Protein, gm.	45
Carbohydrate, gm.	28
Cholesterol, mg.	130
Fiber	high

Swedish Meatballs

This has the mild flavor of a traditional Swedish recipe.
The creamy gravy, with a hint of nutmeg, is wonderful.

Serves 6

Meatballs:

1/2 cup bread crumbs
1/2 cup fat-free evaporated milk
1/2 tablespoon butter or margarine
1/3 cup finely minced onion
1 teaspoon salt
1/4 teaspoon freshly ground pepper
1/8 teaspoon allspice
1/8 teaspoon nutmeg
1 egg, lightly beaten
1 pound extra-lean ground beef

Sauce:

1 cup low-fat chicken broth, divided
3 tablespoons flour
3/4 cup evaporated fat-free milk
Dash nutmeg
2 tablespoons dry sherry wine

Note: A melon baller is helpful in forming small meatballs. This recipe makes 50 small meatballs.

1. In a medium bowl, soak bread crumbs in milk and set aside. In a large skillet, melt butter. Cook onion over medium heat until translucent. Add onion to bread crumbs. Add salt, pepper, allspice, nutmeg, and egg. Mix well. Add meat and stir until well mixed. Form into 3/4-inch balls. Heat skillet and add meatballs. Fry over medium heat until brown on all sides and completely done in the middle. Remove meatballs from skillet and place in large serving bowl.

2. Pour 1/2 cup of chicken broth into pan to deglaze the pan. In a shaker, combine flour and 1/2 cup chicken broth. Pour flour-broth mixture into skillet. Add milk and nutmeg. Bring to a boil, stirring constantly until gravy thickens. Add additional broth if gravy is too thick. Return meatballs to gravy and simmer over low heat for 10 minutes. When ready to serve, add sherry and heat through. Serve over noodles or mashed potatoes.

Nutritional information per serving:

Calories	285
Fat, gm.	12
Protein, gm.	28
Carbohydrate, gm.	15
Cholesterol, mg.	90
Fiber	very low

Sweet-and-Sour Ribs

These are so tender and soooo good!

Serves 6

3 pounds pork spareribs
1 cup ketchup
3/4 cup white vinegar
1/4 cup grape jelly
2 tablespoons molasses
1/4 cup honey
1/4 cup soy sauce
1/2 cup chopped onion
3 cloves garlic, minced
2 teaspoons dry mustard
2 teaspoons ginger
Salt and freshly ground pepper to taste

1. Cut ribs into manageable sections of 4 or 5 bones in each section. In a large bowl, combine all remaining ingredients except salt and pepper. Place all ribs top-side down in a large baking pan that will accommodate them in a single layer. Pour sauce over ribs. Cover pan with plastic wrap and let marinate for about 2 hours.

2. Preheat oven to 350°F. Uncover ribs and turn right-side up in baking pan. Sprinkle with salt and pepper. Cover with aluminum foil and bake for about 1 1/2 hours or until ribs are very tender.

3. Remove ribs from oven and transfer sauce from baking pan to a saucepan. Leave ribs in baking pan and set aside. Boil the sauce until it thickens and is reduced to about 2 cups. Adjust seasoning to taste with salt and pepper. Adjust sweetness or sourness to taste by adding a little bit of white vinegar or brown sugar, if desired. Brush surface of ribs generously with some of the thickened sauce and return to oven. Bake, uncovered, for 20 to 30 minutes or until glazed and very tender. Pass the remaining sauce at the table to be served alongside the ribs.

Nutritional information per serving:

Calories	520
Fat, gm.	30
Protein, gm.	26
Carbohydrate, gm.	36
Cholesterol, mg.	110
Fiber	medium

Swiss Steak

One of those old-time family meals.

Serves 8

3 pounds round steak
¹/2 cup flour
I teaspoon salt
¹/2 teaspoon freshly ground pepper
¹/2 teaspoon paprika
I tablespoon vegetable oil
I large onion, thinly sliced
2 cups low-fat beef broth
30 ounces canned stewed tomatoes
2 tablespoons flour
¹/2 cup water

1. Preheat oven to 300°F. Trim any visible fat from round steak. In a large plastic bag, combine flour, salt, pepper, and paprika. Add steak and mix until it is well coated with the flour. Set aside. In a large, heavy Dutch oven or skillet, heat oil. Add onion and cook over medium heat until translucent. Remove onion slices and set aside. Add meat and cook over medium heat until brown on all sides. Add beef broth and bring to a boil while stirring to loosen browned meat pieces from the bottom of the pan. Add tomatoes and reserved onion. Cover and bake for 2 to 2¹/2 hours or until meat is very tender. Check occasionally and add extra broth or water if it gets too dry.

2. When ready to serve, mix flour and water in a shaker. Add to skillet and bring to a boil, stirring constantly. Add extra water or broth if the mixture gets too thick.

Note: There is lots of sauce with this recipe. It warms up well if you have leftovers.

Nutritional information per serving:

Calories	300
Fat, gm.	15
Protein, gm.	25
Carbohydrate, gm.	15
Cholesterol, mg.	60
Fiber	medium

Tenderloin and Vegetable Kebabs

Create your own colorful kebabs.

Serves 4

1/4 cup red wine vinegar

1/4 cup ketchup

1/4 cup soy sauce

1 tablespoon olive oil

1 tablespoon Dijon mustard

1/4 teaspoon freshly ground pepper

1 small onion, quartered

2 cloves garlic, minced

1 pound beef or pork tenderloin, cut into 1-inch cubes

1/2 pound cherry tomatoes

2 medium red and green bell peppers, cut into 1-inch cubes

1/2 pound mushroom caps

1. In a small bowl, combine vinegar, ketchup, soy sauce, olive oil, mustard, pepper, onion, and garlic. Pour into resealable plastic bag. Add beef cubes. Reseal bag and refrigerate for several hours, turning occasionally.

2. When ready to serve, heat grill. Remove meat from marinade and thread meat onto skewers, alternating with tomatoes, peppers, and mushrooms. Place marinade in small saucepan and bring to a boil. Remove from heat. Grill kebabs over hot grill for 10 to 20 minutes or until meat is cooked to desired doneness. Baste kebabs occasionally with marinade while cooking.

Nutritional information per serving:

Calories	300
Fat, gm.	15
Protein, gm.	25
Carbohydrate, gm.	15
Cholesterol, mg.	60
Fiber	medium

Chapter Seven
Poultry

Apple Cranberry–Topped Chicken Breasts

Baked Chicken Parmesan

Chicken à la King

Chicken and Pea Pods

Chicken Breast with Apricot Curry Sauce

Chicken Breast with Sherry–Sour Cream Sauce

Chicken Divan

Chicken Florentine

Chicken Roulade with Roasted Asparagus and Peppers

Grilled Chicken and Vegetable Stir-Fry

Grilled Ginger Chicken

Honey Mustard Chicken

London Chicken

Plum Chicken

Sassy Salsa Chicken

Swiss Chicken Breasts

Teriyaki Turkey Tenderloin

Apple Cranberry–Topped Chicken Breasts

What a special way to dress up chicken! The sauce is fantastic.

Serves 6

¹/₂ tablespoon vegetable oil
6 boned and skinned chicken breast halves
¹/₂ teaspoon salt
¹/₄ teaspoon freshly ground pepper

Sauce:

15 ounces canned whole cranberry sauce
1 large apple, peeled, cored, and chopped
¹/₂ cup golden raisins
¹/₂ teaspoon cumin
¹/₂ cup chopped pecans

Note: The chicken breasts can be pounded before frying if desired.

In a large nonstick skillet, heat oil. Add chicken and fry over medium heat until brown on all sides and completely done in the middle. Sprinkle with salt and pepper. While chicken is cooking, combine cranberry sauce, apples, raisins, and cumin in a small saucepan. Bring to a boil. Reduce heat and simmer for 5 minutes or until chicken is ready. Thin sauce with water if desired. Stir in pecans. When ready to serve, place chicken on plates and spoon cranberry sauce on top. Serve any remaining sauce on the side.

Nutritional information per serving:

Calories	300
Fat, gm.	6
Protein, gm.	21
Carbohydrate, gm.	41
Cholesterol, mg.	50
Fiber	medium

Baked Chicken Parmesan

What do you do when you want something easy but a little special? Assemble these ahead and bake when you need them. They are good served hot or cold.

Serves 4

¹/₃ cup bread crumbs
¹/₃ cup grated Parmesan cheese
¹/₄ cup chopped fresh parsley
4 tablespoons butter or margarine
¹/₄ teaspoon garlic powder
1 tablespoon Dijon mustard
1 teaspoon Worcestershire sauce
4 boned and skinned chicken breast halves

Preheat oven to 350°F. Butter a 9" x 9" or 7" x 11" baking pan. In a shallow bowl, combine bread crumbs, Parmesan cheese, and parsley. In a small saucepan, melt butter. Stir in garlic powder, mustard, and Worcestershire sauce. Dip chicken breasts in butter mixture and then in crumbs. Place in baking pan. Bake for 45 to 50 minutes or until brown on the outside and completely done in the middle.

Nutritional information per serving:

Calories	260
Fat, gm.	15
Protein, gm.	24
Carbohydrate, gm.	7
Cholesterol, mg.	90
Fiber	very low

Chicken à la King

This looks so creamy and tastes wonderfully rich but it is very low in fat.

Serves 6

3 tablespoons butter or margarine
3 boned and skinned chicken breasts, cut into 1-inch pieces
1 small onion, finely chopped
1/2 pound fresh mushrooms, sliced
1/2 medium red bell pepper, diced
1/4 cup flour
1 cup low-fat chicken broth
1 1/2 cups evaporated fat-free milk
1/4 teaspoon white pepper
1/4 cup chopped fresh parsley
Salt and freshly ground pepper to taste

Note: Fat-free half-and-half may be substituted for the evaporated milk.

In a large heavy saucepan, melt butter. Cook chicken over medium heat until brown on the outside and completely done on the inside. Add onion and cook until translucent. Add mushrooms and bell pepper. Cook until tender. Combine flour and broth in a shaker. Add to pan with the evaporated milk. Bring to a boil, stirring constantly until it thickens. Add additional broth if mixture is too thick or additional flour mixed in broth if it is too thin. Add white pepper and parsley. Adjust seasoning with salt and pepper. Serve on toasted bread, rice, noodles, or puff pastry shells.

Nutritional information per serving without toast:

Calories	200
Fat, gm.	7
Protein, gm.	18
Carbohydrate, gm.	16
Cholesterol, mg.	45
Fiber	low

Chicken and Pea Pods

Chinese meals can get complicated with lots of cutting and chopping.
This one is easy and it's my daughter Vicki's favorite.

Serves 4

1/2 teaspoon ginger
2 teaspoons sugar
2 tablespoons cornstarch
1/2 cup water
1/4 cup soy sauce
1/4 cup dry sherry wine
2 tablespoons vegetable oil
1/4 cup blanched almonds
4 boned and skinned chicken breast halves, cut into 1/2-inch cubes
1 clove garlic, minced
10 ounces frozen pea pods
Salt and freshly ground pepper to taste

In a small bowl, combine ginger, sugar, cornstarch, water, soy sauce, and sherry. Set aside. In a heavy medium skillet or wok, heat oil over medium heat. Add almonds and fry until lightly browned. Remove from pan and set aside. Add chicken to the pan and cook until meat is cooked through. Add garlic and cook for 1 minute. Pour sauce in pan and cook, stirring constantly, until sauce thickens. Add pea pods and cook until tender. Add additional water if sauce becomes too thick. Add salt and pepper to taste. Serve over rice and top with almonds.

Nutritional information per serving without rice:

Calories	275
Fat, gm.	13
Protein, gm.	25
Carbohydrate, gm.	14
Cholesterol, mg.	50
Fiber	high

Chicken Breast with Apricot Curry Sauce

A unique flavor combination.

Serves 4

6 ounces apricot preserves
2 tablespoons Dijon mustard
$^1/_2$ teaspoon curry powder
2 tablespoons water
4 boned and skinned chicken breast halves
$^1/_4$ teaspoon salt
$^1/_4$ teaspoon freshly ground pepper

Note: Instead of baking the chicken, it can be browned in a skillet, then topped with sauce. Partially cover pan and simmer for 15 minutes or until chicken is completely done.

Preheat oven to 350°F. Grease a 7" x 11" baking pan. In a small saucepan, heat apricot preserves, mustard, and curry powder until mixture comes to a boil. Thin with water. Remove from heat and set aside. Place chicken in baking pan. Sprinkle with salt and pepper. Bake for 20 minutes. Spoon sauce on top and bake another 20 minutes or until chicken is completely done.

Nutritional information per serving:

Calories	215
Fat, gm.	2
Protein, gm.	21
Carbohydrate, gm.	28
Cholesterol, mg.	50
Fiber	low

Chicken Breast with Sherry–Sour Cream Sauce

This is a wonderful recipe to double and serve for a large group.
The sauce, served over noodles or mashed potatoes, is rich with homemade flavor.

Serves 4

1 tablespoon butter or margarine
4 boned and skinned chicken breast halves
$^1/_2$ teaspoon salt
$^1/_2$ teaspoon freshly ground pepper
1 large onion, thinly sliced into rings
1 can (10$^3/_4$ ounces) cream of chicken soup
$^1/_3$ cup evaporated fat-free milk
$^1/_3$ cup dry sherry wine
$^1/_3$ cup fat-free sour cream

1. Preheat oven to 325°F. Butter a 7" x 11" or a 9" x 9" baking pan. In a large skillet, melt butter. Fry chicken over medium heat until brown on both sides. Sprinkle with salt and pepper. Remove chicken and place in baking pan. Add onion to skillet and cook until tender. Arrange onion rings on top of chicken. In a small bowl, combine soup, milk, and sherry. Pour over chicken. Cover and bake for 1 hour. Check occasionally and add water or milk if it is getting too dry.

2. Remove chicken and place in large serving bowl. Stir sour cream into sauce. Heat briefly but do not boil. Pour over chicken. Serve with rice, noodles, or mashed potatoes.

Nutritional information per serving:

Calories	240
Fat, gm.	9
Protein, gm.	25
Carbohydrate, gm.	15
Cholesterol, mg.	70
Fiber	medium

Chicken Divan

This is a complete healthy meal, all in one dish, that you can even make ahead.

Serves 6

1 tablespoon cooking oil
6 boned and skinned chicken breast halves
1/2 teaspoon salt
1/4 teaspoon freshly ground pepper
16 ounces frozen or 4 cups fresh broccoli florets
2 cans (10¾ ounces each) cream of chicken soup
1/2 cup fat-free milk
1/2 cup low-fat or fat-free mayonnaise
1/2 teaspoon white pepper
1 tablespoon fresh lemon juice
1/4 teaspoon curry powder
1/2 cup shredded Cheddar cheese
1/4 cup bread crumbs
Butter spray

1. Grease a 9" x 13" baking pan. In a large skillet, heat oil. Add chicken; sprinkle with salt and pepper. Fry over medium heat until chicken is thoroughly cooked and brown on both sides. Set aside. Cook broccoli in boiling water for 2 to 3 minutes or just until tender-crisp. Drain well. Spread broccoli evenly in bottom of baking pan. Top with chicken pieces.

2. In a small bowl combine soup, milk, mayonnaise, white pepper, lemon juice, and curry powder. Mix well and spoon over chicken. Sprinkle with cheese. Top with bread crumbs and spray with butter spray. Cover and refrigerate until ready to bake.

3. Preheat oven to 350°F. Bake for 30 to 35 minutes or until heated through.

Nutritional information per serving:

Calories	300
Fat, gm.	13
Protein, gm.	30
Carbohydrate, gm.	15
Cholesterol, mg.	75
Fiber	medium

Chicken Florentine

This is a very attractive meal and it tastes wonderful!

Serves 4

1/2 cup seasoned bread crumbs
1/4 cup grated Parmesan cheese
4 boned and skinned chicken breast halves
2 tablespoons butter or margarine
1/2 cup finely chopped onion
2 tablespoons flour
1 cup fat-free milk
10 ounces frozen chopped spinach, thawed and squeezed dry
Salt and freshly ground pepper to taste
Butter spray

1. Preheat oven to 350°F. Grease a 7" x 11" baking pan. In a shallow bowl, combine bread crumbs and Parmesan cheese. Coat chicken with crumbs and set aside. In a small saucepan, melt butter. Add onion and cook over medium heat until translucent. Add flour and stir for 2 minutes. Add milk and cook, stirring constantly, until mixture comes to a boil and thickens. Stir in spinach and remove from heat. Add salt and pepper to taste.

2. Pour spinach mixture into baking pan. Place chicken on top. Sprinkle with any remaining bread crumbs. Spray with butter spray. Bake covered for 20 minutes. Remove cover and bake an additional 30 minutes or until chicken is brown and thoroughly cooked.

Nutritional information per serving:

Calories	280
Fat, gm.	9
Protein, gm.	29
Carbohydrate, gm.	21
Cholesterol, mg.	70
Fiber	medium

Chicken Roulade with Roasted Asparagus and Peppers

This is an impressive way to serve chicken for company yet it is deceptively easy.

Serves 4

4 boned and skinned chicken breast halves
1/2 cup extra-virgin olive oil
1 cup chopped fresh basil
1/2 cup chopped fresh parsley
1/4 pound fresh asparagus, about 8 spears
1 large portobello mushroom cap
1 medium canned roasted red bell pepper, cut into thin strips
Salt and freshly ground pepper to taste

1. Preheat oven to 375°F. Place 1 chicken breast half on a piece of heavy plastic wrap. Cover with another piece of plastic wrap. Use a meat mallet to pound out the breast to 1/4-inch thickness. Set aside.

2. In a small food processor or blender, combine olive oil, basil, and parsley. Process until herbs are finely chopped and well blended with the oil. Place asparagus and mushroom cap on a baking sheet. Brush vegetables with 2 tablespoons of the oil-herb mixture. Bake for 10 minutes. Remove from oven and let cool until easy to handle. Cut mushroom cap into thin strips.

3. Arrange 2 stalks of asparagus, mushroom strip, and red pepper strip down the middle of one piece of chicken. Brush chicken and vegetables with small amount (about 1 tablespoon) of the oil-herb mixture. Sprinkle with salt and pepper. Starting at the long side of the chicken piece, roll up into a cylinder shape with the vegetables in the middle. Roll up in the plastic wrap and twist closed at both ends. Wrap tightly with aluminum foil. Place on clean baking pan. Repeat with the other 3 pieces of chicken. Bake chicken (wrapped in both plastic wrap and foil) for 35 to 40 minutes or until completely done.

4. Remove from oven and let stand at room temperature for at least 15 minutes before unwrapping to allow juices to settle into the chicken. Unwrap and cut into 1/2-inch slices. Arrange on a plate and serve with Pistachio Nut and Olive Tapenade (see page 18). This dish may be served warm or cold.

Nutritional information per serving:

Calories	275
Fat, gm.	19
Protein, gm.	22
Carbohydrate, gm.	3
Cholesterol, mg.	50
Fiber	medium

Grilled Chicken and Vegetable Stir-Fry

Combine fresh garden vegetables and chicken for a wonderful outdoor meal on the grill.

Serves 4

4 boned and skinned chicken breasts, cut into 1-inch pieces
$1/3$ cup soy sauce
2 tablespoons honey
1 teaspoon minced fresh garlic
$1/2$ teaspoon minced fresh gingerroot
$1/4$ teaspoon dried red pepper flakes
$1/4$ teaspoon freshly ground black pepper
6 cups fresh vegetables, cut into bite-size pieces
Olive oil spray
1 tablespoon olive or canola oil
$1/4$ cup dry-roasted peanuts

Note: Use any combination of vegetables.

1. Place chicken in large resealable plastic bag. In a small jar, combine soy sauce, honey, garlic, ginger, red pepper flakes, and black pepper. Mix well. Pour into bag with chicken. Refrigerate at least 30 minutes.

2. When ready to prepare the meal, heat grill to medium-hot. Assemble fresh vegetables on large platter. Spray a large grill basket with oil spray. Place vegetables that take the most amount of time to cook into grill basket. Place on grill, cover, and cook until vegetables just begin to get tender. Shake basket frequently to prevent burning. Add any remaining vegetables. Continue to cook until all vegetables are tender.

3. While vegetables are cooking, heat iron skillet on the other half of the grill. Add oil to the pan. Use a slotted spoon or tongs to remove chicken from marinade. Cook over hot heat, stirring frequently until well browned. Add reserved marinade and cook until mixture boils. Add hot vegetables to skillet. Cook for a few minutes longer until mixture is completely heated through. Serve directly from skillet or spoon into serving bowl. Top with peanuts right before serving.

Nutritional information per serving:

Calories	280
Fat, gm.	9
Protein, gm.	27
Carbohydrate, gm.	23
Cholesterol, mg.	50
Fiber	very high

Grilled Ginger Chicken

Sometimes the easiest recipes are the best. This was served at one of our best gourmet group dinners. The key ingredients are the fresh gingerroot and the sesame oil.

Serves 4

4 boned and skinned chicken breast halves
$1/3$ cup soy sauce
2 tablespoons rice wine vinegar
1 medium scallion, minced
1 tablespoon minced fresh gingerroot
1 teaspoon sesame oil
$1/4$ cup extra-light olive oil

1. Place chicken in large resealable plastic bag. Add all remaining ingredients. Reseal bag and mix well. Refrigerate for several hours or overnight.

2. Preheat grill to medium-hot. Remove chicken from marinade. Grill over medium coals until brown on all sides and completely done in the middle. Baste with marinade while grilling. Remove from grill and let stand for 10 minutes. To serve, slice each breast into diagonal slices.

Nutritional information per serving:

Calories	130
Fat, gm.	4
Protein, gm.	21
Carbohydrate, gm.	2
Cholesterol, mg.	50
Fiber	0

Honey Mustard Chicken

A great flavor complement for chicken.

Serves 4

¹/₂ tablespoon cooking oil
4 boned and skinned chicken breast halves
¹/₄ cup butter or margarine, melted
¹/₄ cup honey
¹/₄ cup Dijon mustard
1 teaspoon salt
¹/₄ teaspoon freshly ground pepper
¹/₂ teaspoon curry powder

Preheat oven to 325°F. In a medium skillet, heat oil. Add chicken breasts and brown quickly over medium-hot heat. Remove chicken and place in a 7" x 11" baking pan. (Chicken does not have to be completely done at this point.) In a small bowl, combine butter, honey, mustard, salt, pepper, and curry powder. Mix well. Spoon over chicken. Bake uncovered for 15 minutes. Turn chicken and bake for another 15 minutes or until chicken is completely done. Watch carefully to prevent burning. Spoon sauce over chicken when ready to serve.

Nutritional information per serving:

Calories	240
Fat, gm.	9
Protein, gm.	21
Carbohydrate, gm.	18
Cholesterol, mg.	65
Fiber	0

London Chicken

This is a wonderfully flavored chicken in Marsala wine sauce. It is very good served over cooked noodles.

Serves 4

1 tablespoon butter or margarine
4 boned and skinned chicken breast halves
1/2 pound fresh mushrooms, sliced
1/4 cup Marsala wine
1 can (10¾ ounces) cream of chicken or cream of mushroom soup

Preheat oven to 325°F. Butter a 7" x 11" baking pan. In a large heavy nonstick skillet, heat butter. Add chicken and cook over medium heat until brown on all sides. Remove chicken from pan and place in baking dish. (Chicken does not need to be thoroughly cooked at this point.) Add mushrooms to skillet and cook until tender. Add wine and stir to deglaze the pan. Add soup and blend. Pour soup and mushroom mixture over chicken. Cover and bake for 30 minutes. Uncover pan and bake for another 30 minutes. Check occasionally and add water if it gets too dry.

Nutritional information per serving:

Calories	210
Fat, gm.	9
Protein, gm.	24
Carbohydrate, gm.	8
Cholesterol, mg.	65
Fiber	very low

Plum Chicken

*This is a very attractive way to serve chicken. It has a subtle sweet-sour flavor.
It is easy to make but it looks as though you went to a lot of work.*

Serves 4

1 tablespoon vegetable oil
4 boned and skinned chicken breast halves
$^1/_2$ teaspoon salt
$^1/_4$ teaspoon freshly ground pepper
$^1/_3$ cup plum or cherry jelly
$^1/_4$ cup cider vinegar
1 tablespoon brown sugar
$^1/_8$ teaspoon allspice
4 fresh plums, cut into $^1/_2$-inch slices

In a medium nonstick skillet, heat oil. Add chicken and cook over medium heat until chicken is golden brown on both sides. Sprinkle with salt and pepper. In a small bowl, combine jelly, vinegar, brown sugar, and allspice. Add to the skillet and stir to deglaze the pan (scrape up any browned bits). Partially cover skillet and cook for 10 to 20 minutes or until sauce is slightly reduced and chicken is completely done. Taste and adjust seasoning and add extra sugar, salt, or pepper if desired. Add plums and cook, partially covered, for 5 to 10 minutes or until plums are tender. Arrange chicken on individual plates and top with sauce and plums.

Nutritional information per serving:

Calories	245
Fat, gm.	5
Protein, gm.	21
Carbohydrate, gm.	29
Cholesterol, mg.	50
Fiber	low

Sassy Salsa Chicken

This is a interesting way to serve chicken. Make it mild or hot to suit your taste.

Serves 4

1/4 cup Dijon mustard
2 tablespoons fresh lime juice
1 tablespoon honey
2 tablespoons vegetable oil, divided
1/4 teaspoon paprika
1/2 teaspoon salt
1/4 teaspoon freshly ground pepper
1/4 cup chicken broth
4 boned and skinned chicken breast halves
1 cup salsa, chunky style

1. In a small bowl, combine mustard, lime juice, honey, 1 tablespoon vegetable oil, paprika, salt, pepper, and broth. Pour into a large resealable plastic bag. Place chicken in bag. Reseal and mix well. Refrigerate for several hours.

2. In a large nonstick skillet, heat 1 tablespoon vegetable oil. Remove chicken from bag, reserving marinade. Cook chicken over medium heat, partially covered, until golden brown on both sides. Add reserved marinade. Spoon salsa over chicken pieces. Cover and cook over low heat until chicken is thoroughly done. Thin sauce if necessary with additional chicken broth. Place chicken on platter and ladle sauce on top.

Nutritional information per serving:

Calories	215
Fat, gm.	11
Protein, gm.	22
Carbohydrate, gm.	7
Cholesterol, mg.	50
Fiber	low

Swiss Chicken Breasts

*This is one of those surprise meals that looks so rich but is really low in fat and calories.
Serve the chicken and this wonderful sauce on top of noodles or cooked vegetables.*

Serves 4

$1/4$ cup flour
$1/2$ teaspoon salt
$1/2$ teaspoon freshly ground pepper
$1/2$ teaspoon dill weed
4 boned and skinned chicken breast halves
1 tablespoon butter or margarine
2 tablespoons cornstarch
1 cup low-fat chicken broth
$3/4$ cup fat-free half-and-half
$1/2$ cup white wine
4 ounces reduced-fat processed Swiss cheese
$1/4$ teaspoon paprika
Parsley for garnish

1. Preheat oven to 325°F. Grease a 9" x 9" baking pan or casserole dish. In a plastic bag, mix flour, salt, pepper, and dill weed. Add chicken and toss until well coated. Heat butter in a medium nonstick skillet. Fry chicken over medium heat until brown on both sides. Place chicken in baking pan. (Chicken does not have to be thoroughly cooked at this point.)

2. In a small glass, mix cornstarch and chicken broth. Add to skillet and cook until thickened, stirring constantly to deglaze the pan. Remove from heat. Add half-and-half and wine. Pour sauce over chicken. Cover loosely with foil and bake for 30 minutes or until chicken is done. Remove foil and top with cheese. Sprinkle with paprika. Bake for 5 to 10 minutes until cheese is melted. Place under broiler to brown if desired. Garnish with parsley.

Nutritional information per serving:

Calories	250
Fat, gm.	6
Protein, gm.	33
Carbohydrate, gm.	16
Cholesterol, mg.	70
Fiber	0

Teriyaki Turkey Tenderloin

This is a great marinade that I have used for special occasions for years.

Serves 6

3-pound turkey breast
1/2 cup soy sauce
1/4 cup honey
2 tablespoons dry sherry wine
2 tablespoons vegetable oil
1 teaspoon sesame oil, optional
1 clove garlic, minced
1 small onion, chopped
1/2 teaspoon ginger

Note: This marinade works well with chicken drumsticks, chicken wings, chicken breast, or pork tenderloin. The poultry or meat can also be grilled.

1. Cut turkey breast into strips. Place in a resealable plastic bag. In a small bowl or jar, combine all remaining ingredients. Pour into bag and mix well. Place in refrigerator for several hours.

2. Preheat oven to 325°F. Butter a nonstick baking pan. Remove turkey from marinade. Place into baking pan. Bake for 40 to 60 minutes, turning occasionally, until brown on the outside and thoroughly done on the inside.

Nutritional information per serving:

Calories	235
Fat, gm.	6
Protein, gm.	40
Carbohydrate, gm.	5
Cholesterol, mg.	100
Fiber	0

Chapter Eight
Fish and Seafood

Cajun Cod

This is so simple. The Cajun seasoning adds flavor but it is not excessively hot.

Serves 4

¹/4 cup butter or margarine
2 tablespoons Cajun seasoning*
1 teaspoon minced garlic
¹/2 cup dry vermouth
1 ¹/2 pounds skinless cod fillet, cut into 4 pieces

*Cajun seasonings are usually a mixture of spices such as chili powder, onion powder, paprika, basil, cayenne pepper, black pepper, and garlic.

In a large skillet, melt butter. Stir in Cajun seasoning and garlic. Cook for 2 minutes, stirring constantly. Add vermouth and cook for 3 minutes. Add cod fillets. Cook for 10 minutes per inch of thickness, measured at the thickest part. Fish is done when it flakes easily with a fork.

Nutritional information per serving:

Calories	250
Fat, gm.	12
Protein, gm.	31
Carbohydrate, gm.	5
Cholesterol, mg.	100
Fiber	low

Carrot-Crusted Sea Bass

This is a very moist fish that holds together well with this flavorful coating.

Serves 4

$1/2$ cup dry bread crumbs
$1/4$ cup grated carrot
1 large egg, lightly beaten
$1/4$ cup flour
$1/2$ teaspoon salt
$1/4$ teaspoon freshly ground pepper
1 $1/2$ pounds skinless sea bass fillet
1 tablespoon canola oil

Preheat oven to 350°F. Mix bread crumbs and grated carrots in a shallow bowl. Place egg in another shallow bowl. In a plastic bag, combine flour, salt, and pepper. Place fish in bag. Shake gently until lightly coated. Dip fish into egg and generously coat with bread-crumb mixture. In a large skillet, heat oil. Cook fish over medium heat until golden brown on both sides. Place in oven and bake for 15 to 20 minutes or until fish flakes easily with a fork. Baking time will vary depending on thickness of the fish.

Nutritional information per serving:

Calories	275
Fat, gm.	8
Protein, gm.	35
Carbohydrate, gm.	16
Cholesterol, mg.	115
Fiber	medium

Cinnamon Apricot–Glazed Salmon

Salmon is always good with a touch of sweetness.

Serves 4

2 tablespoons soy sauce
$^{1}/_{2}$ teaspoon ginger
1 large cinnamon stick
12 ounces apricot nectar
1 $^{1}/_{2}$ pounds skinless salmon fillet

Preheat oven broiler. Butter a 9" x 11" baking pan. In a small saucepan, combine soy sauce, ginger, cinnamon stick, and apricot nectar. Bring to a boil, reduce heat, and simmer until reduced to $^{3}/_{4}$ cup. Place salmon fillets in baking pan. Broil for 5 minutes. Brush with apricot mixture. Continue to broil until lightly brown and salmon is completely done on one side. Turn and baste other side with apricot mixture. Broil until lightly brown and fish flakes easily with a fork.

Nutritional information per serving:

Calories	250
Fat, gm.	6
Protein, gm.	34
Carbohydrate, gm.	15
Cholesterol, mg.	90
Fiber	medium

Citrus-Marinated Orange Roughy

The orange, lemon, and soy sauce complements the mild orange roughy.

Serves 4

1/2 cup orange juice
2 tablespoons fresh lemon juice
2 tablespoons soy sauce
1/4 cup ketchup
2 tablespoons canola oil
1/4 teaspoon white pepper
1 1/2 pounds skinless orange roughy fillets
Toasted sesame seeds, optional

1. In a small bowl, combine orange juice, lemon juice, soy sauce, ketchup, canola oil, and pepper. Pour 1/4 cup into a small ceramic or glass bowl and set aside. Pour remaining marinade into a large resealable plastic bag. Add fillets and seal bag. Refrigerate for 30 minutes to 1 hour, turning occasionally.

2. Position broiler rack 4 to 6 inches from heat source. Preheat broiler. Grease a broiler pan. Remove fish from marinade. Discard marinade. Place fillets on broiler pan. Broil for 5 to 10 minutes on each side or until fish begins to brown and it flakes easily with a fork. While broiling, baste with reserved marinade. Sprinkle with sesame seeds if desired

Nutritional information per serving:

Calories	180
Fat, gm.	5
Protein, gm.	26
Carbohydrate, gm.	8
Cholesterol, mg.	35
Fiber	low

Crab Cakes

A special treat but very easy to make.

Serves 4

2 slices white bread, crusts removed
2 tablespoons milk
1 tablespoon low-fat mayonnaise
1 teaspoon Dijon mustard
1 teaspoon Worcestershire sauce
1 teaspoon baking powder
$1/4$ teaspoon salt
$1/8$ teaspoon freshly ground pepper
1 teaspoon seafood seasoning
1 large egg, lightly beaten
1 pound crabmeat, shredded
1 tablespoon canola oil

Note: Old Bay seasoning is one brand of seafood seasoning. It is a mixture of celery salt, pepper, cloves, allspice, ginger, mace, cardamom, cinnamon, and paprika.

Break bread into small pieces and place in large bowl. Add milk and stir to moisten. Add all remaining ingredients except canola oil. Thoroughly mix. Form into 4 to 6 cakes. Heat oil in nonstick skillet. Sauté cakes over medium-low heat for 5 minutes on each side or until lightly brown and done in the middle. Serve with tartar sauce, mustard, or cocktail sauce on the side.

Nutritional information per serving without dipping sauce:

Calories	200
Fat, gm.	7
Protein, gm.	26
Carbohydrate, gm.	8
Cholesterol, mg.	150
Fiber	low

Haddock with Cilantro-Orange Sauce

This is a simple recipe for baking fish with a mild, appealing sauce.

Serves 4

2 pounds halibut or cod fillets
1 tablespoon olive oil
1 medium onion, finely chopped
1/2 teaspoon crushed garlic
1/3 cup chopped fresh cilantro or 2 teaspoons dried
1/4 teaspoon freshly ground pepper
1/4 teaspoon salt
1 cup orange juice
2 tablespoons fresh lemon juice
1 tablespoon lemon zest
1 tablespoon orange zest
1 tablespoon cornstarch
1/4 cup water
4 slices fresh lemon
4 slices fresh orange

1. Preheat oven to 375°F. Place fish in a deep 7" x 11" baking dish. In a small skillet, heat oil. Add onion and cook until translucent. Add garlic, cilantro, pepper, and salt. Cook for 1 minute. Add orange juice, lemon juice, lemon zest, and orange zest. Mix and pour over fish. Bake for 30 to 35 minutes or until fish is completely done. It should flake easily when tested with a fork.

2. Transfer fish to a serving platter and keep warm. Pour sauce from baking pan into a small saucepan. Mix cornstarch and water in a small bowl. Add to saucepan. Bring to a boil, stirring constantly until it thickens. If too thin, add extra cornstarch. If too thick, add extra orange juice. Pour over fish and garnish with lemon and orange slices.

Nutritional information per serving:

Calories	310
Fat, gm.	8
Protein, gm.	49
Carbohydrate, gm.	10
Cholesterol, mg.	75
Fiber	medium

Halibut Steak in Apricot Brandy Marinade

This is so good! It browns beautifully and tastes fantastic. This marinade is also wonderful with salmon.

Serves 4

1/2 cup apricot preserves
2 tablespoons brown sugar
2 tablespoons soy sauce
1/2 teaspoon ginger
2 tablespoons finely chopped onion
3 tablespoons brandy
1 1/2 pounds halibut steak
1 tablespoon vegetable oil

Note: Add extra brandy to the reserved marinade if desired.

1. In a small bowl, combine apricot preserves, brown sugar, soy sauce, ginger, onion, and brandy. Mix well. Pour into a large resealable plastic bag. Add halibut. Seal bag and mix gently. Refrigerate for several hours or overnight.

2. When ready to serve, heat oil in large nonstick skillet. Remove halibut from marinade and place in skillet. Fry over medium heat until lightly browned on the outside and completely done in the middle. Watch carefully to prevent burning. (It will brown quickly because there is sugar in the marinade.)

3. While fish is cooking, place reserved marinade in small saucepan and bring to a boil for 2 minutes. Serve on the side with the fish.

Nutritional information per serving:

Calories	250
Fat, gm.	7
Protein, gm.	36
Carbohydrate, gm.	10
Cholesterol, mg.	55
Fiber	0

Honey Mustard Salmon

This is a great combination of sweet and hot flavors that complements salmon.

Serves 4

1 tablespoon honey
2 tablespoons Dijon mustard
2 tablespoons butter or margarine, melted
1/4 cup dry bread crumbs
1/4 cup chopped pecans
1 tablespoon chopped fresh parsley or
    1 teaspoon dried herbs of your choice
1 1/2 pounds skin-on salmon fillets, cut into 4 pieces

Preheat oven to 400°F. Grease a baking pan or broiler pan. In a small bowl, mix together honey, mustard, and butter. Set aside. In a small food processor, combine bread crumbs, pecans, and parsley. Pulse to mix. Place salmon, skin down, on baking pan. Brush each fillet with honey-mustard mixture. Pat top of each fillet with bread-crumb mixture. Bake for 10 minutes per inch of thickness, measured at thickest part, or until salmon flakes easily when tested with a fork. Watch carefully to prevent burning.

Nutritional information per serving:

Calories	290
Fat, gm.	14
Protein, gm.	34
Carbohydrate, gm.	7
Cholesterol, mg.	100
Fiber	low

Lemon Dijon Sole

Choose any mild white fish and dress it up with this delicious topping.

Serves 4

1 1/2 pounds sole fillets
1/2 teaspoon salt
1/4 teaspoon freshly ground pepper
2 tablespoons fresh lemon juice
1 tablespoon Dijon mustard
2 tablespoons butter or margarine, melted, divided
3 tablespoons low-fat mayonnaise
1/2 teaspoon dry mustard
1/4 cup grated Parmesan cheese
1/4 teaspoon paprika
1 medium lemon, cut into thin slices

1. Grease broiler pan. Place fish on pan. Sprinkle with salt and pepper. In a small bowl, combine lemon juice, Dijon mustard, and 1 tablespoon butter. Brush on fish and let stand for 15 to 20 minutes.

2. Position broiler rack about 4 inches from heat source. Preheat broiler. In another small bowl, combine remaining 1 tablespoon butter, mayonnaise, dry mustard, Parmesan cheese, and paprika. Set aside. Broil fish for about 5 minutes per side or until almost done. Spread mayonnaise mixture on top of fish and broil for 2 to 5 minutes more or until topping is golden brown. Garnish with lemon slices.

Nutritional information per serving:

Calories	230
Fat, gm.	9
Protein, gm.	28
Carbohydrate, gm.	7
Cholesterol, mg.	20
Fiber	low

Potato-Crusted Snapper

If you enjoy pan-fried fish, this one is sure to be a favorite.

Serves 4

1 1/2 pounds skinless, boneless red snapper or pollack fillets
1/2 cup fat-free milk
1 egg, lightly beaten
Dash hot pepper sauce
1/2 teaspoon salt
1/4 teaspoon freshly ground pepper
1 teaspoon Worcestershire sauce
1 tablespoon canola oil
1 cup potato flakes

Place fish in a large resealable plastic bag. In a small bowl, combine milk, egg, pepper sauce, salt, pepper, and Worcestershire sauce. Mix well. Pour into plastic bag with fish. Set aside. In a large nonstick skillet, heat oil. Place potato flakes in a shallow bowl. Remove fish from bag, one piece at a time, and dredge in potato flakes. Place fish pieces in skillet. Cook over medium heat until golden brown on all sides and completely done in the middle.

Nutritional information per serving:

Calories	230
Fat, gm.	6
Protein, gm.	36
Carbohydrate, gm.	8
Cholesterol, mg.	65
Fiber	low

Scallop and Shrimp Marsala

This is for the seafood lover.

Serves 4

2 tablespoons canola oil
8 ounces fresh mushrooms, sliced
1/2 cup flour
1/2 teaspoon salt
1/4 teaspoon white pepper
1/2 pound sea scallops
1 pound cooked shrimp, peeled and deveined
2 cups diced fresh plum tomatoes
1/2 cup Marsala wine

In a large nonstick skillet, heat oil. Add mushrooms and cook until tender. Remove mushrooms from pan and set aside. Combine flour, salt, and pepper in a plastic bag. Add scallops and shrimp. Shake gently to coat. Add 1 layer of scallops and shrimp to skillet. Cook for about 5 minutes, until lightly browned. Remove from pan. Cook remaining scallops and shrimp. Remove all shrimp and scallops from pan and set aside. Drain and discard any liquid from skillet. Add tomatoes to skillet and cook for 1 minute. Stir in reserved mushrooms, scallops, and shrimp. Add wine and bring to a boil. Simmer for 2 minutes or until sauce thickens. Serve over pasta if desired.

Nutritional information per serving without pasta:

Calories	300
Fat, gm.	9
Protein, gm.	19
Carbohydrate, gm.	34
Cholesterol, mg.	190
Fiber	medium

Shrimp and Artichokes in Garlic Tomato Sauce

Easy to make but full of flavor.

Serves 4

$^1/_2$ tablespoon olive oil
1 medium onion, finely chopped
3 cloves garlic, minced
1 tablespoon finely chopped jalapeño
1 pound cooked shrimp, shelled and tails removed
14 ounces artichoke hearts, drained and quartered
30 ounces canned diced Italian tomatoes
$^1/_2$ cup finely chopped fresh cilantro
$^1/_2$ cup vegetable or chicken broth
Salt and freshly ground pepper to taste
Shredded Parmesan cheese, optional

In a large skillet, heat oil. Add onion and cook until lightly brown. Add garlic, jalapeño pepper, and shrimp. Cook for 3 minutes over medium heat. Add artichokes, tomatoes, and cilantro. Bring to a boil. Reduce heat and simmer for 10 to 15 minutes or until it reaches desired consistency. Add vegetable or chicken broth to thin if needed. Add salt and pepper to taste. Serve over warm pasta. Top with Parmesan cheese if desired.

Nutritional information per serving without pasta:

Calories	260
Fat, gm.	4
Protein, gm.	30
Carbohydrate, gm.	26
Cholesterol, mg.	220
Fiber	very high

Shrimp and Pepper Stir-Fry

This is sure to be a favorite. The sauce is wonderful.
This recipe could also be made with chicken or pork in place of the shrimp.

Serves 4

1/3 cup apricot preserves
3/4 cup fat-free chicken broth
2 tablespoons soy sauce
1 tablespoon cornstarch
1 tablespoon canola oil
2 large red bell peppers, thinly sliced
1/2 pound mushrooms, sliced
1/2 cup green onions, diced
2 cloves garlic, minced
1 pound shrimp, peeled and deveined

Note: Frozen cooked shrimp can be used in place of raw shrimp.

In small bowl or jar, combine apricot preserves, chicken broth, soy sauce, and cornstarch. Mix well and set aside. In a large non-stick skillet, heat oil. Add peppers, mushroom, onions, and garlic. Cook over medium heat until tender. Remove from pan and set aside. Add shrimp to skillet and cook over medium heat for 3 to 4 minutes or until shrimp turns pink. Discard any excess liquid from pan. Stir in broth mixture. Bring to a boil and cook until sauce thickens. Add pepper and mushroom mixture. Heat through. Serve with rice.

Nutritional information per serving without rice:

Calories	255
Fat, gm.	5
Protein, gm.	25
Carbohydrate, gm.	27
Cholesterol, mg.	175
Fiber	medium

Chapter Nine
Side Dishes

Apple Apricot Bread Dressing

Creamy Scalloped Potatoes

Four-Bean Casserole

Fried Rice

German Potato Salad

Gnocchi

Greek Spinach Phyllo Squares

Hash Brown Potato Casserole

Homemade Baked Beans

Make-Ahead Gratin Potatoes

Onion Pie

Parsley Dumplings

Rice with Green Onions and Mushrooms

Roasted Herb Potato Medley

Saffron Wild Rice Pilaf

Wild Rice and Mushroom Stuffing

Yellow Rice with Golden Raisins

Apple Apricot Bread Dressing

*This has a wonderful combination of flavors and it is lower in fat
and calories than most bread dressings or stuffings.*

Serves 6

1 tablespoon canola oil
1 large onion, finely chopped
$^1/_2$ cup dried apricot halves, each cut into 4 pieces
1 large cooking apple (Golden Delicious, for example), peeled,
   cored, and chopped
$^1/_2$ teaspoon cinnamon
$^1/_4$ teaspoon cloves
$^1/_4$ teaspoon savory or thyme
$^1/_4$ teaspoon salt
$2^1/_2$ cups fat-free chicken broth
4 cups herb-seasoned stuffing cubes

Preheat oven to 350°F. Butter a 2-quart ovenproof bowl. In a medium skillet, heat oil. Add onion and cook over medium heat until lightly brown. Add apricot pieces, apples, cinnamon, cloves, savory, and salt. Cook for 5 minutes. Add chicken broth. Bring to a boil. Reduce heat and simmer for 5 minutes. In a large bowl, combine fruit mixture and stuffing cubes. Gently mix with a spoon. Place mixture in ovenproof bowl. Cover and bake for 40 minutes. Uncover and bake for 20 more minutes.

Nutritional information per serving:

Calories	210
Fat, gm.	3
Protein, gm.	6
Carbohydrate, gm.	39
Cholesterol, mg.	0
Fiber	medium

Creamy Scalloped Potatoes

My friend Mary has been making these potatoes for years.
For a simple supper, serve with a ring of bologna or pork chops.

Serves 4

1 can (10³/4 ounces) cream of mushroom soup
¹/2 cup fat-free milk
¹/2 teaspoon salt
¹/4 teaspoon white pepper
5 medium potatoes, peeled and thinly sliced
1 medium onion, thinly sliced
Dash paprika

Preheat oven to 375°F. Butter a 1¹/2-quart casserole. In a large bowl, combine soup, milk, salt, and pepper. Add potatoes and onion. Gently stir to mix. Spoon into casserole. Sprinkle with paprika. Cover and bake for 1 to 1¹/2 hours or until potatoes are tender.

Nutritional information per serving:

Calories	140
Fat, gm.	2
Protein, gm.	5
Carbohydrate, gm.	26
Cholesterol, mg.	5
Fiber	medium

Four-Bean Casserole

What would a summer cookout be without this bean casserole?

Serves 15

8 bacon slices

1 large onion, finely chopped

3/4 cup brown sugar

1 teaspoon dry mustard

1 teaspoon salt

1/2 teaspoon garlic powder

1 teaspoon Worcestershire sauce

1/2 cup cider vinegar

15 ounces canned kidney beans, drained

30 ounces canned butter beans, drained

15 ounces canned lima beans, drained

15 ounces canned baked beans

Note: The variety of beans can be changed to suit your taste.

Preheat oven to 325°F. In a medium skillet, fry bacon until crisp. Remove bacon from pan, crumble, and set aside. Add onion to skillet and cook until translucent. Pour off excess bacon fat and discard. Add brown sugar, dry mustard, salt, garlic powder, Worcestershire, and vinegar. Simmer for 10 minutes. Spoon mixture into a 2-quart casserole. Add the beans and the reserved bacon. Mix gently. Bake uncovered for 1 hour.

Nutritional information per serving:

Calories	175
Fat, gm.	2
Protein, gm.	8
Carbohydrate, gm.	32
Cholesterol, mg.	5
Fiber	very high

Fried Rice

This is a very special fried rice recipe. It is so flavorful and it makes enough for several meals.
It can be made ahead and reheated in the microwave or oven.

Serves 10

$^1/_3$ cup butter or margarine
3 cups long-grain white rice
5$^1/_2$ cups fat-free beef broth
8 slices bacon
2 medium onions, chopped
3 stalks celery, diced
1 pound fresh mushrooms, sliced
$^1/_3$ cup soy sauce

In a large heavy nonstick skillet or saucepan, melt butter. Add rice and fry over medium-hot heat, stirring frequently, until light brown. Add broth and cover pan. Reduce heat and simmer for 20 to 30 minutes or until rice is tender and broth has been absorbed. While rice is cooking, fry bacon in medium skillet until crisp. Remove bacon from skillet and crumble. Set aside. Add onions and celery to the bacon drippings. Cook until tender. Drain excess fat and discard. Add mushrooms to the skillet and cook, stirring frequently, until tender. When rice is done, combine rice with bacon, onions, celery, and mushrooms. Add soy sauce and stir until well mixed. Taste and add additional soy sauce if desired.

Nutritional information per serving:

Calories	260
Fat, gm.	9
Protein, gm.	4
Carbohydrate, gm.	41
Cholesterol, mg.	20
Fiber	low

German Potato Salad

A little bit of bacon provides a lot of flavor. Your grandmother may have used a lot more of the bacon drippings but it is healthier and tastes just as good with less.

Serves 8

6 medium potatoes
6 slices bacon
2 tablespoons bacon fat
1 cup finely chopped onion
2 tablespoons flour
1 cup water
²/₃ cup cider vinegar
¹/₃ cup sugar
¹/₂ teaspoon salt
¹/₄ teaspoon white pepper
Salt and freshly ground pepper to taste

In a large saucepan, boil potatoes in water just until tender. Chill under cold running water. Drain. Peel and slice. Place in large bowl and set aside. In a medium skillet, fry bacon until crisp. Remove and crumble. Place in bowl with potatoes. Pour bacon drippings into custard cup and return 2 tablespoons to the skillet. Cook onion in skillet over medium heat until translucent. Stir in flour and cook for 2 minutes, stirring constantly. Add 1 cup water and bring to a boil, stirring constantly until mixture thickens. Add vinegar, sugar, salt, and pepper. Pour over potatoes and bacon. Adjust seasoning with salt and pepper. Serve warm.

Nutritional information per serving:

Calories	145
Fat, gm.	5
Protein, gm.	3
Carbohydrate, gm.	21
Cholesterol, mg.	10
Fiber	medium

Gnocchi

*Gnocchi are small dumplings poached in boiling water and garnished with cheese and butter.
My friend's Italian grandmother served these with a spicy tomato sauce.*

Serves 8

1 cup flour
1 teaspoon salt
1/4 teaspoon garlic powder
1/4 teaspoon dry mustard
1 cup water
1/2 cup butter or margarine
4 eggs
2 tablespoons butter or margarine, melted
1/4 cup grated Parmesan cheese

1. In a small bowl, combine flour, salt, garlic powder, and dry mustard. Set aside. In a heavy medium saucepan, combine water and 1/2 cup butter. Bring to a boil. Add dry ingredients all at once, stirring until mixture forms a ball that does not separate. Remove from heat. Add eggs, one at a time, beating well after each addition.

2. Drop teaspoons of the mixture into a medium saucepan of boiling water. Cook for 5 minutes, keeping water boiling gently. Remove balls with slotted spoon and drain well on a rack.

3. Preheat oven broiler. Place gnocchi in a shallow 1 1/2-quart baking dish. Top with 2 tablespoons melted butter and sprinkle with cheese. Place under broiler and heat until heated through. Watch carefully to prevent burning.

Nutritional information per serving:

Calories	220
Fat, gm.	17
Protein, gm.	5
Carbohydrate, gm.	12
Cholesterol, mg.	139
Fiber	0

Greek Spinach Phyllo Squares

I used to avoid using phyllo dough because it seemed to be too much trouble, but this recipe really turned out to be easy. My guests were impressed and it was fabulously flaky.

Serves 12

1 tablespoon butter or margarine
1 medium onion, finely chopped
3 eggs, lightly beaten
16 ounces fat-free ricotta cheese
20 ounces frozen chopped spinach, thawed and squeezed dry
1/2 cup chopped fresh parsley
1/4 teaspoon nutmeg
1 1/2 teaspoons salt
1/4 teaspoon freshly ground black pepper
1/4 teaspoon red pepper flakes
10 phyllo dough sheets, thawed, room temperature
1/2 cup olive oil

Preheat oven to 350°F. Butter a 9" x 13" baking pan. In a small skillet, melt butter. Add onion and cook until translucent. In a large bowl, combine eggs, ricotta cheese, spinach, parsley, nutmeg, salt, black and red pepper, and onion. Fit 1 layer of phyllo pastry into pan. Brush with olive oil. Add 4 more sheets of phyllo, brushing with oil between each layer. Spoon spinach mixture over phyllo. Cover spinach mixture with another layer of phyllo and brush with oil. Add 4 more sheets, brushing each layer with oil. Bake for 40 to 50 minutes or until lightly browned.

Note: To cut down on the fat in this recipe, use an olive oil spray in place of brushing the olive oil on each layer of phyllo. When working with phyllo, read the directions on the box. It is important to keep the sheets covered as you work because they become dry and brittle very quickly.

Nutritional information per serving:

Calories	195
Fat, gm.	12
Protein, gm.	9
Carbohydrate, gm.	13
Cholesterol, mg.	50
Fiber	low

Hash Brown Potato Casserole

At any large potluck, there will usually be a pan of these tasty creamy potatoes. This is a lower-fat version.

Serves 15

2 pounds frozen, loose packed, hash brown potatoes
$1/2$ cup finely chopped onion
1 can (10¾ ounces) cream of chicken soup
1 teaspoon salt
$1/2$ teaspoon freshly ground pepper
1$1/2$ cups fat-free sour cream
2 cups shredded reduced-fat Cheddar cheese
1 cup corn flake crumbs

Preheat oven to 350°F. If using a glass or nonstick pan, preheat oven to 325°F. Butter a 9" x 13" baking pan. In a large bowl, combine potatoes, onion, soup, salt, pepper, sour cream, and cheese. Stir to mix well. Spoon into pan. Sprinkle with corn flakes. Bake for 60 minutes or until lightly browned.

Nutritional information per serving:

Calories	200
Fat, gm.	10
Protein, gm.	7
Carbohydrate, gm.	20
Cholesterol, mg.	15
Fiber	low

Homemade Baked Beans

It's fun and economical to make your own baked beans.

Serves 12

1 pound (2¹/₂ cups) dried navy beans
2 teaspoons baking soda
¹/₄ cup brown sugar
¹/₂ cup ketchup
3 cups fat-free chicken broth
1 large onion, finely chopped
1 teaspoon dry mustard
1 tablespoon Worcestershire sauce
2 teaspoons salt
¹/₂ pound lean ham, diced
2 tablespoons barbecue sauce, optional

1. Wash beans and throw out any stones. Place beans and baking soda in a large soup pot and cover with water. Bring to a boil and boil for 2 minutes. Cover, remove from heat, and let stand for at least 1 hour or overnight.

2. Pour off water. Add all remaining ingredients except barbecue sauce. Bring to a boil. Place in a 4-quart casserole. Cover and bake at 275°F for 4 to 6 hours or until beans are tender. Check occasionally and add additional broth or water if beans get too dry. Add barbecue sauce for extra flavor if desired.

Nutritional information per serving:

Calories	180
Fat, gm.	1
Protein, gm.	13
Carbohydrate, gm.	30
Cholesterol, mg.	10
Fiber	very high

Make-Ahead Gratin Potatoes

It always helps to prepare some dishes ahead of time before a family gathering.

Serves 6

12 ounces evaporated fat-free milk
1/3 cup fat-free milk
1 teaspoon minced garlic
1 teaspoon salt
1/2 teaspoon white pepper
1/8 teaspoon nutmeg
3 pounds potatoes, peeled and thinly sliced
1/2 cup shredded reduced-fat Cheddar cheese
1/2 cup shredded Parmesan cheese
1 tablespoon flour
1/2 teaspoon paprika

1. Butter a 9-inch pie pan or a 2-quart casserole dish. In a large saucepan, combine evaporated milk, fat-free milk, garlic, salt, white pepper, and nutmeg. Add potatoes to pan. Bring to boil over medium heat. Reduce heat and boil gently for 10 minutes, stirring occasionally. Mix together Cheddar, Parmesan, and flour in a small bowl. Remove potatoes from heat and spoon half of potatoes into baking pan. Sprinkle half of cheese mixture over potatoes. Add remaining potatoes and milk mixture. Top with remaining cheese. Sprinkle with paprika. Cover with aluminum foil and refrigerate until ready to bake.

2. When ready to bake, preheat oven to 350°F. Bake for 20 minutes, covered. Remove cover and bake for another 20 to 30 minutes or until potatoes are very tender.

Nutritional information per serving:

Calories	235
Fat, gm.	3
Protein, gm.	13
Carbohydrate, gm.	39
Cholesterol, mg.	10
Fiber	medium

Onion Pie

This is best made with Vidalia onions when they are available. It is delicious and can be served in place of potatoes with grilled steak or hamburgers. It is very easy to make with a prepared pie crust, yet it is an impressive side dish.

Serves 8

9-inch refrigerated unbaked pie crust
1 egg white, lightly beaten
1 tablespoon butter or margarine
2 cups sliced onion
1 cup grated reduced-fat Swiss cheese
1 cup evaporated fat-free milk
2 eggs
1/4 teaspoon salt
1/2 teaspoon dry mustard
1/8 teaspoon cayenne pepper
2 tablespoons grated Parmesan cheese
1/4 teaspoon paprika

1. Preheat oven to 400°F. Place pie crust in pie pan. Brush with egg white. Prick sides and bottom of crust. Bake for 5 minutes. Set aside. In a medium nonstick skillet, melt butter. Add onion and cook over medium heat until translucent and very soft. Spoon into pie shell. Sprinkle with Swiss cheese.

2. In a small bowl, combine milk, eggs, salt, dry mustard, and cayenne pepper. Mix well. Pour over onions and cheese. Top with Parmesan cheese and sprinkle with paprika. Bake for 10 minutes at 400°F and then reduce heat to 325°F. Bake an additional 20 to 25 minutes or until a knife inserted in the center comes out clean.

Note: Leftovers warm up beautifully in the oven.

Nutritional information per serving:

Calories	200
Fat, gm.	10
Protein, gm.	10
Carbohydrate, gm.	18
Cholesterol, mg.	55
Fiber	low

Parsley Dumplings

Dumplings are a part of the past that is often forgotten in the rush of making dinner.
But try these because they are so easy.

Serves 8

2 cups flour
1 tablespoon baking powder
1 teaspoon salt
1 tablespoon finely chopped fresh parsley
²/₃ cup fat-free milk
1 egg, lightly beaten
2 tablespoons butter or margarine, melted

In a medium bowl, combine flour, baking powder, salt, and parsley. Stir to mix. In a small bowl, mix milk, egg, and butter together. Pour liquid mixture into dry ingredients. Stir just until mixed. Batter should be stiff but moist. Add additional milk or flour if needed, a little at a time. Drop batter by teaspoons into hot simmering broth, soup, or gravy. Cover and cook for 20 minutes.

Nutritional information per serving:

Calories	145
Fat, gm.	3
Protein, gm.	4
Carbohydrate, gm.	25
Cholesterol, mg.	30
Fiber	0

Rice with Green Onions and Mushrooms

*This is a flavorful rice recipe. The original recipe used much more butter
but it has been adapted to use just a small amount.*

Serves 4

1 tablespoon butter or margarine
1/2 pound fresh mushrooms, sliced
1/2 cup chopped green onions
1 teaspoon Italian seasoning or oregano
1/4 teaspoon white pepper
1/4 teaspoon salt
1 cup long-grain white rice
2 cups fat-free beef broth

Note: Chicken broth can be substituted for the beef broth.

Preheat oven to 400°F. Butter a 1 1/2-quart casserole with a cover. Melt butter in medium skillet. Add mushrooms, onions, Italian seasoning, white pepper, and salt. Cook until tender. Spoon into casserole. Add rice and broth. Cover. Bake for 60 minutes or until rice is tender and broth has been absorbed.

Nutritional information per serving:

Calories	170
Fat, gm.	3
Protein, gm.	2
Carbohydrate, gm.	34
Cholesterol, mg.	10
Fiber	low

Roasted Herb Potato Medley

The fresh herbs make this potato dish a special treat.

Serves 10

1/3 cup olive oil
1/3 cup balsamic vinegar
1/4 cup chopped shallots
2 tablespoons chopped fresh thyme
2 tablespoons chopped fresh rosemary
2 teaspoons ground fennel seeds
2 pounds small red potatoes, quartered
2 pounds russet potatoes, peeled and cubed

1. Preheat oven to 400°F. Grease 2 large baking sheets. In a small bowl or pint jar, combine oil, vinegar, shallots, thyme, rosemary, and fennel seeds. Pour into a large bowl or large resealable plastic bag. Add potatoes and toss to coat. Use a slotted spoon to transfer potatoes to prepared baking sheets in single layer. Reserve oil mixture. Roast potatoes for 1 hour or until tender and golden brown. Stir and turn potatoes occasionally during baking. Remove from oven and return potatoes to reserved oil mixture. Toss to mix.

2. If desired, this can be prepared ahead of time. Cover oil-coated potatoes and refrigerate. When ready to serve, rewarm in 400°F oven for 20 minutes or until heated through, stirring occasionally.

Nutritional information per serving:

Calories	290
Fat, gm.	7
Protein, gm.	3
Carbohydrate, gm.	54
Cholesterol, mg.	0
Fiber	medium

Saffron Wild Rice Pilaf

A pilaf usually consists of rice, onions, raisins, and spices. This recipe uses a combination of wild rice and white rice, and it is seasoned with the elegant saffron. The pilaf warms up beautifully, so this recipe is large enough for several meals.

Serves 12

Large pinch (about 50 threads) saffron
2 tablespoons warm water
1 cup wild rice
4 cups water
1 tablespoon chicken bouillon
1 tablespoon butter or margarine
1 medium onion, finely chopped
1 cup long-grain white rice
2 cups fat-free chicken broth
1 cup golden raisins
1 cup toasted sliced almonds

Note: Sautéed mushrooms can be added to this recipe.

1. In a small custard cup, combine saffron with warm water. Set aside. Wash wild rice. In a medium saucepan, combine wild rice, water, and bouillon. Bring to a boil. Reduce heat, cover, and boil gently for 45 minutes or until rice is tender. Drain and discard any remaining liquid.

2. While wild rice is cooking, melt butter in a medium saucepan. Add onion and cook over medium heat until translucent. Add white rice to saucepan and cook until lightly browned, stirring frequently. Add chicken broth and reserved saffron and water. Cover pan. Reduce heat and simmer for 20 minutes or until rice is tender and liquid has been absorbed. When both wild rice and white rice are done, mix together. Stir in raisins. When ready to serve, top with almonds.

Nutritional information per serving:

Calories	210
Fat, gm.	7
Protein, gm.	5
Carbohydrate, gm.	32
Cholesterol, mg.	5
Fiber	medium

Wild Rice and Mushroom Stuffing

This is a wonderful, flavorful dish. The small amount of Italian sausage provides lots of flavor with a limited amount of fat. Using a full pound of sausage in this recipe would add an extra 200 calories per serving.

Serves 6

1/2 cup wild rice
3 cups low-fat chicken broth, divided
1/2 cup long-grain white rice
1/4 pound reduced-fat Italian sausage, crumbled
1 medium onion, finely chopped
2 stalks celery, finely chopped
1/2 pound fresh mushrooms, sliced
2 tablespoons dry sherry wine
1/3 cup chopped fresh parsley
Salt and freshly ground pepper to taste

Note: The chicken broth can be replaced with chicken bouillon. Substitute 1 cup water and 1 teaspoon chicken bouillon for each cup of chicken broth.

1. Wash wild rice. In a medium saucepan, combine wild rice and 2 cups of chicken broth. Bring to a boil. Cover, reduce heat, and boil gently for 45 minutes or until rice is tender. Drain off and discard any excess broth. In another small saucepan, combine white rice and 1 cup of chicken broth. Bring to a boil. Cover, reduce heat, and simmer for 20 minutes or until rice is tender.

2. While rice is cooking, cook sausage in a large skillet over medium heat. Fry until brown and completely done. Add onion and celery and cook until onion is translucent. Drain off any excess fat. Add mushrooms and sherry. Cook until tender. In a large serving bowl, combine wild rice, white rice, sausage-mushroom mixture, and parsley. Add salt and pepper to taste.

Nutritional information per serving:

Calories	175
Fat, gm.	6
Protein, gm.	7
Carbohydrate, gm.	23
Cholesterol, mg.	15
Fiber	medium

Yellow Rice with Golden Raisins

This yellow rice is mildly seasoned with an unusual combination of sweet spices.

Serves 6

1 tablespoon olive oil
1 cup long-grain rice
¼ teaspoon cloves
¼ teaspoon cardamom
¼ teaspoon cinnamon
¼ teaspoon turmeric
½ teaspoon salt
1 teaspoon minced garlic
2 cups fat-free chicken broth or vegetable broth
½ cup golden raisins
¼ cup chopped fresh chives

In a large, heavy saucepan, heat oil. Add rice, cloves, cardamom, cinnamon, turmeric, and salt. Cook over medium heat, stirring constantly, until rice is lightly brown. Add garlic and cook for 1 minute. Remove from heat and carefully add chicken broth. Return to heat and bring to a boil. Reduce heat, cover pan, and boil gently for 20 minutes or until rice is tender and liquid has been absorbed. Add raisins and chives. Stir to mix.

Nutritional information per serving:

Calories	175
Fat, gm.	2
Protein, gm.	3
Carbohydrate, gm.	36
Cholesterol, mg.	0
Fiber	medium

Chapter Ten
Vegetables

Apricot-Glazed Carrots

Asparagus with Lemon Mustard Dressing

Baked Stuffed Potatoes

Broccoli with Cheese Sauce

Butternut Squash and Apple Bake

Carrot, Potato, and Onion Gratin

Corn Custard

Cranberry Yam Bake

Crusty Mashed Potato Balls

Garden Vegetables with Mustard Vinaigrette

Green Beans and Mushrooms

Green Beans with Roasted Peppers and Pine Nuts

Harvard Beets

Hot German Coleslaw

Maple-Glazed Carrots

Mashed Rutabaga

Mixed Vegetables and Swiss Cheese

Parsnips and Carrots in Lemon Mustard Sauce

Potato and Broccoli Bake

Potatoes Romanoff

Red Cabbage Au Gratin

Sweet-and-Sour Red Cabbage

Sweet Potato Casserole

Sweet Potatoes and Apples in Orange Ginger Sauce

Swiss Green Beans

Winter Squash with Maple Mustard Sauce

Zippy Carrots

Zucchini Skillet Medley

Apricot-Glazed Carrots

With this recipe, the carrots taste great hot or cold.

Serves 6

1 ¹/₂ pounds baby carrots
1 tablespoon butter or margarine
¹/₃ cup apricot preserves
¹/₄ teaspoon nutmeg
¹/₄ teaspoon salt
1 tablespoon lemon zest
1 tablespoon fresh lemon juice

In a large saucepan, cook carrots in boiling water just until tender. Drain in colander. In the same saucepan, melt butter and stir in preserves. Add nutmeg, salt, lemon zest, and lemon juice. Add carrots and toss until well coated and heated through.

Nutritional information per serving:

Calories	105
Fat, gm.	2
Protein, gm.	1
Carbohydrate, gm.	21
Cholesterol, mg.	5
Fiber	medium

Asparagus with Lemon Mustard Dressing

This is an elegant yet simple way to serve asparagus. It is a favorite recipe in my son-in-law's family.
The best part is that it can be made ahead of time.

Serves 6

2 pounds fresh asparagus
1 cup plain low-fat yogurt, drained
1/4 cup fat-free or low-fat mayonnaise
1/4 cup Dijon mustard
2 tablespoons fresh lemon juice
1 teaspoon lemon zest
1 1/2 tablespoons honey

....

Note: To drain yogurt, place yogurt in a very fine strainer or a coffee filter. Allow liquid to drain off for several hours in the refrigerator. Discard liquid and use the thickened yogurt in the recipe.

Wash and snap the ends off the asparagus. In a large saucepan, cook asparagus in salted boiling water for 2 to 3 minutes or just until tender. Do not overcook. Chill under cold running water. Drain well and pat dry with paper towel. In a small bowl combine yogurt, mayonnaise, mustard, lemon juice, lemon zest, and honey. Arrange asparagus in shallow serving bowl. Spoon dressing on top and mix gently. Refrigerate until ready to serve. Serve cold.

Nutritional information per serving:

Calories	75
Fat, gm.	1
Protein, gm.	4
Carbohydrate, gm.	13
Cholesterol, mg.	2
Fiber	medium

Baked Stuffed Potatoes

These have been a family favorite for years. They are perfect for holiday and company dinners because they can be made ahead. No mashing potatoes at the last minute.

Serves 12

8 large baking potatoes
³/₄ cup fat-free milk
2 cups shredded reduced-fat Cheddar cheese, divided
3 green onions, finely chopped
¹/₂ teaspoon white pepper
Salt to taste
6 slices bacon, fried and crumbled, optional

1. Preheat oven to 425°F. Wash potatoes and pierce each with a fork. Bake for 1 hour or until fully cooked. Test inside tenderness by poking with a fork. The inside should be tender and the outside crisp.

2. Remove from oven and immediately cut each potato in half lengthwise, being careful of the hot steam. (Use hot pads or oven gloves.) Scoop out insides with a large spoon, keeping the shells intact. Place potato flesh in a large bowl. Add milk and beat well with electric mixer. Add extra milk if needed to make potatoes light and fluffy. Add 1 cup of the cheese, onions, white pepper, and salt to taste. Mix thoroughly.

3. Fill 12 of the scooped-out shells with mashed potato mixture. Discard shells that do not get filled. Sprinkle top of stuffed potatoes with remaining cheese and bacon. At this point, the potatoes can be covered and refrigerated or frozen until ready to use. When ready to serve, heat potatoes in oven at 350°F until heated through, about 15 to 20 minutes.

Note: These freeze beautifully. Thaw out before rewarming. They will taste like you just made them.

Nutritional information per serving:

Calories	100
Fat, gm.	1
Protein, gm.	7
Carbohydrate, gm.	16
Cholesterol, mg.	5
Fiber	high

Broccoli with Cheese Sauce

Cheese sauce usually means high fat and calories. Not this recipe. It is low in fat and tastes fantastic.
my daughter had her first college apartment, she called the first week to ask, "How do you make that cheese sauce
we put on broccoli?" The following recipe is further adapted so that it can be prepared ahead of time.

Serves 6

1 pound (4 cups) fresh broccoli florets
2 tablespoons butter or margarine
3 tablespoons flour
1 1/2 cups fat-free milk
1/4 teaspoon white pepper
2 ounces fat-free processed American cheese
Salt to taste
2 tablespoons grated Parmesan cheese
1 tablespoon seasoned bread crumbs

1. Butter a 1 1/2-quart casserole. In a saucepan, cook broccoli in boiling water for 2 minutes. Chill under cold running water. Drain well, dry with a paper towel, and arrange in casserole. In a small saucepan, melt butter. Add flour and cook over medium heat, stirring constantly for 2 minutes. Add milk and cook, stirring constantly, until it comes to a boil and thickens. Add white pepper and American cheese. Cook, stirring constantly, until cheese melts. Add salt to taste. Cool to room temperature and pour over broccoli. Sprinkle with Parmesan cheese and bread crumbs. Refrigerate if serving at a later time.

2. When ready to serve, preheat oven to 350°F. Bake for 20 minutes or until heated through and broccoli is tender.

Nutritional information per serving:

Calories	110
Fat, gm.	4
Protein, gm.	8
Carbohydrate, gm.	11
Cholesterol, mg.	15
Fiber	medium

Butternut Squash and Apple Bake

This is so good you could almost serve it for dessert. It has an apple pie flavor with sweet mashed squash on top. My guests rave about it.

Serves 8

1 medium butternut squash (1 1/2 pounds)
1 tablespoon butter or margarine
1/2 teaspoon salt
1/4 teaspoon freshly ground pepper
1 tablespoon brown sugar
2 medium apples, peeled and cored
1/4 teaspoon cinnamon
2 tablespoons sugar

Topping:

1 cup corn flakes, slightly crushed
1/4 cup chopped pecans
1 tablespoon butter, melted
1 tablespoon brown sugar

1. Peel squash and cut in half lengthwise. Remove seeds and cut in large pieces. Place in a large pan with 2 inches of water. Cover and steam for 20 to 30 minutes or until squash is tender. Drain well. Add 1 tablespoon butter, salt, pepper, and brown sugar. Mash with electric mixer. Set aside.

2. Preheat oven to 350°F. Butter a 9-inch round pie pan. Thinly slice apples and arrange in pan. Sprinkle with cinnamon and sugar. Spread squash over apples. In a small bowl combine topping ingredients. Sprinkle over squash. Bake for 25 to 30 minutes or until apples are tender.

Nutritional information per serving:

Calories	125
Fat, gm.	4
Protein, gm.	1
Carbohydrate, gm.	22
Cholesterol, mg.	10
Fiber	low

Carrot, Potato, and Onion Gratin

This crusty golden vegetable casserole can be put together ahead of time and baked later. The caramelized onions give it a sweet unusual flavor.

Serves 6

1 tablespoon butter or margarine
2 large onions, finely sliced
4 medium potatoes, peeled and thinly sliced
4 large carrots, peeled and thinly sliced
1 teaspoon salt, divided
1/2 teaspoon freshly ground pepper, divided
1 1/2 cups shredded Swiss cheese
1/2 cup low-fat chicken broth
Butter spray

....
Note: In place of Swiss, you could use Gruyère cheese or another cheese of your choice. If desired, add more cheese on top after the baking time and place under the broiler until it melts.

1. Butter a 9" x 9" baking dish or a 1 1/2-quart casserole. In a large nonstick skillet, melt butter. Add onions and cook over medium heat for 20 to 30 minutes or until very tender, lightly browned, and caramelized. In a large pan, cook potatoes in boiling salted water for 5 minutes. Add carrots and cook another 2 minutes. Drain well.

2. Preheat oven to 350°F. Arrange a third of the potatoes, carrots, and onions in bottom of baking dish. Sprinkle with salt and freshly ground pepper. Sprinkle with a third of the cheese. Repeat layering with remaining vegetables, salt, and pepper, and top with remaining cheese. Pour chicken broth over vegetables. Spray with butter spray. Cover tightly and bake for 60 minutes or until broth is absorbed and vegetables are tender.

Nutritional information per serving:

Calories	200
Fat, gm.	10
Protein, gm.	10
Carbohydrate, gm.	17
Cholesterol, mg.	30
Fiber	high

Corn Custard

Make this ahead and rewarm it when you want a special vegetable side dish.

Serves 4

15 ounces canned corn, drained
$1/2$ cup evaporated fat-free milk
1 large egg, lightly beaten
$1/4$ teaspoon salt
$1/4$ teaspoon white pepper
$1/4$ teaspoon thyme
1 teaspoon minced garlic

Note: Frozen corn can be substituted for the canned corn.

Preheat oven to 375°F. Butter 4 ovenproof custard cups. In a large bowl, combine all ingredients. Stir to mix. Divide corn mixture between custard cups. Place cups in a large baking pan. Add 1 to 2 inches of water. Bake for 40 to 50 minutes or until a knife inserted in the center of custard comes out clean. Remove from oven and let cool for 10 minutes. Loosen edges of custards with a knife. To serve, invert onto individual plates.

Nutritional information per serving:

Calories	130
Fat, gm.	2
Protein, gm.	6
Carbohydrate, gm.	23
Cholesterol, mg.	45
Fiber	high

Cranberry Yam Bake

Some people call them yams and others call them sweet potatoes. Use either one.
They are essentially the same great, nutritious vegetable. The cranberries add interest and zest.

Serves 6

2 tablespoons flour
$^1/_2$ cup brown sugar
$^1/_2$ cup quick-cooking oats, uncooked
3 tablespoons butter or margarine, melted
$^1/_2$ teaspoon cinnamon
$^1/_4$ teaspoon nutmeg
2 cups fresh or frozen cranberries
29 ounces canned yams or sweet potatoes, drained

Preheat oven to 350°F. Butter a 1 $^1/_2$-quart casserole. In a medium bowl, combine flour, brown sugar, oats, butter, cinnamon, and nutmeg. Stir until well mixed. Add cranberries and yams. Toss gently. Spoon into casserole. Bake for 45 to 55 minutes or until cranberries have popped and are tender.

Nutritional information per serving:

Calories	275
Fat, gm.	6
Protein, gm.	4
Carbohydrate, gm.	51
Cholesterol, mg.	5
Fiber	high

Crusty Mashed Potato Balls

If you are a potato lover, you will love these. They are a little messy to make but they can be made ahead of time and baked when you are ready to serve.

Serves 6

5 medium potatoes, peeled and cubed
1/4 cup grated Parmesan cheese
2 tablespoons fat-free or low-fat cream cheese
1 tablespoon dry onion soup mix
1/4 teaspoon white pepper
1/4 cup fat-free milk
Salt and freshly ground pepper to taste
1 egg, lightly beaten
2 cups corn flake crumbs

1. In a medium saucepan, cook potatoes in salted water until tender. Drain. Add Parmesan cheese, cream cheese, dry onion soup mix, white pepper, and milk. Beat with electric mixer until fluffy. Add extra milk if needed to thin. Add salt and pepper to taste.

2. Preheat oven to 400°F. Grease a baking sheet. Shape mashed potatoes into 2-inch balls. Dip in egg and roll in corn flake crumbs. Place on baking sheet. Makes about 15 balls. Bake for 10 to 15 minutes or until lightly browned and crispy.

Nutritional information per serving:

Calories	125
Fat, gm.	2
Protein, gm.	5
Carbohydrate, gm.	22
Cholesterol, mg.	35
Fiber	low

Garden Vegetables with Mustard Vinaigrette

An attractive, healthy way to prepare vegetables ahead of time.
This may easily become one of your favorite ways to serve fresh vegetables.

Serves 6

3 large carrots, peeled and cut into 3-inch julienne slices
1 teaspoon cider vinegar
$1/2$ pound fresh mushrooms, thickly sliced
3 medium zucchini, cut into 3-inch julienne slices

Dressing:

3 tablespoons extra-virgin olive oil
2 tablespoons Dijon mustard
2 tablespoons white wine vinegar
1 clove garlic, minced
1 tablespoon sugar
$1/4$ teaspoon salt
Freshly ground pepper to taste

Note: Vegetables can be arranged attractively on a platter or tossed in a bowl. Other fresh vegetables such as broccoli, asparagus, or cauliflower can also be used.

In a small saucepan, blanch carrots in boiling water for 2 minutes. Add vinegar and mushrooms. Boil for 30 seconds more. Rinse under cold running water. Drain well. Combine carrots, mushrooms, and zucchini in a large resealable plastic bag. In a small jar, combine olive oil, mustard, vinegar, garlic, sugar, and salt. Mix well. Pour over vegetables and mix gently. Refrigerate for several hours or overnight. Add freshly ground pepper to individual servings.

Nutritional information per serving:

Calories	105
Fat, gm.	7
Protein, gm.	2
Carbohydrate, gm.	9
Cholesterol, mg.	0
Fiber	high

Green Beans and Mushrooms

Sometimes it is nice to dress up an ordinary vegetable.

Serves 6

1 pound fresh green beans, snip ends
1 tablespoon butter or margarine
1 small red onion, thinly sliced
1/2 pound fresh mushrooms, sliced
1 clove garlic, minced
1/2 teaspoon dill weed
1/4 teaspoon salt
Freshly ground pepper to taste
2 tablespoons slivered almonds, toasted

In a medium saucepan, cook green beans in salted water until tender. While beans are cooking, melt butter in medium skillet. Add onion and cook over medium heat until translucent. Add mushrooms, garlic, dill weed, and salt. Cook until tender. When beans are done, drain water and add onion and mushroom mixture. Stir to blend. Add pepper to taste. Spoon into serving bowl and top with almonds.

Nutritional information per serving:

Calories	75
Fat, gm.	3
Protein, gm.	3
Carbohydrate, gm.	9
Cholesterol, mg.	10
Fiber	high

Green Beans with Roasted Peppers and Pine Nuts

This is a great way to dress up green beans.

Serves 6

1 pound fresh green beans, ends trimmed
1 medium red bell pepper
1 medium yellow bell pepper
1 teaspoon olive oil
1/2 teaspoon crushed garlic
1/4 teaspoon freshly ground pepper
1 teaspoon fresh lemon juice
2 tablespoons grated Parmesan cheese
2 tablespoons pine nuts, toasted

Note: Roasted peppers can be purchased in a jar if you prefer not to make them.

1. Preheat broiler. Grease a baking sheet. In a large saucepan, cook green beans in salted water until tender-crisp. Drain and chill to stop cooking process. Set aside. While beans are cooking, cut red and yellow peppers into quarters and remove seeds. Press down flat on baking sheet. Place a few inches below broiler unit and broil until the skin is totally blackened. Remove and place in a small paper or plastic bag for 10 minutes. Peel off and discard blackened skin. Cut peppers into thin strips.

2. In a medium skillet, heat oil. Add garlic and cook for 1 minute. Add green beans, roasted peppers, black pepper, and lemon juice. Cook over medium heat just until heated through. Top with grated cheese and cover pan for 1 minute or until cheese is melted. Place in serving bowl and top with pine nuts.

Nutritional information per serving:

Calories	75
Fat, gm.	3
Protein, gm.	3
Carbohydrate, gm.	9
Cholesterol, mg.	0
Fiber	high

Harvard Beets

These were a favorite on farm dinner tables.
They added a little zip and lots of color to meals.

Serves 6

30 ounces canned sliced beets, drained and juice reserved
2 tablespoons sugar
2 tablespoons cornstarch
1/3 cup vinegar
1 tablespoon butter or margarine

Measure 1/2 cup of liquid from the canned beets and pour into medium saucepan. (Discard remaining juice.) Add sugar, cornstarch, and vinegar. Stir until smooth. Bring to a boil over medium heat, stirring constantly, until thickened. Stir in butter and beets. Heat through.

Nutritional information per serving:

Calories	80
Fat, gm.	2
Protein, gm.	1
Carbohydrate, gm.	15
Cholesterol, mg.	5
Fiber	medium

Hot German Coleslaw

The taste of this fabulous coleslaw will remind you of good German potato salad with a hot bacon dressing.

Serves 4

4 slices bacon, diced
1/2 cup chopped sweet onion
1/2 tablespoon flour
1/3 cup white wine vinegar
2 tablespoons sugar
2 tablespoons fat-free chicken broth or water
4 cups shredded cabbage
Salt and freshly ground pepper to taste

In a large skillet, fry bacon until crisp. Discard all but 2 tablespoons of bacon drippings. Add onion to skillet and cook in drippings over medium heat until lightly brown. Whisk in flour and cook for 2 minutes, stirring constantly. Add vinegar, sugar, and broth. Bring to a boil. Add cabbage and toss to wilt, about 5 minutes. Add salt and pepper to taste.

Nutritional information per serving:

Calories	100
Fat, gm.	3
Protein, gm.	3
Carbohydrate, gm.	15
Cholesterol, mg.	5
Fiber	medium

Maple-Glazed Carrots

A great way to dress up carrots.

Serves 4

1 pound baby carrots
1 tablespoon butter or margarine
$1/4$ cup maple syrup
$1/4$ teaspoon ginger
$1/8$ teaspoon nutmeg
2 teaspoons orange zest

Cook carrots in water in medium saucepan just until crisp-tender. Drain well. Add all remaining ingredients. Simmer, uncovered, until liquid is reduced and carrots are glazed with sauce.

Nutritional information per serving:

Calories	120
Fat, gm.	3
Protein, gm.	1
Carbohydrate, gm.	23
Cholesterol, mg.	10
Fiber	low

Mashed Rutabaga

Rutabaga may not be the most popular vegetable in the world but I learned to love it served with pork roast. This recipe makes it a little bit sweet and very tasty.

Serves 6

1 large rutabaga (1 ¹/₂ pounds)
¹/₃ cup brown sugar
1 tablespoon butter or margarine
¹/₄ cup fat-free milk
¹/₄ cup fat-free sour cream
Salt and freshly ground pepper to taste
2 tablespoons dry bread crumbs
Butter spray

Note: Rutabagas have a bitter bite. Add more sugar if desired.

Preheat oven to 350°F. Butter a 1-quart casserole dish. Peel rutabagas and cut into chunks. In a medium saucepan, cook rutabagas in salted water for 45 to 60 minutes or until very tender. Drain. Add brown sugar, butter, and milk. Beat with an electric mixer until light and fluffy. Add extra milk if need to thin. Add sour cream and mix. Add salt and pepper to taste. Spoon into casserole dish and top with bread crumbs. Spray with butter spray. Bake for 15 minutes or until heated through.

Nutritional information per serving:

Calories	100
Fat, gm.	2
Protein, gm.	2
Carbohydrate, gm.	18
Cholesterol, mg.	10
Fiber	medium

Mixed Vegetables and Swiss Cheese

Choose the vegetables you like best for this recipe. It is a way to combine vegetables from the farmer's market or your garden with any others you have on hand.

Serves 4

2 cups fresh or frozen mixed vegetables, cut into bite-size pieces
1 cup shredded Swiss cheese
1 egg
$1/2$ cup fat-free milk
$1/2$ teaspoon basil
$1/2$ teaspoon salt
$1/4$ teaspoon white pepper
$1/4$ teaspoon paprika

Preheat oven to 350°F. Butter a 1-quart casserole. In a large bowl, combine vegetables and cheese. In a small bowl, combine egg, milk, basil, salt, and white pepper. Beat well. Pour into vegetables and stir until blended. Pour into casserole. Sprinkle with paprika. Bake for 45 to 55 minutes or until lightly browned and knife inserted in the middle comes out clean.

Nutritional information per serving:

Calories	155
Fat, gm.	6
Protein, gm.	12
Carbohydrate, gm.	13
Cholesterol, mg.	60
Fiber	high

Parsnips and Carrots in Lemon Mustard Sauce

The sauce is so easy but it adds a lot of flavor to the vegetables.
Other vegetable combinations may be used.

Serves 4

2 cups peeled and julienne-sliced parsnips
2 cups peeled and julienne-sliced carrots

Sauce:

$^1/_2$ cup fat-free sour cream
1 teaspoon fresh lemon juice
2 teaspoons Dijon mustard
1 tablespoon brown sugar
Dash dill weed

In a medium saucepan, cook parsnips and carrots in salted boiling water just until tender. Drain well. While vegetables are cooking, combine all sauce ingredients in a small saucepan. Stir to mix and warm over low heat. Pour sauce over cooked vegetables and spoon into serving bowl.

Nutritional information per serving:

Calories	100
Fat, gm.	0
Protein, gm.	2
Carbohydrate, gm.	23
Cholesterol, mg.	5
Fiber	high

Potato and Broccoli Bake

This is a good recipe if you would like to make your potatoes and vegetables ahead of time.
Put it together and refrigerate it until ready to bake.

Serves 8

2 tablespoons butter or margarine
2 tablespoons flour
$1/2$ teaspoon salt
$1/4$ teaspoon white pepper
$1/8$ teaspoon nutmeg
$1 1/2$ cups fat-free milk
3 ounces fat-free processed American cheese
16 ounces (4 cups) frozen chopped potatoes, loose packed
10 ounces frozen chopped broccoli, thawed
2 tablespoons grated Parmesan cheese
2 tablespoons seasoned bread crumbs
Butter spray

Note: If you make the recipe ahead and refrigerate it, increase baking time to 40 minutes.

1. Preheat oven to 350°F. Butter a 9" x 9" or a 7" x 11" baking pan. In a medium saucepan, melt butter. Stir in flour and cook over medium heat for 3 minutes, stirring constantly. Add salt, pepper, nutmeg, and milk. Bring to a boil, stirring constantly until mixture thickens. Add cheese and stir until melted. Remove from heat. Stir in potatoes.

2. Spoon half of potato mixture into baking pan. Top with broccoli. Spoon remaining potato mixture on top. Cover and bake for 30 minutes. Remove cover and top with Parmesan cheese and bread crumbs. Spray with butter spray. Broil for 5 minutes or until lightly browned on top.

Nutritional information per serving:

Calories	130
Fat, gm.	3
Protein, gm.	8
Carbohydrate, gm.	17
Cholesterol, mg.	10
Fiber	medium

Potatoes Romanoff

These potatoes are my family's favorites. I also like serving them for company meals because I can make them ahead of time. There is no need to mash potatoes at the last minute. It is a lifesaver for Thanksgiving dinner.

Serves 4

4 medium potatoes, peeled
$1/3$ cup fat-free milk
$1/3$ cup fat-free sour cream
4 small green onions, diced
$3/4$ cup shredded reduced-fat Cheddar cheese, divided
$1/2$ teaspoon salt
$1/4$ teaspoon white pepper
Dash paprika

1. Butter a 1-quart casserole. Boil potatoes in water until fork-tender. Drain. Place potatoes in large bowl. Add milk and beat with electric mixer. Add extra milk if needed for a lighter consistency. Add sour cream, onions, $1/2$ cup of shredded cheese, salt, and pepper. Taste mixture and add extra salt and pepper if desired. Spoon into casserole. Top with remaining $1/4$ cup of cheese and sprinkle with paprika. Refrigerate until ready to serve.

2. When ready to serve, preheat oven to 350°F. Bake for 20 to 30 minutes or just until heated through.

Nutritional information per serving:

Calories	180
Fat, gm.	2
Protein, gm.	11
Carbohydrate, gm.	30
Cholesterol, mg.	10
Fiber	medium

Red Cabbage Au Gratin

If you like cabbage, you will love this dish.

Serves 8

1 small red cabbage (about 2¹/2 pounds), cut into bite-size pieces
1 tablespoon butter or margarine
1 tablespoon flour
1 cup milk
¹/4 teaspoon salt
¹/4 teaspoon freshly ground black pepper
¹/4 teaspoon curry powder
Dash cayenne pepper
2 cups grated Swiss cheese
2 tablespoons white wine
¹/2 cup seasoned bread crumbs, toasted

Preheat oven to 350°F. Butter a 9" x 13" baking pan. Place cabbage in a large saucepan. Boil in salted water for 5 to 10 minutes or until just tender. Drain and set aside. In a medium saucepan, melt butter. Add flour and cook for 2 minutes. Add milk, salt, pepper, curry powder, and cayenne pepper. Bring to a boil and stir until thickened. Add cheese and stir until melted. Add wine. Combine cabbage and white sauce. Spoon into baking dish. Top with bread crumbs. Bake for 15 to 20 minutes or until heated through.

Nutritional information per serving:

Calories	220
Fat, gm.	12
Protein, gm.	12
Carbohydrate, gm.	16
Cholesterol, mg.	15
Fiber	medium

Sweet-and-Sour Red Cabbage

This has a subtle sweet-sour taste and a rich red color. The port wine adds extra flavor.

Serves 8

1 large head of red cabbage
1/2 cup cider vinegar
1/2 cup water
1/2 cup brown sugar
1/2 cup port wine
4 medium apples, peeled, cored, and diced

Thinly shred cabbage and place in large cooking pan. Add vinegar, water, and brown sugar. Cover pan and bring to a boil. Reduce heat, cover, and gently boil for 30 to 40 minutes or until cabbage is tender. Stir occasionally. Add port wine and apples. Cook for another 10 minutes or until apples are tender. Taste and add extra sugar or vinegar to suit your preference.

Note: The length of time it takes to cook the cabbage depends on the size of the pieces and the variety of cabbage.

Nutritional information per serving:

Calories	105
Fat, gm.	0
Protein, gm.	1
Carbohydrate, gm.	25
Cholesterol, mg.	0
Fiber	medium

Sweet Potato Casserole

This was adapted from an old recipe that used lots more butter, sugar, and nuts. That recipe had 555 calories and 25 grams of fat per serving. Many older recipes used more fat than was necessary. This is a great way to get lots of vitamin A.

Serves 8

46 ounces canned sweet potatoes, drained
2 eggs
$^1/_4$ cup sugar
$^3/_4$ cup evaporated fat-free milk
$^1/_2$ teaspoon salt
$^1/_4$ teaspoon nutmeg
2 tablespoons butter or margarine, melted
$^1/_4$ cup brown sugar
$^1/_4$ cup chopped walnuts

Preheat oven to 350°F. Butter a 1-quart casserole dish. In a large bowl, combine sweet potatoes and eggs. Mash with an electric mixer. Add sugar, milk, salt, nutmeg, and butter. Spoon into casserole. Sprinkle with brown sugar and nuts on top. Bake for 45 to 55 minutes or until set.

Nutritional information per serving:

Calories	200
Fat, gm.	4
Protein, gm.	5
Carbohydrate, gm.	35
Cholesterol, mg.	55
Fiber	high

Sweet Potatoes and Apples in Orange Ginger Sauce

This is a delightful combination of flavors.

Serves 6

Sauce:

1 cup orange juice
1 tablespoon cornstarch
2 tablespoons brown sugar
$^1/_2$ teaspoon allspice
$^1/_4$ teaspoon ginger
$^1/_4$ teaspoon salt
$^1/_2$ cup diced mixed dried fruit

Fruit and Vegetables:

2 large sweet potatoes, peeled and diced
3 large carrots, peeled and diced
1 tablespoon butter or margarine
1 large sweet onion, chopped
2 large Granny Smith apples, peeled and sliced
Salt and freshly ground pepper to taste

1. In a small saucepan, combine all sauce ingredients. Stir until well mixed. Cook over medium heat, stirring constantly until mixture comes to a boil and thickens. Remove from heat and set aside.

2. Bring salted water to boil in a medium saucepan. Cook sweet potatoes and carrots until tender, about 10 minutes. Drain well and set aside.

3. While potatoes are cooking, melt butter in large nonstick skillet. Cook onion over medium-high heat until lightly browned. Add apples and cook until just tender-crisp. Remove from heat. Add cooked potatoes and carrots. Add sauce and stir gently until heated through. If dish is made ahead, cover and refrigerate until ready to serve. Add salt and pepper to taste.

Nutritional information per serving:

Calories	155
Fat, gm.	2
Protein, gm.	2
Carbohydrate, gm.	33
Cholesterol, mg.	5
Fiber	high

Swiss Green Beans

This is a great recipe to make with canned green beans. It is creamy and cheesy but low in fat.
I like to take it to potlucks because it is easy to make and everyone loves it.

Serves 8

1 tablespoon butter
1 tablespoon flour
1/2 cup fat-free milk
1/8 teaspoon white pepper
2 ounces fat-free processed Swiss cheese
3/4 cup shredded Swiss cheese, divided
1/2 cup fat-free sour cream
45 ounces canned green beans, drained
2 tablespoons seasoned bread crumbs

Notes: The blending of fat-free and regular cheese works well in this recipe. The processed fat-free cheese melts beautifully but it doesn't taste like real Swiss cheese. Adding regular cheese adds the great cheese flavor to this dish.

This is a good dish to make ahead and refrigerate until ready to bake. Increase baking time to 30 minutes if it has been refrigerated.

Preheat oven to 325°F. Butter a 1-quart casserole dish. In a small skillet, melt butter. Add flour and cook for 2 minutes, stirring constantly. Add milk and bring to a boil, stirring constantly until mixture thickens. Add white pepper, fat-free Swiss cheese, and 1/2 cup Swiss cheese. Stir until cheeses melt. Remove from heat and add sour cream. Pour into casserole dish. Add beans and stir gently to mix. Top with remaining cheese and bread crumbs. Bake for 20 minutes or until heated through.

Nutritional information per serving:

Calories	110
Fat, gm.	4
Protein, gm.	8
Carbohydrate, gm.	11
Cholesterol, mg.	20
Fiber	low

Winter Squash with Maple Mustard Sauce

Even those who don't care for squash may like this one.

Serves 6

2 pounds winter squash

1/4 cup maple syrup

2 tablespoons butter or margarine, melted

1 tablespoon Dijon mustard

1/4 teaspoon allspice

Dash cloves

Salt and freshly ground pepper to taste

1 medium roasted red bell pepper, diced

Note: Any winter squash such as butternut, acorn, or spaghetti squash can be used in this recipe.

Preheat oven to 350°F. Cut squash in half. Scoop out and discard seeds. Place cut-side down in a baking pan. Add 1 inch of water. Bake for 45 minutes or until tender. Remove from oven and let cool until easy to handle. Gently scoop out squash with a fork. Place in a large bowl. Add maple syrup, butter, mustard, allspice, cloves, salt, and pepper. Beat with electric mixer or blend in food processor. Stir in peppers.

Nutritional information per serving:

Calories	120
Fat, gm.	4
Protein, gm.	2
Carbohydrate, gm.	19
Cholesterol, mg.	10
Fiber	medium

Zippy Carrots

Sometimes simple is best.

Serves 4

3 cups peeled and sliced carrots
1 tablespoon butter
2 tablespoons brown sugar
1 tablespoon Dijon mustard
$1/4$ teaspoon salt

In a medium saucepan, cook carrots in a small amount of boiling water just until tender. Remove from heat and drain. While carrots are cooking, melt butter in a medium skillet. Add brown sugar, mustard, and salt. Add cooked carrots and heat, stirring constantly for 3 minutes or until glazed.

Nutritional information per serving:

Calories	75
Fat, gm.	3
Protein, gm.	1
Carbohydrate, gm.	11
Cholesterol, mg.	10
Fiber	medium

Zucchini Skillet Medley

This is my friend Mary's favorite way to prepare fresh vegetables.
Serve it on the side with grilled meat or make it a meatless main dish.

Serves 4

1 tablespoon olive oil
1 medium onion, thinly sliced
2 large carrots, peeled and finely sliced
$1/2$ teaspoon dill weed
1 clove garlic, minced
$1/2$ medium green bell pepper, diced
4 cups sliced unpeeled zucchini ($1/4$-inch-thick slices)
$1/4$ cup water or broth
$1/2$ cup chopped, seeded tomatoes
Salt and freshly ground pepper to taste
$1/2$ cup grated Parmesan cheese

Heat oil in a large skillet. Add onions and cook until translucent. Add carrots, dill weed, garlic, bell pepper, zucchini, and water. Cover pan and cook until vegetables are tender. Stir occasionally. When ready to serve, add tomatoes and season with salt and pepper and heat through. Sprinkle cheese on top.

Nutritional information per serving:

Calories	120
Fat, gm.	6
Protein, gm.	6
Carbohydrate, gm.	10
Cholesterol, mg.	10
Fiber	high

Chapter Eleven
Breads

Almond–Poppy Seed Bread

Apple Pancakes

Banana Nut Bread

Blueberry Coffeecake

Blueberry Muffins

Buttermilk Baking Powder Biscuits

Cranberry Nut Muffins

Double-Corn Corn Bread

Fresh Lemon-Glazed Bread

Golden Corn Bread

Lemon Bread

Norwegian Potato Lefse

Oatmeal Cherry Muffins

Orange Marmalade–Pecan Bread

Play Dough

Plum Coffeecake

Popovers

Pumpkin Bread

Raspberry Streusel Muffins

Streusel-Filled Coffeecake

Zucchini Bread

Almond–Poppy Seed Bread

Surprise a friend with a tasty gift. This recipe is large enough for 2 large loaves or 8 tiny gift-size loaves.

Serves 30

3 cups flour
1 1/2 teaspoons salt
1 1/2 teaspoons baking powder
2 1/2 cups sugar
3 tablespoons poppy seeds
3 eggs
1 cup vegetable oil
1 1/2 cups fat-free milk
2 teaspoons vanilla extract
1 teaspoon almond extract
1 teaspoon butter extract, optional
2 tablespoons sugar

Optional Glaze:

1/4 cup orange juice
1/3 cup sugar
1/2 teaspoon vanilla extract
1/2 teaspoon almond extract

1. In a small saucepan, heat all glaze ingredients. Pour warm glaze over bread as soon as it comes out of the oven. Let bread cool in the pans.

2. Preheat oven to 350°F. If using glass or nonstick pans, preheat oven to 325°F. Grease two 5" x 9" loaf pans. In a large bowl, combine flour, salt, baking powder, sugar, and poppy seeds. Stir to blend, then make a well in the middle. In another small bowl, combine eggs, oil, milk, vanilla, and flavoring extracts. Mix well and pour into dry ingredients. Stir with a spoon just until well mixed. Spoon into pans. Sprinkle with sugar. Bake for 60 to 70 minutes or until light brown and set in the middle. Remove from pans and cool on a rack. If adding the optional glaze, keep bread in the pan and drizzle glaze on top.

Nutritional information per serving without glaze:

Calories	190
Fat, gm.	8
Protein, gm.	2
Carbohydrate, gm.	28
Cholesterol, mg.	16
Fiber	low

Apple Pancakes

These are so much better than the frozen pancakes you put in your toaster.

Serves 4

4 medium apples, peeled and thinly sliced
2 tablespoons sugar
$1/2$ teaspoon cinnamon
I cup flour
3 teaspoons baking powder
I egg, lightly beaten
I cup fat-free milk
I tablespoon butter or margarine, melted
Butter-flavored cooking spray

Note: Serve with Caramel Cinnamon Sauce (page 254) or dust with powdered sugar.

1. Place apples, sugar, and cinnamon in a small bowl. Stir until mixed. Place in microwave for 2 to 3 minutes or just until apples are tender. Set aside. In a medium bowl, combine flour, baking powder, egg, milk, and butter. Stir until smooth. Add apples to batter and stir gently.

2. Heat a nonstick skillet over medium heat. Coat pan lightly with cooking spray. Pour batter in hot pan to form 4-inch circles. Turn when bubbles form and bottom is lightly browned. Cook the second side until golden brown.

Nutritional information per serving:

Calories	280
Fat, gm.	5
Protein, gm.	7
Carbohydrate, gm.	52
Cholesterol, mg.	55
Fiber	low

Banana Nut Bread

This homebaked American favorite is given as a gift more than any other bread.

Serves 20

1 cup sugar

1/3 cup vegetable oil

2 eggs

2 tablespoons fat-free milk

1/4 teaspoon salt

1 teaspoon baking soda

1/2 teaspoon baking powder

1/4 teaspoon nutmeg

3 medium bananas, mashed

1 3/4 cups flour

1/2 cup chopped pecans or walnuts

Preheat oven to 325°F. Grease a 5" x 9" loaf pan. In a large bowl, combine sugar, oil, eggs, and milk. Beat well. Add salt, baking soda, baking powder, and nutmeg. Blend well. Stir in bananas. Add flour and nuts. Stir just until blended. Spoon into pan. Bake for 45 to 60 minutes or until set in the middle and light brown. Do not overbake. Remove from pan and cool on a rack.

Note: To make small loaves for gifts, use four 2" x 4" pans.

Nutritional information per serving:

Calories	135
Fat, gm.	5
Protein, gm.	2
Carbohydrate, gm.	21
Cholesterol, mg.	20
Fiber	low

Blueberry Coffeecake

This is easy enough to make quickly for a special breakfast or brunch. It is great served warm or cold.

Serves 12

1/2 cup butter or margarine
I cup sugar
2 eggs
I teaspoon baking powder
I teaspoon baking soda
1/2 teaspoon salt
1/2 cup low-fat buttermilk
1/2 cup fat-free sour cream
I teaspoon vanilla extract
2 cups flour
2 cups fresh or frozen loose-pack blueberries

Topping:

1/2 cup sugar
1/3 cup flour
1/2 teaspoon cinnamon
1/2 teaspoon nutmeg
1/4 cup butter or margarine

Heat oven to 325°F. Grease a 9" x 13" baking pan. In a large bowl, beat butter and sugar until light and fluffy. Add eggs and beat well. Add baking powder, baking soda, salt, buttermilk, sour cream, and vanilla. Mix well. Add flour and beat at low speed until blended. Spoon into pan. Top with blueberries. In a small bowl, combine sugar, flour, cinnamon, nutmeg, and butter. Sprinkle over blueberries. Bake for 35 to 45 minutes or until cake is light brown and a toothpick inserted in the middle comes out clean.

Note: Prepare half a recipe for an 8" x 8" pan.

Nutritional information per serving:

Calories	325
Fat, gm.	12
Protein, gm.	4
Carbohydrate, gm.	50
Cholesterol, mg.	65
Fiber	very low

Blueberry Muffins

These were my blue ribbon winners at the county fair when I was 10 years old. They are very light and tender.

Serves 12

1 ½ cups flour
⅔ cup sugar
½ teaspoon salt
1 tablespoon baking powder
1 egg, lightly beaten
½ cup fat-free milk
¼ cup canola oil
1 cup fresh blueberries or unthawed frozen blueberries

Preheat oven to 375°F or 350°F if using nonstick pans. Grease 12 muffin tins. In a large bowl, combine flour, sugar, salt, and baking powder. Stir to mix. Add egg, milk, and oil. Stir with a spoon just until moistened but not smooth. Gently stir in blueberries. Spoon into muffin tins, filling ⅔ full. Bake for 15 to 20 minutes.

Note: The secret I learned from exhibiting these muffins at the Dane County Fair is not to mix them too much. Vigorous stirring causes big tunnels to form inside the muffins. The dough should look lumpy and bumpy when you spoon it into the muffin tins. The judges at the fair examined the muffins by breaking them open, and if they saw tunnels, I lost my chance for a blue ribbon.

Nutritional information per serving:

Calories	150
Fat, gm.	5
Protein, gm.	2
Carbohydrate, gm.	25
Cholesterol, mg.	15
Fiber	medium

Buttermilk Baking Powder Biscuits

Remember these with butter and honey? They are delicate and crusty. In the days before commercial baking powder, homemakers made their own by combining cream of tartar with baking soda.

Makes 18 small biscuits

2 cups flour
$1/2$ teaspoon salt
2 teaspoons baking powder
$1/2$ teaspoon baking soda
2 teaspoons sugar
$1/3$ cup butter-flavored shortening
$1/3$ cup buttermilk

1. Preheat oven to 425°F. In a medium bowl, combine flour, salt, baking powder, baking soda, and sugar. Mix with a fork. Add shortening. Using a pastry blender or knife, cut in shortening until mixture resembles coarse cornmeal. Add buttermilk and stir with a fork just until blended.

2. Turn dough onto lightly floured countertop and knead lightly 8 times. Pat or roll dough $1/2$ inch thick. Cut with a biscuit cutter or a glass. Bake on ungreased cookie sheet for 10 to 15 minutes or until light brown.

Note: These are wonderful served with honey butter. Mix 4 tablespoons of butter at room temperature with 1 tablespoon of honey.

Nutritional information per serving:

Calories	85
Fat, gm.	4
Protein, gm.	2
Carbohydrate, gm.	11
Cholesterol, mg.	0
Fiber	0

Cranberry Nut Muffins

These were always special in the fall when cranberries were harvested in Wisconsin.
I now keep cranberries in my freezer so I can make these muffins at any time of the year.

Serves 16

$^1/_4$ cup butter or margarine

1 $^1/_4$ cups sugar

2 eggs

2 teaspoons baking powder

$^1/_2$ teaspoon salt

$^1/_2$ cup fat-free milk

2 cups flour

2 cups coarsely chopped cranberries

1 cup chopped walnuts

Note: Chop fresh or frozen cranberries in a food processor or in a nut chopper.

Preheat oven to 350°F. Grease 16 muffin tins. In a large bowl, mix butter and sugar together. Add eggs and beat well. Add baking powder, salt, and milk. Beat well. Stir in flour with a spoon. Stir in cranberries and walnuts. Spoon into muffin tins, filling ¾ full. Bake for 25 to 30 minutes or until light brown. Remove from tins and cool on racks.

Nutritional information per serving:

Calories	170
Fat, gm.	4
Protein, gm.	3
Carbohydrate, gm.	30
Cholesterol, mg.	30
Fiber	low

Double-Corn Corn Bread

Corn bread has a reputation for being dry but this one is supermoist and so good.

Serves 20

1 box (8 ounces) corn muffin mix
8 ounces canned corn, drained
8 ounces creamed corn
1 cup fat-free sour cream
2 large eggs, lightly beaten
4 tablespoons butter or margarine, melted

Preheat oven to 350°F. Butter a 7" x 11" baking pan. In a large mixing bowl, combine all ingredients. Stir until well mixed. Spoon into pan. Bake for 40 to 45 minutes or until set in the middle and lightly browned.

Nutritional information per serving:

Calories	95
Fat, gm.	4
Protein, gm.	2
Carbohydrate, gm.	13
Cholesterol, mg.	25
Fiber	low

Fresh Lemon-Glazed Bread

If you like lemon, you will love this bread.

Serves 16

1 cup sugar

$^1/_3$ cup vegetable oil

2 eggs

$^1/_2$ cup fat-free milk

1 teaspoon baking powder

$^1/_2$ teaspoon salt

1 tablespoon fresh lemon zest

1 $^1/_2$ cups flour

1 tablespoon poppy seeds, optional

Lemon Glaze:

3 tablespoons fresh lemon juice

$^1/_3$ cup sugar

1. Preheat oven to 350°F. If using a glass or nonstick pan, preheat oven to 325°F. Butter a 5" x 9" loaf pan. In a large bowl, combine sugar, oil, eggs, and milk. Beat well. Add baking powder, salt, and lemon zest. Stir until mixed. Stir in flour and poppy seeds. Pour into loaf pan. Bake for 45 to 60 minutes or until toothpick inserted in the center comes out clean.

2. Toward the end of the baking period, combine lemon juice and sugar in a small saucepan. Stir over medium heat until sugar is dissolved and mixture comes to a rolling boil.

3. When bread is done, remove from oven and spoon lemon juice mixture over bread. Allow bread to cool in the pan.

Nutritional information per serving:

Calories	155
Fat, gm.	5
Protein, gm.	2
Carbohydrate, gm.	26
Cholesterol, mg.	20
Fiber	low

Golden Corn Bread

Try this with a chili supper.

Serves 8

³/₄ cup cornmeal

³/₄ cup flour

3 tablespoons sugar

1 teaspoon baking powder

¹/₂ teaspoon baking soda

¹/₂ teaspoon salt

3 tablespoons butter or margarine, melted

1 cup buttermilk

1 egg, lightly beaten

¹/₂ cup frozen or canned corn

Preheat oven to 375°F. If using a glass or nonstick pan, preheat oven to 350°F. Butter an 8" x 8" baking pan. In a large bowl, combine cornmeal, flour, sugar, baking powder, baking soda, and salt. Stir to blend. Add butter, buttermilk, and egg. Stir just until well mixed. Add corn and stir. Spoon into pan. Bake for 20 to 30 minutes or until light brown and a toothpick inserted in the middle comes out clean.

Nutritional information per serving:

Calories	170
Fat, gm.	5
Protein, gm.	4
Carbohydrate, gm.	27
Cholesterol, mg.	35
Fiber	medium

Lemon Bread

This is a super-easy recipe for a delicious sweetbread. It is my sister's very favorite recipe from my first book, The Cancer Survival Cookbook. *She and her husband make it fresh twice a week and enjoy it on their way to work every morning.*

Serves 20

4 eggs
1 box (18 ounces) lemon cake mix (with pudding in mix)
1 box (3 ounces) instant lemon pudding mix
1/2 cup plain yogurt
1 cup hot water
1 tablespoon poppy seeds, optional

Preheat oven to 325°F. Grease 2 large or 3 small loaf pans. In a large mixing bowl, beat eggs. Add cake mix, pudding mix, and yogurt. Mix together. Add hot water and mix well. Stir in poppy seeds if desired. Pour into loaf pans. Bake for 50 to 60 minutes for large pans or 40 to 50 minutes for small pans. Remove from pan and cool on rack.

Nutritional information per serving:

Calories	150
Fat, gm.	4
Protein, gm.	3
Carbohydrate, gm.	25
Cholesterol, mg.	35
Fiber	low

Norwegian Potato Lefse

My Aunt Florence and Uncle Oley always made lefse for family reunion dinners. I always thought it was too difficult to make but when I tried it, I was surprised that it was actually easy and fun to prepare.

Serves 8

5 medium potatoes, peeled and boiled
2 tablespoons butter or margarine
2 tablespoons evaporated fat-free milk
1 1/2 cups flour, divided
1 teaspoon salt
1 tablespoon sugar

1. In a large bowl, combine cooked potatoes, butter, and milk. Mash potatoes. Measure out 3 cups and place in medium bowl. Cool to room temperature. Add 1 1/4 cups flour, salt, and sugar. If mixture is sticky, add additional 1/4 cup flour.

2. Form dough into 2-inch balls. Cover and chill.

3. Take balls out of the refrigerator one at a time and roll out each on a floured pastry sheet to about 8 inches in diameter. Turn and use more flour if necessary and roll out very thin to about 10 inches.

4. Heat a nonstick griddle or nonstick skillet. Cook each lefse piece over medium heat on ungreased grill until speckled brown.

5. Turn over and cook until speckled brown again. Cool and wrap in plastic wrap. Refrigerate or freeze until ready to use.

Note: Use as a wrap to make sandwiches or simply spread lightly with butter and roll up to eat. A Norwegian tradition is to dip them in sugar and cinnamon.

Nutritional information per serving:

Calories	190
Fat, gm.	4
Protein, gm.	5
Carbohydrate, gm.	34
Cholesterol, mg.	10
Fiber	low

Oatmeal Cherry Muffins

These are unusual, great-tasting muffins.

Serves 12

1 cup quick-cooking oatmeal
1 cup low-fat vanilla or plain yogurt
1/2 cup vegetable oil
3/4 cup brown sugar
1 egg, lightly beaten
1 cup flour
3/4 tablespoon salt
1/2 teaspoon baking soda
1 teaspoon baking powder
1/2 cup dried cherries

Note: Raisins or dried cranberries can be substituted for the dried cherries.

Preheat oven to 375°F or 350°F if using nonstick pans. Grease 12 muffin tins. In a large bowl combine oatmeal and yogurt. Add oil, brown sugar, and egg. Beat well with a spoon. In a small bowl, mix flour, salt, baking soda, and baking powder. Add the flour mixture to the oatmeal mixture and stir just until blended. Fold in dried cherries. Fill muffin tins half full. Bake for 20 minutes or until light brown.

Nutritional information per serving:

Calories	215
Fat, gm.	10
Protein, gm.	4
Carbohydrate, gm.	27
Cholesterol, mg.	15
Fiber	low

Orange Marmalade–Pecan Bread

This is a wonderful quick bread! The appearance is lovely with a golden brown crust and it has a subtle sweet flavor.

Serves 14

2 cups flour
2 teaspoons baking powder
$1/2$ cup sugar
$1/2$ teaspoon salt
2 eggs, lightly beaten
$2/3$ cup evaporated fat-free milk
$1/3$ cup shortening, melted
$1/2$ cup chopped pecans
$1/2$ cup orange marmalade

1. Preheat oven to 350°F or 325°F if using glass or nonstick pans. Grease one 9" x 5" loaf pan or five small 4" x 2" baking pans. In a large bowl, combine flour, baking powder, sugar, and salt. Stir to mix. Add eggs, milk, and shortening. Stir gently just until blended. Add pecans and marmalade. Stir gently. Avoid any extra stirring because that will toughen the bread.

2. Pour batter into pan(s). Bake large loaf for 45 to 55 minutes and small loaves for 30 to 35 minutes or until light brown and a toothpick inserted in the middle comes out clean. Do not overbake. Remove from pan and place on a rack. It is best served fresh and warm.

Nutritional information per serving:

Calories	195
Fat, gm.	7
Protein, gm.	3
Carbohydrate, gm.	30
Cholesterol, mg.	25
Fiber	very low

Play Dough

This is a true "recipe with memories". When I was going through my old recipes, I came across this one filed under "Breads." I remember making Play Dough with my children when they were young.

½ cup salt
1 cup flour
1 teaspoon cream of tartar
1 tablespoon vegetable oil
1 cup water
Food coloring, optional

In a small heavy saucepan, combine all ingredients. Cook over medium heat, stirring constantly, until mixture forms into a ball. Remove from heat and turn out onto a board. Cool for a few minutes. Knead for 5 minutes. Keeps for weeks in a covered bowl.

Plum Coffeecake

This old German recipe is impressive if served at the table or on a buffet. It is absolutely beautiful.

Serves 10

¾ cup sugar
¼ cup butter or margarine
1 egg
½ cup fat-free milk
2 teaspoons baking powder
½ teaspoon salt
1½ cups flour
3 large fresh plums, pitted and thinly sliced

Topping:

2 tablespoons butter or margarine
½ cup brown sugar
3 tablespoons flour
½ teaspoon cinnamon
½ cup chopped walnuts

1. Preheat oven to 375°F. If using a glass or nonstick pan, preheat oven to 350°F. Butter a 7" x 11" or 9" x 9" baking pan. In a medium bowl, combine sugar and butter. Beat well. Add egg and beat. Add milk, baking powder, and salt. Beat until well blended. Stir in flour. Spread dough in pan. Top with rows of plums.

2. In a small saucepan, melt butter. Add brown sugar, flour, cinnamon, and nuts. Stir to mix. Sprinkle over plums. Bake for 25 to 35 minutes or until light brown and set in the middle.

Nutritional information per serving:

Calories	250
Fat, gm.	8
Protein, gm.	3
Carbohydrate, gm.	42
Cholesterol, mg.	40
Fiber	low

Popovers

When I was a child, popovers were wonderfully mysterious. How could these delicate crispy shells be as light as balloons? Surprise your family or guests with a treat from the past. They really aren't hard to make.

Serves 6

3 eggs, room temperature
1 cup fat-free milk
2 tablespoons butter or margarine, melted
1/2 teaspoon salt
1 cup flour

Preheat oven to 450°F. Heavily grease 12 muffin tins or 6 popover pan cups. In a small bowl, beat eggs until foamy. Add milk, butter, and salt and beat until blended. Add flour and beat 10 seconds or just until blended. Pour batter into pans, filling each cup half full. Bake for 15 minutes. Reduce oven temperature to 350°F and bake for another 20 to 30 minutes or until browned and firm. If popovers brown too quickly on the bottom, reduce oven temperature to 325°F. A few minutes before removing from oven, prick with a fork to let steam escape.

Note: Serve with a mixture of butter and honey.

Nutritional information per serving:

Calories	130
Fat, gm.	4
Protein, gm.	6
Carbohydrate, gm.	18
Cholesterol, mg.	95
Fiber	0

Pumpkin Bread

So moist, great flavor, and a rich source of vitamin A.

Serves 16

2 eggs
$1/2$ cup vegetable oil
$1/3$ cup fat-free milk
1 cup canned pumpkin
$11/2$ cups sugar
$13/4$ cups flour
1 teaspoon salt
1 teaspoon baking soda
1 teaspoon cinnamon
$1/2$ teaspoon nutmeg
$1/4$ teaspoon cloves
1 cup chopped walnuts or pecans

Preheat oven to 350°F. If using glass or nonstick pans, preheat oven to 325°F. Grease a 5" x 9" loaf pan. In a large bowl, combine eggs, oil, milk, and pumpkin. Mix well. In another medium bowl, combine all remaining ingredients. Mix until blended. Add dry ingredients to egg mixture. Mix well. Pour into pan and bake for 1 hour and 10 minutes or until loaf is firm in the middle, light brown, and beginning to pull away from the sides. Remove from pan and cool on a rack.

Nutritional information per serving:

Calories	205
Fat, gm.	8
Protein, gm.	3
Carbohydrate, gm.	31
Cholesterol, mg.	25
Fiber	low

Raspberry Streusel Muffins

Raspberry muffins are a real treat. They are worth a little extra effort.

Serves 16

1/2 cup sugar
2 cups flour
1 tablespoon baking powder
1/2 teaspoon cinnamon
1/2 teaspoon salt
1 cup fat-free milk
1 egg
1/2 cup butter or margarine, melted
1 teaspoon vanilla extract
1 1/2 cups fresh or frozen loose-pack raspberries

Topping:

1/4 cup flour
1/4 cup quick-cooking oats
1/4 cup sugar
1/2 teaspoon cinnamon
3 tablespoons butter or margarine

1. Preheat oven to 375°F. If using a nonstick pan, preheat oven to 350°F. Grease 16 muffin tins. In a large bowl, combine sugar, flour, baking powder, cinnamon, and salt. Stir to mix. In another small bowl, combine milk, egg, butter, and vanilla. Mix well. Pour into dry ingredients. Stir just until blended. Dough will still appear lumpy. Gently stir in raspberries. Spoon into muffin tins, filling half full.

2. In a small bowl, combine topping ingredients. Sprinkle muffins with streusel. Bake for 20 minutes or until light brown and toothpick inserted in the middle comes out clean. Cool on racks.

Nutritional information per serving:

Calories	165
Fat, gm.	7
Protein, gm.	2
Carbohydrate, gm.	23
Cholesterol, mg.	30
Fiber	low

Streusel-Filled Coffeecake

There is something about the aroma of a cinnamon streusel coffeecake baking in the morning that says,
"Life is good." This is one coffeecake that doesn't skimp on the streusel.

Serves 10

1 1/2 cups flour
3 teaspoons baking powder
1/4 teaspoon salt
3/4 cup sugar
1/3 cup shortening
1 egg, lightly beaten
3/4 cup fat-free milk
1 teaspoon vanilla extract

Filling and Topping:

2 tablespoons flour
2 teaspoons cinnamon
1/2 teaspoon nutmeg
1/2 cup brown sugar
2 tablespoons butter or margarine, melted
1/2 cup chopped walnuts

Note: Double the recipe for a 9" x 13" pan.

1. Preheat oven to 350°F. If using a glass or nonstick pan, preheat oven to 325°F. Butter and flour an 8" x 8" baking pan. In a medium bowl, combine flour, baking powder, salt, and sugar. Add shortening and cut in with a pastry blender or knife until it resembles coarse cornmeal. Add egg, milk, and vanilla. Blend with a spoon. Spread half the batter in the baking pan. Set aside.

2. In a small bowl, combine flour, cinnamon, nutmeg, brown sugar, butter, and nuts. Stir until blended. Sprinkle half of this mixture over cake batter. With a spoon, drop remaining batter on top. Batter will be thick but can be smoothed out with a knife. Sprinkle remaining streusel over the top. Bake for 25 to 30 minutes or until lightly browned.

Nutritional information per serving:

Calories	260
Fat, gm.	10
Protein, gm.	4
Carbohydrate, gm.	39
Cholesterol, mg.	25
Fiber	low

Zucchini Bread

This recipe is flavorful and moist but is lower in fat and calories than many quick-bread recipes. Make several batches when zucchinis are plentiful because the bread freezes well. Note the healthy wheat germ in this recipe.

Serves 20

3 eggs
1/2 cup vegetable oil
3/4 cup sugar
1 teaspoon baking powder
2 teaspoons baking soda
1 tablespoon cinnamon
1 teaspoon salt
2 teaspoons vanilla extract
1/4 cup orange juice
2 cups flour
2 cups shredded zucchini
1/2 cup wheat germ
1 cup raisins, optional
1 cup chopped walnuts, optional

Preheat oven to 375°F. If using glass or nonstick pans, preheat oven to 350°F. Butter a 5" x 9" loaf pan. In a large bowl, beat eggs. Add oil, sugar, baking powder, baking soda, cinnamon, salt, vanilla, and orange juice. Beat well. Stir in flour. Stir in zucchini and wheat germ. Add raisins and nuts if desired. Spoon into pan. Bake for 50 to 60 minutes or until light brown and set in the middle. Cool in pan for 10 minutes and remove. Cool on racks.

Note: This makes a very large loaf or the batter can be divided among several smaller loaves.

Nutritional information per serving:

Calories	165
Fat, gm.	6
Protein, gm.	3
Carbohydrate, gm.	25
Cholesterol, mg.	25
Fiber	low

Chapter Twelve
Sauces and Salsas

Barbecue Sauce

Basic Mustard

Caramel Cinnamon Sauce

Corn Relish

Homemade Onion Soup Mix

Homemade Taco Seasoning Mix

Melba Sauce

Mustard and Horseradish Sauce

Pesto

Pesto—Low-Fat

Rhubarb Sauce

Sherry Mushroom Sauce

Shrimp Cocktail Sauce

Swedish Fruit Sauce

Warm Blueberry Sauce

White Sauce

Barbecue Sauce

This sauce has a great robust flavor. It is so good on ribs.

Serves 8

$^1/_2$ tablespoon vegetable oil
1 medium onion, finely chopped
1 $^1/_2$ cups ketchup
6 ounces beer
$^1/_3$ cup brown sugar
$^1/_3$ cup cider vinegar
1 tablespoon Worcestershire sauce
1 tablespoon soy sauce
$^1/_2$ teaspoon chili powder
1 tablespoon Dijon mustard
Tabasco sauce to taste

In a medium saucepan, heat vegetable oil. Add onion and cook over medium heat until translucent. Add all remaining ingredients except Tabasco sauce. Bring to a boil. Reduce heat and simmer for 30 to 45 minutes or until mixture reaches desired consistency. Add Tabasco sauce to taste. Store in covered jar in the refrigerator.

Nutritional information per serving:

Calories	90
Fat, gm.	1
Protein, gm.	1
Carbohydrate, gm.	20
Cholesterol, mg.	0
Fiber	low

Basic Mustard

Mustard making is easy and fun and it is something Grandma used to do.
Your own mustard can be packed in an attractive jar or crock to use as an inexpensive holiday gift.

Serves 16

1 cup mustard powder
¹/3 cup cool water
¹/3 cup cider vinegar
1 tablespoon honey
¹/2 teaspoon salt

Note: Change the flavor of the mustard by substituting sugar or maple syrup for the honey. Try other vinegars such as balsamic or tarragon vinegar. Add spices and herbs of your choice such as tarragon, basil, dill, or hot peppers.

Mustard-making tips:
• Use glass, stainless steel, or ceramic utensils and containers. Aluminum gives mustard an odd flavor.
• For a standard thickness, use 8 parts mustard powder to 7 parts liquid.
• Mustard is very sharp when first mixed and then mellows with age. Refrigeration nearly stops the mellowing process. For a nippy but not overpowering mustard, store at room temperature for 4 to 8 weeks (4 weeks for hot mustard and 8 weeks for mild), and then refrigerate.

In a small jar, combine mustard powder and water. Mix and let stand for 10 to 15 minutes. Add vinegar, honey, and salt. Mix well. Add small amount of additional water if it is too thick. Cover and store at room temperature for 4 to 6 weeks and then store in refrigerator.

Nutritional information per serving:

Calories	5
Fat, gm.	0
Protein, gm.	0
Carbohydrate, gm.	1
Cholesterol, mg.	0
Fiber	0

Caramel Cinnamon Sauce

Serve this warm cinnamon syrup over pancakes, waffles, French toast, or apple desserts.

Serves 8

$^1/_2$ *cup light brown sugar*
$^1/_2$ *cup sugar*
$^1/_2$ *cup evaporated fat-free milk*
1 tablespoon butter or margarine
$^1/_4$ *teaspoon cinnamon*
$^1/_2$ *teaspoon vanilla extract*
2 teaspoons brandy, optional

In a small saucepan, combine brown sugar, sugar, evaporated milk, butter, and cinnamon. Bring to a boil, stirring constantly, over medium heat. Boil gently for 3 minutes. Remove from heat. Add vanilla and brandy. Stir to blend. Serve warm. Makes 1 cup.

Nutritional information per serving:

Calories	105
Fat, gm.	1
Protein, gm.	1
Carbohydrate, gm.	23
Cholesterol, mg.	5
Fiber	0

Corn Relish

This everyday zesty vegetable dish used to be popular in farm kitchens.
It can be made in bigger batches because it keeps for at least 2 weeks in the refrigerator.

Serves 10

1 tablespoon cornstarch
1/4 cup cold water
1/2 cup cider vinegar
1/2 cup sugar
4 cups frozen corn
1/3 cup finely chopped celery
1/4 cup finely chopped green onions
1/3 cup finely chopped green bell pepper
2 tablespoons chopped pimientos
1 teaspoon turmeric
1/2 teaspoon dry mustard

In a medium saucepan, mix cornstarch and water. Stir until dissolved. Add all remaining ingredients. Bring to a boil, stirring constantly until mixture thickens. Simmer for 3 minutes. Remove from heat. Spoon into serving bowl. Cover and refrigerate until ready to serve.

Nutritional information per serving:

Calories	100
Fat, gm.	0
Protein, gm.	2
Carbohydrate, gm.	23
Cholesterol, mg.	0
Fiber	medium

Homemade Onion Soup Mix

Use this blend of ingredients for any recipe that calls for a package of onion soup mix.

Makes 1 cup

¾ cup minced dry onion flakes
⅓ cup beef bouillon or beef soup base
1 tablespoon onion powder
¼ teaspoon celery salt
¼ teaspoon sugar

1. Preheat oven to 400°F. Sprinkle onion flakes on baking sheet and bake for 2 to 5 minutes or just until onions are toasted. In a small bowl, combine onions and all remaining ingredients. Stir to mix. Store in resealable plastic bag.

2. Use 5 tablespoons to equal the amount in 1 commercial dry onion-soup packet.

Homemade Taco Seasoning Mix

You can make your own taco seasoning with the spices you have in your cupboard.

Makes ¹/₂ cup

2 tablespoons chili powder
2 tablespoons paprika
1 ¹/₂ tablespoons cumin
1 tablespoon onion powder
1 teaspoon garlic powder
¹/₄ teaspoon cayenne pepper

1. In a custard cup, combine all ingredients. Stir to mix. Store in resealable plastic bag.

2. Use 2 tablespoons of the mixture to season 1 pound of ground beef for tacos. It is also a good seasoning to use in chili and refried beans.

Melba Sauce

This classic sauce makes an ordinary dish of ice cream extraordinary.

Serves 6

¹/₄ cup currant jelly
10 ounces frozen raspberries in syrup, thawed, divided
1 tablespoon cornstarch
1 tablespoon water
1 teaspoon fresh lemon juice

In a small heavy saucepan, melt jelly over medium heat. Add the juice from the thawed raspberries, along with half of the whole raspberries. In a cup mix cornstarch and water. Pour into pan. Cook mixture over medium heat, stirring constantly, until it comes to a boil and thickens. Remove from heat and cool to room temperature. Add remaining raspberries and lemon juice. Place in covered jar in the refrigerator until ready to serve.

Nutritional information per serving:

Calories	80
Fat, gm.	0
Protein, gm.	0
Carbohydrate, gm.	20
Cholesterol, mg.	0
Fiber	medium

Mustard and Horseradish Sauce

When you want to add some zest to a meat or vegetable dish, try this.

Serves 8

$1/2$ cup fat-free or low-fat mayonnaise
$1/2$ cup fat-free sour cream
1 tablespoon Dijon mustard
1 tablespoon yellow mustard
$1/2$ teaspoon dry mustard
1 teaspoon horseradish
1 tablespoon white wine vinegar
$1/2$ teaspoon Worcestershire sauce
Hot pepper sauce to taste
Salt to taste

Combine all ingredients in a food processor. Blend until smooth. Adjust seasonings with hot pepper sauce, salt, or extra horseradish to suit your taste.

Nutritional information per serving:

Calories	20
Fat, gm.	0
Protein, gm.	0
Carbohydrate, gm.	5
Cholesterol, mg.	3
Fiber	0

Pesto

Pesto is so good, but it is also high in fat and calories.
A little can go a long way. Mix it with cooked pasta for a quick meal.

Serves 6

1 cup chopped fresh basil
2 tablespoons pine nuts
2 cloves garlic, minced
2 tablespoons grated Parmesan cheese
1/2 cup extra-virgin olive oil

Place basil, pine nuts, and garlic in food processor. Blend until finely minced. Add cheese and oil. Process until blended. Store in covered jar in the refrigerator.

Nutritional information per serving:

Calories	190
Fat, gm.	20
Protein, gm.	1
Carbohydrate, gm.	1
Cholesterol, mg.	0
Fiber	very low

Pesto—Low-Fat

This is a low-fat adaptation of the traditional recipe.

Serves 8

3 cloves garlic, minced
2 tablespoons pine nuts
1 1/2 cups chopped fresh basil leaves
1/4 cup chopped fresh parsley
1/2 cup grated Parmesan cheese
1 tablespoon extra-virgin olive oil
1/2 cup fat-free Italian Parmesan salad dressing

Combine all ingredients in food processor. Blend until finely minced. Add extra salad dressing if needed to thin.

Nutritional information per serving:

Calories	65
Fat, gm.	4
Protein, gm.	3
Carbohydrate, gm.	4
Cholesterol, mg.	0
Fiber	low

Rhubarb Sauce

This is a sauce you can enjoy for breakfast, lunch, or dinner.
Eat it as is or spoon it over frozen yogurt or ice cream.

Serves 6

4 cups sliced fresh or frozen rhubarb (1-inch slices)
3/4 cup sugar
1/4 cup water
2 teaspoons orange zest, optional
1/2 teaspoon vanilla extract

In a heavy saucepan, combine all ingredients except vanilla. Bring to a boil. Reduce heat, partially cover pan, and simmer for 5 minutes or until rhubarb is tender. Add vanilla. Taste and add additional sugar if desired.

Nutritional information per serving:

Calories	110
Fat, gm.	0
Protein, gm.	0
Carbohydrate, gm.	28
Cholesterol, mg.	0
Fiber	low

Sherry Mushroom Sauce

This creamy sauce can be served with vegetarian dishes.
It is also good with poultry and fish.

Serves 6

2 tablespoons butter or margarine, divided
$1/2$ pound fresh mushrooms, sliced
$1/4$ cup chopped onion
1 tablespoon flour
1 cup fat-free half-and-half
$1/2$ teaspoon salt
$1/4$ teaspoon white pepper
$1/8$ teaspoon tarragon
$1/2$ cup fat-free milk, optional
2 tablespoons sherry

Note: Evaporated fat-free milk can be substituted for the fat-free half-and-half. Vegetable broth or chicken broth may be used in place of the milk to thin the sauce.

In a medium heavy saucepan, melt 1 tablespoon butter. Add mushrooms and onion and cook until mushrooms are tender. Add additional tablespoon butter. Add flour and cook, stirring constantly, over medium heat for 2 minutes. Add half-and-half and bring to a boil, stirring constantly. Add salt, white pepper, and tarragon. Thin with milk if desired. Add sherry when ready to serve.

Nutritional information per serving:

Calories	90
Fat, gm.	4
Protein, gm.	3
Carbohydrate, gm.	10
Cholesterol, mg.	10
Fiber	low

Shrimp Cocktail Sauce

You can make your own to suit your own taste and there will be one less bottle of sauce to keep in the refrigerator.

Serves 10

2 cups ketchup
2 tablespoons fresh lemon juice
2 tablespoons horseradish
2 tablespoons minced onion
1 tablespoon Worcestershire sauce
$^1/_2$ teaspoon dry mustard
Tabasco sauce to taste

Note: For more zest, replace half of the ketchup with bottled chili sauce.

In a small bowl, combine all ingredients. Store in covered jar and refrigerate.

Nutritional information per serving:

Calories	60
Fat, gm.	0
Protein, gm.	1
Carbohydrate, gm.	14
Cholesterol, mg.	0
Fiber	very low

Swedish Fruit Sauce

This sauce, also called hedelmokiisseli, *is often served in Swedish or Finnish homes with rice pudding, frozen yogurt, or ice cream.*

Serves 12

1 ¹/₂ cups dried pitted prunes
1 ¹/₂ cups dried apricot halves
¹/₂ cup seedless raisins
4 cups water
¹/₂ fresh lemon, cut into wedges
1 cinnamon stick
³/₄ cup sugar
3 tablespoons tapioca

Note: Use a combination of any dried fruits of your choice.

In a large saucepan, soak prunes, apricots, and raisins in water for several hours or overnight. Add lemon, cinnamon stick, sugar, and tapioca. Place over medium heat and bring mixture to a boil. Reduce heat, partially cover, and simmer for about 40 minutes or until fruit is tender. Add additional water to thin if sauce is too thick. Sauce is best served warm.

Nutritional information per serving:

Calories	175
Fat, gm.	0
Protein, gm.	1
Carbohydrate, gm.	43
Cholesterol, mg.	0
Fiber	high

Warm Blueberry Sauce

Serve this healthy sauce (full of flavonoids) over ice cream, yogurt, pancakes, or waffles.

Serves 12

1/4 cup water
1 tablespoon cornstarch
1/3 cup brown sugar
2 tablespoons fresh lemon juice
1/2 teaspoon cinnamon
1/4 teaspoon nutmeg
Dash cloves
2 teaspoons lemon zest
2 cups fresh blueberries

In a small saucepan, mix water and cornstarch. Add brown sugar, lemon juice, cinnamon, nutmeg, and cloves. Bring to a boil over medium heat, stirring constantly. Remove from heat and cool for 10 to 15 minutes. Thin with water if mixture is too thick. Add lemon zest and blueberries. Serve warm.

Note: This can be made ahead and refrigerated. Warm it in a small saucepan over low heat and add additional water to thin if necessary.

Nutritional information per serving:

Calories	130
Fat, gm.	0
Protein, gm.	0
Carbohydrate, gm.	32
Cholesterol, mg.	0
Fiber	low

White Sauce

This recipe is the basis of many sauces, including that important cheese sauce for vegetables.

Thin White Sauce:

1 tablespoon butter or margarine

1 tablespoon flour

1 cup cold milk

Medium White Sauce:

2 tablespoons butter or margarine

2 tablespoons flour

1 cup cold milk

Thick White Sauce:

3 tablespoons butter or margarine

4 tablespoons flour

1 cup cold milk

Notes: For a reduced-fat cheese sauce, add fat-free processed cheese, such as American, Cheddar, or Swiss.

Be sure to cook the butter and flour, stirring constantly with a wooden spoon, until the flour is completely cooked. The milk should be cold or at room temperature when you add it to the hot flour and butter mixture. This will prevent lumps from forming.

In a heavy saucepan, melt butter. Using a wooden spoon or a wire whip, blend in flour. Cook over medium heat, stirring constantly, for 2 to 3 minutes. Add cold milk all at once and stir constantly over medium heat until mixture comes to a boil and thickens. Boil gently for 1 minute, stirring constantly. Add salt and white pepper to taste.

Chapter Thirteen
Breakfast and Brunch

Bacon and Spinach Breakfast Pizza

Even the kids will look forward to eating this breakfast!

Serves 6

10 ounces refrigerated pizza dough
^{1}/$_2$ tablespoon canola oil
1 medium onion, finely chopped
10 ounces frozen spinach, thawed and squeezed dry
1 teaspoon Italian seasoning
2 medium tomatoes, seeded and chopped
8 slices cooked bacon, cut into ^{1}/$_2$-inch pieces
Shredded cheese for topping

Preheat oven to 400°F. Grease a 15-inch pizza pan or a baking sheet. Unroll dough and place in pan. Press out dough to fit pan. Bake for 8 to 10 minutes or until edges begin to brown. Remove from heat and set aside. In a medium skillet, heat oil. Add onion and cook over medium heat until lightly brown. Turn off heat. Add spinach and Italian seasoning. Stir to mix. Distribute spinach mixture on top of pizza crust. Distribute tomatoes and bacon evenly over spinach. Top with cheese. Bake for 8 to 10 minutes or until cheese is melted and pizza is heated through.

Nutritional information per serving:

Calories	195
Fat, gm.	5
Protein, gm.	8
Carbohydrate, gm.	29
Cholesterol, mg.	5
Fiber	medium

Baked Breakfast Apples and Raisins

Remember the wonderful smells of warm apples and cinnamon?

Serves 4

2 large cooking apples (Golden Delicious, for example),
   peeled, cored, and diced
2 tablespoons Splenda or sugar
1/4 teaspoon cinnamon
1/2 cup golden raisins
2 tablespoons apple or orange juice
1/4 cup raspberry jam, warmed

Preheat oven to 350°F. Butter 4 individual baking dishes. In a medium bowl, combine apples, Splenda, cinnamon, raisins, and juice. Stir to mix. Divide between prepared baking dishes. Drizzle 1 tablespoon jam on top of each. Cover with foil and bake for 10 to 20 minutes or until apples are tender.

Nutritional information per serving:

Calories	160
Fat, gm.	0
Protein, gm.	1
Carbohydrate, gm.	40
Cholesterol, mg.	0
Fiber	medium

Breakfast Potato and Canadian Bacon Casserole

Make this the day before and serve it for breakfast or brunch.

Serves 6

3 cups frozen shredded hash brown potatoes
1 cup shredded Monterey jack cheese, divided
4 ounces green chilies, diced
1/2 cup chopped green onions
6 ounces Canadian bacon, diced
4 large eggs
1/4 teaspoon salt
1/4 teaspoon white pepper
12 ounces evaporated fat-free milk

Butter a 9" x 9" baking pan. Arrange hash brown potatoes on bottom of pan. Sprinkle with ¾ cup cheese, chilies, onions, and Canadian bacon. In a medium bowl, combine eggs, salt, pepper, and milk. Beat well. Pour over potato mixture. Top with remaining cheese. This dish may be covered and refrigerated for several hours or overnight. When ready to bake, preheat oven to 350°F. Bake uncovered for 40 to 60 minutes or until center is set. Let stand for 10 minutes before serving.

Nutritional information per serving:

Calories	250
Fat, gm.	10
Protein, gm.	20
Carbohydrate, gm.	20
Cholesterol, mg.	155
Fiber	low

Crème Brûlée French Toast

If you love the taste of brown sugar and cinnamon, this is the recipe for you. It is easy to make ahead and it will be ready to bake when you need it for a special family or company breakfast.

Serves 6

4 tablespoons butter or m̶

$^1/_2$ cup brown sugar

1 tablespoon corn syrup

1 large cooking apple (Golden Delicious, for example), peeled, cored, and very thinly sliced

2 tablespoons cinnamon and sugar mixture, divided

6 thick slices French bread

3 large eggs

$^1/_2$ cup fat-free half-and-half

$^1/_2$ cup fat-free milk

1 teaspoon vanilla extract

1 tablespoon Grand Marnier, optional

$^1/_4$ teaspoon salt

....

Notes: A cinnamon-sugar mixture can be made with 2 tablespoons sugar and $^1/_8$ teaspoon cinnamon. Stir until well mixed.

To make 1$^1/_2$ times the recipe, use a 9" x 13" baking pan.

....

1. Butter a 7" x 11" baking pan. In a small s̶ ̶ ̶mbine butter, brown sugar, and corn syrup. Heat until butter is melted. Bring to a boil and boil gently for 3 minutes. Pour into baking pan. Arrange apple slices in a single layer on top of brown sugar mixture. Sprinkle with 1 tablespoon cinnamon and sugar mixture. Trim crusts from French bread and arrange on top of apples. In a small bowl, combine eggs, half-and-half, milk, vanilla, Grand Marnier, and salt. Beat until well mixed. Pour over bread. If making ahead, cover with plastic wrap and refrigerate for several hours or overnight.

2. When ready to bake, preheat oven to 350°F. Sprinkle with remaining 1 tablespoon cinnamon and sugar mixture. Bake uncovered for 40 to 45 minutes or until puffed and edges are golden in color. Serve immediately.

Nutritional information per serving:

Calo̶	360
Fat̶	12
Pr̶ ̶in, gm.	8
Carbohydrate, gm.	56
Cholesterol, mg.	110
Fiber	medium

Fancy Baked Apple Pancakes

Serve this for breakfast on a special occasion.

Serves 2

1 tablespoon butter or margarine, divided
2 medium cooking apples (Golden Delicious, for example), peeled, cored, and sliced
$1/4$ cup Splenda or sugar
$1/4$ teaspoon cinnamon
$1/8$ teaspoon nutmeg
$1/8$ teaspoon cardamom, optional
1 large egg
$1/4$ cup fat-free milk
$1/4$ cup flour
$1/4$ teaspoon salt

1. Preheat oven to 400°F. In a small ovenproof skillet, melt $1/2$ tablespoon butter. Add apples and cook over medium heat until apples begin to get tender. In a small bowl, combine Splenda, cinnamon, nutmeg, and cardamom. Sprinkle over apples. Transfer apples to a plate or bowl and set aside.

2. Combine egg, milk, flour, and salt in a small bowl. Beat until smooth. Add $1/2$ tablespoon butter to the ovenproof skillet. Melt over medium heat. Pour batter into skillet. Place skillet in oven and bake for 10 minutes. Remove from oven and top with apple-cinnamon mixture. Return to oven and bake for another 10 minutes or until the pancake is lightly browned and puffy. Serve immediately.

Nutritional information per serving:

Calories	235
Fat, gm.	8
Protein, gm.	5
Carbohydrate, gm.	35
Cholesterol, mg.	100
Fiber	medium

Salmon Mushroom Quiche

If you enjoy salmon, you will love this quiche seasoned with dill weed and thyme.

Serves 6

$1/2$ tablespoon butter or margarine
$1/2$ cup chopped green onions
$1/2$ pound sliced mushrooms
6 ounces salmon fillet
1 teaspoon fresh lemon juice
$1/2$ teaspoon dill weed
9-inch unbaked pie crust
12 ounces evaporated fat-free milk
4 eggs
1 teaspoon salt
$1/4$ teaspoon white pepper
$1/2$ teaspoon thyme
$1/2$ cup shredded Swiss cheese

Preheat oven to 375°F. In a medium skillet, heat butter. Add onions and mushrooms. Cook until tender. Transfer to a bowl and set aside. Place salmon in skillet and cook over medium heat until brown on both sides and cooked through. Flake salmon with a fork and place in bowl with mushrooms. Add lemon juice and dill weed. Blend gently. Spoon into pie crust. In a large bowl, combine milk, eggs, salt, white pepper, and thyme. Beat well. Pour into pie crust. Top with cheese. Bake for 40 to 50 minutes or until set in the middle. Let stand for 10 minutes before serving.

Nutritional information per serving:

Calories	300
Fat, gm.	15
Protein, gm.	19
Carbohydrate, gm.	23
Cholesterol, mg.	150
Fiber	medium

Spinach and Bacon Strata

The blend of spinach, bacon, cheese, and Italian seasoning make this a delicious brunch or supper dish.

Serves 6

¹/₄ cup butter or margarine, plus extra for greasing
2 cups seasoned croutons, crushed
3 eggs, lightly beaten
1 cup small-curd, low-fat cottage cheese
1 cup grated low-fat Cheddar cheese
¹/₂ cup fat-free milk
¹/₂ cup finely chopped onion
¹/₂ teaspoon freshly ground black pepper
¹/₂ teaspoon Italian seasoning
¹/₂ teaspoon crushed garlic
10 ounces frozen spinach, thawed and squeezed dry
8 slices cooked bacon, crumbled
¹/₃ cup grated Parmesan cheese

Note: This can be prepared ahead and baked when you need it or it can be baked and refrigerated. Warm it up in the oven to serve. It also works well to warm it piece by piece. Cut the number of pieces you need and place on a baking sheet. Bake at 350°F until heated through. The crust gets crispy this way.

Preheat oven to 350°F. Grease a 9-inch deep pie pan with butter. Place crushed croutons in bottom of pan. Melt butter and drizzle over croutons. In a large bowl, combine eggs, cottage cheese, Cheddar, milk, onion, pepper, Italian seasoning, and garlic. Mix well. Stir in spinach and bacon. Spoon on top of croutons. Cover pan with foil. Bake for 35 minutes. Remove cover and sprinkle with Parmesan cheese. Return to oven and continue baking for 15 to 20 minutes or until set in the middle. Let stand for 5 minutes before serving.

Nutritional information per serving:

Calories	340
Fat, gm.	22
Protein, gm.	22
Carbohydrate, gm.	14
Cholesterol, mg.	135
Fiber	medium

Chapter Fourteen
Cookies and Bars

Best-Ever Sugar Cookies

This is the perfect, old-fashioned, crisp sugar cookie.

Serves 60

1 cup butter
$2/3$ cup vegetable oil
1 cup sugar
1 cup powdered sugar
2 eggs
1 teaspoon vanilla extract
1 teaspoon salt
1 teaspoon baking soda
1 teaspoon cream of tartar
$4 1/4$ cups flour
$1/4$ cup colored sugar for dipping

1. Grease a baking sheet. In a large bowl, cream butter, vegetable oil, sugar, and powdered sugar until light. Add eggs and vanilla. Mix well. Add salt, baking soda, and cream of tartar. Blend well. Stir in flour. Chill dough.

2. Preheat oven to 325°F. Roll dough into 1-inch balls. Dip in sugar. Place on cookie sheet and flatten with bottom of a glass or cookie press. Bake for 8 to 15 minutes or until cookies begin to brown. Watch carefully.

Nutritional information per serving:

Calories	100
Fat, gm.	5
Protein, gm.	1
Carbohydrate, gm.	12
Cholesterol, mg.	15
Fiber	0

Butterfingers

My daughter Vicki recommends a warning label on these bars: "Caution: These are addictive!"

Serves 20

4 cups quick-cooking oats
$1/2$ cup corn syrup
1 cup brown sugar
$2/3$ cup butter or margarine, melted

Topping:
$1/2$ cup peanut butter
1 cup semisweet chocolate chips

1. Preheat oven to 325°F. Butter a 10" x 15" nonstick baking pan. In a large bowl, combine oats, corn syrup, brown sugar, and butter. Stir with a wooden spoon until well mixed. Press mixture into baking pan. Bake for 8 to 10 minutes or just until mixture is bubbly in the middle. Do not brown or overbake. Remove from oven and let cool for 10 to 15 minutes.

2. In a small nonstick skillet, combine peanut butter and chocolate chips. Melt over the lowest heat. Spread on top of baked bars.

Note: It is important not to overbake the oatmeal layer.

Nutritional information per serving:

Calories	245
Fat, gm.	12
Protein, gm.	4
Carbohydrate, gm.	31
Cholesterol, mg.	115
Fiber	medium

Caramel Apple Pecan Bars

This is a sweet, very moist, and dense bar with a caramel apple flavor. It is surprisingly low in fat.

Serves 30

1 box (18 ounces) yellow cake mix
4 eggs
1/2 cup caramel topping
1/2 cup brown sugar
1 cup dark corn syrup
1/4 teaspoon allspice
2 teaspoons vanilla extract
1 1/2 cups chopped pecans
2 1/2 cups finely chopped, peeled apples

Preheat oven to 325°F. Grease a 9" x 13" baking pan. In a large bowl, combine cake mix, eggs, caramel topping, brown sugar, corn syrup, allspice, and vanilla. Beat well with electric mixer. Stir in pecans and apples. Bake for 40 to 45 minutes or until lightly browned and set in the middle.

Note: This is good served with a dollop of whipped cream.

Nutritional information per serving:

Calories	165
Fat, gm.	4
Protein, gm.	2
Carbohydrate, gm.	30
Cholesterol, mg.	25
Fiber	very low

Chocolate Chip Pan Cookies

This is the easy way to have chocolate chip cookies.
I like to make these at the summer cottage when I don't want to work too hard.

Serves 24

1 cup butter-flavored shortening
3/4 cup sugar
3/4 cup brown sugar
2 eggs
1 teaspoon vanilla extract
1 teaspoon baking soda
1 teaspoon salt
2 1/4 cups flour
1 1/2 cups semisweet chocolate chips

Preheat oven to 350°F. Butter a 10" x 15" baking pan. In a large bowl, combine shortening, sugar, and brown sugar. Beat well. Add eggs and beat well. Add vanilla, baking soda, and salt. Beat well. Stir in flour. Stir in chocolate chips. Spoon into baking pan. Bake for 15 to 20 minutes or until lightly browned. Do not overbake.

Note: If you don't have a 10" x 15" pan, use two 9" x 9" pans.

Nutritional information per serving:

Calories	215
Fat, gm.	12
Protein, gm.	2
Carbohydrate, gm.	25
Cholesterol, mg.	15
Fiber	low

Chocolate-Covered Blueberry Clusters

Try it; you'll like it. This is an understatement. The combination of chocolate and blueberries is an incredible treat. Even my husband, who isn't that much of a chocolate or a fruit lover, can't resist them if they are in the refrigerator.

Serves 30

1 cup semisweet chocolate chips
1 tablespoon shortening
2 cups blueberries

In a small nonstick skillet, melt chocolate chips and shortening over lowest heat. Stir to mix. Add blueberries and stir gently until well coated. Drop by teaspoons in clusters of three onto waxed paper or paper plates. Store in the refrigerator.

Note: Hide these well if you want to keep a few for yourself.

Nutritional information per serving:

Calories	40
Fat, gm.	2
Protein, gm.	0
Carbohydrate, gm.	5
Cholesterol, mg.	0
Fiber	low

Chocolate Kiss Cookies

When my daughter was out of the country for a semester in college, she asked me to send her favorite cookies. I sent these airmail, special delivery, with love.

Serves 70

1 cup peanut butter
1 cup butter or margarine
1 cup sugar
1 cup brown sugar
2 eggs
1 teaspoon vanilla extract
1 teaspoon baking soda
1 teaspoon baking powder
1 teaspoon salt
2 tablespoons milk
2¾ cups flour
¼ cup sugar for dipping
70 chocolate kisses, miniature peanut butter cups,
   or pecan halves

Preheat oven to 375°F. In a large mixing bowl, combine peanut butter, butter, sugar, and brown sugar. Beat until fluffy. Add eggs and beat well. Add vanilla, baking soda, baking powder, salt, and milk. Mix well. Add flour and mix. Roll into 1-inch balls and dip in sugar. Place on ungreased cookie sheets. Bake for 8 to 10 minutes. Remove from oven and immediately press a chocolate kiss, peanut butter cup, or a pecan half in the middle of each cookie. Return to oven for 1 to 5 minutes or until cookie is lightly browned. Do not overbake. Let stand on cookie sheet for 2 to 3 minutes and remove cookies to a wire rack to cool.

Nutritional information per cookie with chocolate kiss:

Calories	115
Fat, gm.	6
Protein, gm.	2
Carbohydrate, gm.	13
Cholesterol, mg.	10
Fiber	very low

Chocolate–Peanut Butter Swirl Bars

The chocolate and peanut butter combination is a real treat.

Serves 24

1/2 cup peanut butter
1/3 cup margarine or shortening
3/4 cup brown sugar
3/4 cup sugar
2 eggs
1 teaspoon baking soda
1/4 teaspoon salt
2 teaspoons vanilla extract
1 cup flour
1/2 cup quick-cooking oats
1/3 cup chopped peanuts, optional
1 cup chocolate chips

1. Preheat oven to 350°F. If using a glass or nonstick pan, preheat oven to 325°F. Butter a 9" x 13" baking pan. In a medium bowl, combine peanut butter, margarine, brown sugar, and white sugar. Beat with electric mixer until light and fluffy. Add eggs and beat well. Add baking soda, salt, and vanilla. Mix well. Stir in flour, oats, and peanuts. Spread in baking pan. Sprinkle with chocolate chips. Place in oven for 3 minutes to melt the chips.

2. Remove pan from oven and run a knife through the softened chips to marble chocolate through the batter. Return to oven and bake 15 to 20 minutes or until lightly browned and set in the middle. Do not overbake.

Nutritional information per serving:

Calories	160
Fat, gm.	7
Protein, gm.	3
Carbohydrate, gm.	21
Cholesterol, mg.	15
Fiber	low

Cranberry Chip Cookies

These are a little different and so good.

Serves 40

¹/2 cup sugar
¹/2 cup butter-flavored shortening
2 eggs
1 teaspoon vanilla extract
1 cup flour
1 teaspoon baking powder
¹/2 teaspoon salt
1 cup quick cooking oats
1 cup chocolate chips
¹/2 cup dried cranberries
¹/2 cup flaked coconut

Preheat oven to 350°F. Grease cookie sheet. In a large bowl, cream sugar and shortening together. Add eggs and vanilla. Mix well. Add flour, baking powder, and salt. Mix well. Stir in oats, chocolate chips, dried cranberries, and coconut. Drop by teaspoons onto cookie sheet. Bake for 9 to 12 minutes or until lightly browned. (The cookies do not spread.)

Nutritional information per cookie:

Calories	80
Fat, gm.	4
Protein, gm.	1
Carbohydrate, gm.	10
Cholesterol, mg.	10
Fiber	low

Fudge Brownies

These brownies taste as fudgy and good as traditional brownies but part of the butter is replaced by a fat-free fruit purée baking alternative.

Serves 24

4 ounces unsweetened baking chocolate squares

1/4 cup butter or margarine

2 cups sugar

3 eggs

1 1/2 teaspoons vanilla extract

1/2 cup fruit purée baking alternative

1 cup flour

1 cup chopped nuts, optional

Note: The fruit purée is usually found with shortenings and oils in the grocery store aisle. In place of the fruit purée baking alternative, substitute butter or margarine.

Preheat oven to 350°F. If using a glass or nonstick pan, preheat oven to 325°F. Butter a 9" x 13" pan. In a small nonstick skillet, melt chocolate squares over the very lowest heat. Remove from heat and set aside. In a medium bowl, combine butter, sugar, eggs, and vanilla. Beat well. Add melted chocolate and mix well. Stir in fruit purée. Stir in flour and nuts. Spoon into pan. Bake for 25 to 30 minutes or just until set in the middle. Do not overbake.

Nutritional information per serving without nuts:

Calories	150
Fat, gm.	5
Protein, gm.	2
Carbohydrate, gm.	25
Cholesterol, mg.	30
Fiber	medium

Lemon Squares

Soft and sweet on a tender crust.

Serves 16

Crust:

1 cup flour
1/2 cup butter or margarine
1/4 cup powdered sugar

Filling:

2 eggs
1 cup sugar
2 tablespoons flour
1/2 teaspoon baking powder
1/4 cup fresh lemon juice
2 teaspoons lemon zest

Topping:

2 tablespoons powdered sugar

1. Preheat oven to 350°F or 325°F if using a nonstick pan. In a small bowl, combine 1 cup flour, butter, and 1/4 cup powdered sugar. Press into a glass or nonstick 7" x 11" or 9" x 9" baking pan. Bake for 20 minutes.

2. Meanwhile in the same small bowl, combine eggs, sugar, flour, baking powder, lemon juice, and lemon zest. Mix with beater until smooth. Pour over baked crust. Bake for 20 to 25 minutes longer or until lightly browned. Cool. Place powdered sugar in a small strainer and sprinkle on top.

Nutritional information per serving:

Calories	150
Fat, gm.	6
Protein, gm.	2
Carbohydrate, gm.	22
Cholesterol, mg.	40
Fiber	0

Macaroon Nests with Jellybeans

Make these cute cookies for Easter.

Serves 50

1/3 cup butter or margarine

3/4 cup sugar

3 ounces low-fat cream cheese

1 egg

2 teaspoons vanilla extract

1 tablespoon apricot brandy or regular brandy

2 teaspoons baking powder

1/2 teaspoon salt

1 1/2 cups flour

5 cups (14 ounces) flaked coconut, divided

1/2 cup jellybeans

Preheat oven to 350°F. In a large bowl, cream butter, sugar, and cream cheese. Add egg, vanilla, brandy, baking powder, and salt. Mix well. Add flour and mix until blended. Stir in 4 cups coconut. Shape dough into small 3/4-inch balls and roll in remaining coconut. Place on ungreased baking sheet and press fingertip into the middle of each cookie to make a nest. Bake for 8 to 12 minutes or until lightly browned. Remove from oven and press a jellybean into the nest of each cookie. Cool on wire rack.

Nutritional information per serving:

Calories	65
Fat, gm.	3
Protein, gm.	1
Carbohydrate, gm.	9
Cholesterol, mg.	10
Fiber	very low

Molasses Cookies

Do you remember coming home from school to the smell of fresh molasses cookies?

Serves 60

1 cup butter-flavored shortening
1 1/2 cups sugar
1/2 cup molasses
2 eggs
1 teaspoon salt
2 1/2 teaspoons baking soda
2 teaspoons ginger
1/2 teaspoon nutmeg
1/4 teaspoon cloves
1 teaspoon cinnamon
4 cups flour
1/4 cup sugar for garnish

Preheat oven to 350°F. Grease baking sheet. In a large bowl, cream shortening and sugar. Add molasses and mix well. Add eggs and mix well. Add salt, baking soda, ginger, nutmeg, cloves, and cinnamon and mix well. Add flour and mix on low speed until blended. Roll dough into small balls and dip tops in sugar. Place on baking sheet and bake for 8 to 10 minutes or just until done. Do not overbake. Cool on wire rack.

Nutritional information per serving:

Calories	90
Fat, gm.	3
Protein, gm.	1
Carbohydrate, gm.	14
Cholesterol, mg.	5
Fiber	very low

No-Bake Chocolate Oatmeal Balls

No need to heat up the oven. Easy enough for kids to make.

Serves 50

1 cup sugar
1/4 cup unsweetened cocoa
1/4 cup butter or margarine
1/4 cup fat-free milk
1/4 cup peanut butter
1 teaspoon vanilla extract
2 cups quick-cooking oats
1/2 cup chopped pecans

In a small saucepan, combine sugar, cocoa, butter, and milk. Cook over medium heat, stirring constantly, until mixture comes to a rolling boil. Boil for 1 minute. Remove from heat. Add peanut butter and stir until blended. Add vanilla, oats, and pecans. Stir until well mixed. Drop by teaspoons onto a plate and form into small balls. Refrigerate until firm. Place in a plastic bag and store in the refrigerator.

Nutritional information per ball:

Calories	45
Fat, gm.	2
Protein, gm.	1
Carbohydrate, gm.	6
Cholesterol, mg.	2
Fiber	low

Oatmeal Fudge Bars

This is like an oatmeal cookie sandwich with fabulous fudge filling.
A local carry-out deli features these bars and they run out every day.

Serves 40

1 cup butter-flavored shortening
2 cups brown sugar
2 eggs
2 teaspoons vanilla extract
1 teaspoon salt
1 teaspoon baking soda
2 1/2 cups flour
3 cups oatmeal

Filling:

12 ounces semisweet chocolate chips
14 ounces fat-free sweetened condensed milk
2 tablespoons butter or margarine
1/2 teaspoon salt
2 teaspoons vanilla extract
1 cup chopped walnuts, optional

1. Preheat oven to 350°F or 325°F for a nonstick pan. Grease a 10" x 15" baking pan. In a large bowl, combine shortening and sugar. Beat well. Add eggs and beat. Mix in vanilla, salt, and baking soda. Stir in flour and oatmeal. The batter will be very stiff. Set aside.

2. In a small saucepan, combine chocolate chips, condensed milk, butter, and salt. Cook over medium heat until chips have melted and mixture is smooth. Remove from heat. Stir in vanilla and nuts if desired.

3. To assemble bars, press 3/4 of the oatmeal mixture into baking pan. Cover with filling. Crumble and dot with remaining 1/4 of oatmeal mixture. Bake for 20 to 25 minutes or until very lightly browned. Do not overbake.

Note: If you do not have a 10" x 15" pan, use two 9" x 9" pans. To prepare half a recipe, use one 9" x 9" or one 7" x 11" baking pan.

Nutritional information per serving:

Calories	200
Fat, gm.	9
Protein, gm.	3
Carbohydrate, gm.	27
Cholesterol, mg.	10
Fiber	medium

Peanut Butter–Corn Flake Nuggets

Wow! These are so good and you can put them together in minutes.
They are best eaten in small servings or the calories will add up quickly.

Serves 30

$^1/_2$ cup sugar
$^1/_2$ cup corn syrup
$^3/_4$ cup peanut butter
1 tablespoon butter or margarine
1 teaspoon vanilla extract
3 cups corn flakes
1 cup chocolate chips

1. Butter a 9" x 13" pan. In a medium saucepan, combine sugar and corn syrup. Place over high heat. Stir constantly and bring to a rolling boil. Remove immediately from heat. Add peanut butter, butter, and vanilla. Stir until smooth. Stir in corn flakes. Spoon into buttered pan. Work quickly or mixture will harden. Pat mixture smoothly into pan with back of spatula.

2. In a small nonstick skillet melt chocolate chips over the lowest heat. Spread over bars. Cut into 30 small nuggets.

Nutritional information per serving:

Calories	95
Fat, gm.	4
Protein, gm.	2
Carbohydrate, gm.	13
Cholesterol, mg.	0
Fiber	very low

Special Chocolate Chip–Oatmeal Cookies

This recipe substitutes puréed white canned beans for half of the shortening. The beans add extra fiber and nutrients but do not change the flavor. The cookies have half of the usual fat but they taste just like normal chocolate chip cookies.

Serves 100

1 can (15 ounces) northern white beans, drained and rinsed
4 eggs
1 cup shortening
1 1/2 cups brown sugar
1 1/2 cups sugar
2 teaspoons salt
2 teaspoons baking soda
2 teaspoons vanilla extract
3 1/4 cups flour
2 cups quick-cooking oats
12 ounces chocolate chips

1. Preheat oven to 375°F. Grease 2 large air-bake cookie sheets. In a food processor, blend drained beans and eggs until smooth. Set aside. In a large mixing bowl, cream shortening, brown sugar, and sugar until light. Add beans and egg mixture. Beat until well mixed. Add salt, baking soda, and vanilla. Mix well. Add flour and blend until smooth. Stir in oats and chocolate chips.

2. Drop by teaspoons onto baking sheet. Bake for 8 to 10 minutes or just until cookies are turning brown. Do not overbake. Remove cookies from baking sheet and cool on wire rack.

3. Place cookies in plastic bags as soon as they are cool and hide them.

Nutritional information per cookie:

Calories	80
Fat, gm.	3
Protein, gm.	1
Carbohydrate, gm.	12
Cholesterol, mg.	7
Fiber	0.5 gm.

Traditional Peanut Butter Cookies

For peanut butter lovers.

Serves 60

1 cup butter or butter-flavored shortening
1 cup sugar
1 cup brown sugar
1 cup peanut butter
2 eggs
1 teaspoon vanilla extract
1 teaspoon baking soda
1 teaspoon baking powder
$1/2$ teaspoon salt
$2^{1}/_{2}$ cups flour

Preheat oven to 350°F. Grease cookie sheet. In a medium bowl cream butter, sugar, and brown sugar with electric mixer. Add peanut butter and mix well. Add eggs, vanilla, baking soda, baking powder, and salt. Mix well. Add flour and mix on low speed. Roll into small balls, place on cookie sheet, and flatten with the tines of a fork. Bake for 10 to 15 minutes or just until done. Do not overbake. Cool on wire rack.

Nutritional information per serving:

Calories	95
Fat, gm.	5
Protein, gm.	2
Carbohydrate, gm.	10
Cholesterol, mg.	15
Fiber	very low

Chapter Fifteen
Desserts

Apple Rum Dum

Apple Streusel Pie

Blitz Torte

Bread Pudding with Brandy Sauce

Buttermilk Coconut Pie

Cherry Torte

Chocolate Coconut Delight

Cran-Apple Crisp

Cranberry and Raspberry Streusel Pie

Cranberry Pudding

Cream Puffs

Crème Brûlée

Easy Cocoa Cake

Fruit Cocktail Torte

Gingerbread Cake

Lazy Daisy Cake

Lemon Meringue Pie

Maple Nut Pie

Oatmeal Cake with Coconut Frosting

Orange Zucchini Cake

Poppy Seed Torte

Rhubarb Cake

Rhubarb Crunch

Rhubarb Custard Pie

Sour Cream Apple Pie

Strawberries Romanoff

Wash Day Cake

Apple Rum Dum

Cinnamon, nutmeg, and apples just go together. My original recipe card for this is so yellow, I can hardly read it but I can still see the three stars. That means it is really good. It was first served by my friend Nancy Walker at one of our dinner and bridge evenings more than 25 years ago.

Serves 8

1/4 cup butter or margarine
I cup sugar
I egg
I teaspoon baking soda
1/2 teaspoon salt
1/2 teaspoon cinnamon
1/4 teaspoon nutmeg
I cup flour
2 medium cooking apples, peeled, cored, and finely chopped
1/2 cup chopped walnuts, optional

1. Preheat oven to 350°F. If using glass or nonstick pan, preheat oven to 325°F. Butter an 8" x 8" baking pan. In a large bowl, beat butter and sugar together. Add egg and beat well. Add baking soda, salt, cinnamon, and nutmeg. Beat well. Stir in flour. Add apples and nuts and stir gently until blended. Spoon into pan. Bake for 30 to 40 minutes or until light brown and knife inserted in the middle comes out clean.

2. Serve with warm Caramel Cinnamon Sauce (page 254).

Nutritional information per serving:

Calories	225
Fat, gm.	6
Protein, gm.	2
Carbohydrate, gm.	41
Cholesterol, mg.	40
Fiber	low

Apple Streusel Pie

I love this recipe. It tastes so good and it is easy to make. It is a pie without a high-fat crust.

Serves 8

6 cups peeled cooking apple slices
1 teaspoon cinnamon
1/2 teaspoon nutmeg
1 cup sugar
3/4 cup fat-free milk
1/2 cup reduced-fat baking mix (Bisquick)
2 eggs
2 tablespoons butter or margarine, melted

Streusel:

1 cup reduced-fat baking mix (Bisquick)
1/3 cup brown sugar
3 tablespoons butter or margarine
1/2 cup chopped walnuts

1. Preheat oven to 325°F. Butter a deep 9-inch pie pan. In a large bowl, combine apples with cinnamon and nutmeg. Spoon into pie pan. In the same bowl, combine sugar, milk, 1/2 cup baking mix, eggs, and butter. Mix well with electric beater. Pour over apples.

2. In a small bowl, combine 1 cup baking mix, brown sugar, and butter. Using a pastry blender or a knife, cut in butter until mixture resembles coarse cornmeal. Sprinkle on top of batter in pie pan. Top with nuts. Bake for 50 to 60 minutes or until lightly browned and apples are tender.

Note: It works well to use a glass pan because you can see when the pie gets golden brown on the bottom.

Nutritional information per serving:

Calories	350
Fat, gm.	11
Protein, gm.	4
Carbohydrate, gm.	59
Cholesterol, mg.	65
Fiber	medium

Blitz Torte

This important family recipe is my father's traditional birthday cake. He has requested it every year that I can remember and this year is no exception. He will be 87 and of course he will have his special cake.

Serves 12

4 eggs, separated
1 3/4 cups sugar, divided
1/2 cup butter or margarine
1/4 cup evaporated fat-free milk
1 cup flour
3 teaspoons baking powder
1 teaspoon vanilla extract
1/4 cup chopped pecans
2 tablespoons sugar

Custard:

3 tablespoons flour
1/3 cup sugar
1 cup evaporated fat-free milk
1 egg
2 teaspoons vanilla extract

1. Preheat oven to 325°F. Grease and flour two 9-inch round baking pans. Separate eggs and place the whites in a medium bowl. Beat egg whites until foamy with electric beater. Gradually add 1 cup sugar while continuing to beat until very stiff. Set aside.

2. In another bowl, combine 3/4 cup sugar and butter. Beat well. Add egg yolks and beat. Add milk, flour, baking powder, and vanilla. Beat well. Divide batter between the pans. Divide whipped egg whites between the pans. Spread evenly. Sprinkle with nuts and sugar. Bake for 35 minutes. Remove from oven. Loosen cake by running a knife around the edges.

3. While cake is cooling, prepare custard. In a small saucepan, mix flour and sugar. Gradually stir in milk. Add egg and cook over medium heat, stirring constantly, until mixture coats the spoon and is thickened. Stir in vanilla. Refrigerate until ready to use.

4. When cakes are cool, carefully remove from pan and place 1 cake on a serving platter with meringue side up. Spread cooled custard over the meringue. Place second cake on top with meringue side up.

Nutritional information per serving:

Calories	300
Fat, gm.	10
Protein, gm.	5
Carbohydrate, gm.	48
Cholesterol, mg.	100
Fiber	very low

Bread Pudding with Brandy Sauce

Is there anything more comforting and warm than bread pudding?

Serves 12

3 eggs, lightly beaten
12 ounces evaporated fat-free milk
1 cup fat-free milk
3/4 cup brown sugar
3/4 cup sugar
1 teaspoon cinnamon
1/2 teaspoon nutmeg
1 tablespoon vanilla extract
2 tablespoons butter or margarine, melted
10 slices day-old or slightly dry white bread, cut into cubes
1/2 cup chopped pecans, optional
1 cup raisins, optional

Sauce:

2 cups fat-free half-and-half
1/3 cup sugar
3 tablespoons cornstarch
1 tablespoon vanilla extract
3 tablespoons brandy

1. Preheat oven to 325°F. Butter a 9" x 13" baking pan or a 1 1/2-quart casserole. In a large bowl, combine eggs, evaporated milk, milk, brown sugar, sugar, cinnamon, nutmeg, vanilla, and butter. Beat until well mixed. Add bread and stir gently. Add nuts and raisins if desired. Pour into pan or casserole. Place baking pan in a larger pan of warm water in the oven. Bake for 1 hour or until lightly browned and a toothpick inserted in the middle comes out clean.

2. In a small saucepan, combine half-and-half, sugar, and cornstarch. Stir until well mixed. Cook over medium heat, stirring constantly, until mixture comes to a boil and thickens. Remove from heat. Stir in vanilla and brandy. Serve warm sauce over the warm bread pudding.

Nutritional information per serving without nuts or raisins:

Calories	265
Fat, gm.	4
Protein, gm.	7
Carbohydrate, gm.	50
Cholesterol, mg.	50
Fiber	low

Buttermilk Coconut Pie

This is a very old recipe that is super easy to make.

Serves 10

1 1/4 cups sugar
2 tablespoons flour
1/2 cup butter or margarine, melted
3 eggs, lightly beaten
1/2 cup low-fat buttermilk
1 teaspoon vanilla extract
1 cup flaked coconut
9-inch unbaked pie crust

Preheat oven to 325°F. In a medium bowl, combine sugar and flour. Add butter, eggs, buttermilk, vanilla, and coconut. Mix well. Pour into unbaked pie shell. Bake for 60 to 70 minutes or until set.

Nutritional information per serving:

Calories	295
Fat, gm.	16
Protein, gm.	3
Carbohydrate, gm.	35
Cholesterol, mg.	80
Fiber	low

Cherry Torte

An easy recipe from the '50s.

Serves 16

Crust:

2 cups graham cracker crumbs

$1/4$ cup sugar

$1/3$ cup butter or margarine

Filling:

3 ounces fat-free cream cheese, room temperature

1 cup powdered sugar

8 ounces crushed pineapple, drained

2 cups low-fat whipped topping

1 cup miniature marshmallows

Topping:

20 ounces cherry pie filling

In a 9" x 13" pan, mix graham cracker crumbs, sugar, and butter. Pat firmly into pan. Set aside. In a medium bowl, beat cream cheese and sugar. Stir in crushed pineapple, whipped topping, and marshmallows. Pour over crust. Spoon pie filling evenly over filling. Cover with plastic wrap and refrigerate for several hours or until ready to serve.

Nutritional information per serving:

Calories	205
Fat, gm.	6
Protein, gm.	2
Carbohydrate, gm.	36
Cholesterol, mg.	10
Fiber	low

Chocolate Coconut Delight

*If you have ever dreamed of a soft, luscious coconut dessert that is simple to make,
your dream just came true. This is one of my favorite desserts and it was served by
Ron and Sharon when we were first welcomed into our church's young couples group years ago.*

Serves 12

6 ounces semisweet chocolate chips

1/4 cup butter or margarine

1 1/2 cups sugar

3 tablespoons cornstarch

2 eggs

12 ounces evaporated fat-free milk

1/4 teaspoon salt

1 teaspoon vanilla extract

1 1/2 cups flaked coconut

1/2 cup chopped pecans

Preheat oven to 325°F. Butter a 7" x 11" or 9" x 9" baking pan. In a small nonstick skillet, melt chocolate chips over the lowest heat. In a medium mixing bowl, combine butter, sugar, cornstarch, eggs, milk, salt, and vanilla. Beat well. Add melted chocolate. Mix well. Pour into baking pan. Sprinkle coconut and nuts on top. Bake for 40 to 50 minutes or until top puffs and cracks slightly. Let cool for 2 hours before serving. Serve with frozen yogurt or ice cream on top.

Note: This is great served warm but if it is left over in the refrigerator, I can't resist sneaking "tiny" bites. It is also good cold!

Nutritional information per serving:

Calories	260
Fat, gm.	10
Protein, gm.	4
Carbohydrate, gm.	38
Cholesterol, mg.	40
Fiber	medium

Cran-Apple Crisp

Cranberries and apples make a great combination.

Serves 10

4 large cooking apples, peeled and chopped
1 1/2 teaspoons fresh lemon juice
2 cups fresh or frozen cranberries
1 cup sugar
1 1/2 cups oats
1 cup chopped walnuts
1/2 cup butter or margarine, melted
1/3 cup brown sugar

Note: When cranberries are in season, buy extra bags and store them in the freezer to use all year. Do not thaw the cranberries before adding them to this recipe.

Preheat oven to 350°F or 325°F if using glass or nonstick pan. Butter a 7" x 11" baking pan. In a medium bowl, combine apples, lemon juice, cranberries, and sugar. Spoon into baking pan. In a small bowl, combine oats, nuts, butter, and brown sugar. Mix well. Sprinkle over the fruit. Bake for 60 minutes or until apples are tender and top is light brown.

Nutritional information per serving:

Calories	280
Fat, gm.	11
Protein, gm.	3
Carbohydrate, gm.	43
Cholesterol, mg.	25
Fiber	high

Cranberry and Raspberry Streusel Pie

This is a very easy pie to make, yet it makes such a big hit with family and friends. It is beautiful and delicious.

Serves 8

2 cups fresh or frozen cranberries, chopped
1 cup sugar
2 tablespoons tapioca
1/4 teaspoon salt
2 teaspoons vanilla extract
12 ounces frozen loose-pack raspberries
9-inch unbaked pie crust

Topping:
1/4 cup flour
1/4 cup brown sugar
1 tablespoon butter or margarine

Preheat oven to 425°F. In a large bowl, mix chopped cranberries, sugar, tapioca, salt, and vanilla. Gently stir in raspberries. Pour into unbaked pie crust. In a small bowl, combine flour, brown sugar, and butter. Cut in butter with a fork until it resembles fine cornmeal. Sprinkle over pie. Bake for 10 minutes. Reduce oven temperature to 325°F and bake for another 45 to 50 minutes or until pie is bubbly. Pie will set when it is cooled to room temperature.

Nutritional information per serving:

Calories	300
Fat, gm.	7
Protein, gm.	2
Carbohydrate, gm.	58
Cholesterol, mg.	5
Fiber	high

Cranberry Pudding

This will warm the heart!

Serves 10

1/2 cup sugar
1 1/2 tablespoons butter or margarine
1/2 cup evaporated fat-free milk
1 1/2 teaspoons baking powder
1 cup flour
1 cup fresh or frozen cranberries, chopped

Sauce:

1 cup sugar
2 tablespoons flour
1/2 cup butter or margarine
1/2 cup evaporated fat-free milk
1 teaspoon vanilla extract
1 tablespoon brandy, optional

Note: Fat-free milk can be substituted for the evaporated fat-free milk.

1. Preheat oven to 350°F or 325°F for a nonstick pan. Butter a 9" x 9" baking pan. In a medium bowl, cream sugar and butter together. Add milk, baking powder, and flour. Beat until smooth. Stir in cranberries. Pour into baking pan. Bake for 40 minutes.

2. In a small saucepan, combine sugar and flour. Add butter and milk. Cook, stirring constantly, until mixture comes to a boil and thickens slightly. Remove from heat. Stir in vanilla and brandy if desired. Serve warm over pudding.

Nutritional information per serving:

Calories	290
Fat, gm.	11
Protein, gm.	3
Carbohydrate, gm.	45
Cholesterol, mg.	30
Fiber	very low

Cream Puffs

I remember going to the Wisconsin State Fair when I was a child and we always stood in a long line to get cream puffs. They were made with real whipped cream. This recipe uses a custard that tastes creamy and wonderful but is almost fat-free.

Serves 15

1 cup water
1/2 cup butter or margarine
1/4 teaspoon salt
1 cup flour
4 eggs

Filling:

1 box (1 ounce) sugar-free, fat-free instant vanilla pudding mix
1 1/4 cups fat-free milk
1 cup light frozen whipped topping
1 teaspoon vanilla extract

Optional Topping:

1/2 cup semisweet chocolate chips

1. Preheat oven to 400°F. Grease and flour 2 large baking sheets. In a medium heavy saucepan, heat water, butter, and salt until it boils. Remove from heat and add flour. Stir with a wooden spoon until mixture forms a ball. Add eggs one at a time, beating each with a wooden spoon until it is well mixed. Drop batter on baking sheets forming 15 small balls. Keep balls several inches from each other to allow for expansion. Bake for 40 minutes. Turn off oven and bake for another 20 minutes. Remove from oven and cool puffs on racks.

2. For filling combine pudding mix and milk in a medium bowl. Beat with electric mixer for 2 minutes. Stir in whipped topping and vanilla. Cover bowl and refrigerate until ready to use. Fill cream puffs when ready to serve.

3. For optional topping, melt chocolate chips in nonstick skillet over lowest heat. Drizzle over cream puffs.

Nutritional information per serving with topping:

Calories	160
Fat, gm.	9
Protein, gm.	3
Carbohydrate, gm.	17
Cholesterol, mg.	60
Fiber	0

Crème Brûlée

I wanted to be able to savor every bite of a Crème Brûlée without guilt. It is usually classified as a sinful dessert because the traditional recipe uses lots of heavy cream. My adaptation is just as creamy but it has only a touch of fat and not many calories.

Serves 6

$^1/_2$ cup fat-free milk

1 tablespoon cornstarch

12 ounces canned evaporated fat-free milk

$^1/_2$ cup sugar

$^3/_4$ cup fat-free half-and-half

4 egg yolks

1 tablespoon vanilla extract

1 tablespoon brandy

3 tablespoons sugar, for topping

Note: If fat-free half-and-half is unavailable, substitute regular milk. Hint: It is important to chill the custard before caramelizing the sugar on top.

1. Preheat oven to 350°F. Place six 1-cup ramekins or custard cups in 2 large pans. In a medium heavy saucepan, combine fat-free milk and cornstarch. Mix until smooth. Add evaporated milk and sugar. Cook over medium heat, stirring occasionally, until mixture comes to a boil. Remove from heat. In a small bowl, combine fat-free half-and-half with the egg yolks. Beat lightly. Add a small amount of the hot milk into the egg mixture while stirring. Pour the egg mixture into the saucepan. Add vanilla and brandy. Stir to mix.

2. Divide mixture among the 6 ramekins. Pour hot water into the large pans to make a water bath for the custard. Carefully place pans in oven. Bake for 30 minutes or until custard is set. Remove ramekins from water bath. Refrigerate for several hours or until completely cold.

3. When ready to serve, sprinkle 1 to 2 teaspoons of sugar on top of each serving. Using a small butane-fuel torch, heat sugar until it caramelizes and turns light brown.

Nutritional information per serving:

Calories	200
Fat, gm.	3
Protein, gm.	8
Carbohydrate, gm.	36
Cholesterol, mg.	145
Fiber	0

Easy Cocoa Cake

This recipe was developed in the days when people just dropped in unexpectedly to visit.
You could go to the kitchen and throw together a warm dessert in minutes, even if you were out of eggs and milk.

Serves 10

1 1/2 cups flour
1 cup sugar
3 tablespoons cocoa
1 teaspoon baking soda
1/2 teaspoon salt
1/3 cup vegetable oil
1 tablespoon white vinegar
1 teaspoon vanilla extract
1 cup cold water
1/4 cup powdered sugar

Preheat oven to 350°F. If using a glass or nonstick pan, preheat oven to 325°F. Butter an 8" x 8" or a 7" x 11" baking pan. In a medium bowl, combine flour, sugar, cocoa, baking soda, and salt. Stir to mix. Add oil, vinegar, vanilla, and water. Mix with a spoon until well blended. Pour into pan. Bake for 30 to 35 minutes or until middle of cake springs back when lightly touched. Place powdered sugar in a small fine strainer and sprinkle over cake.

Note: In place of powdered sugar, the cake can be frosted.

Nutritional information per serving:

Calories	225
Fat, gm.	7
Protein, gm.	2
Carbohydrate, gm.	38
Cholesterol, mg.	0
Fiber	low

Fruit Cocktail Torte

This is one of my mother's favorites. She still throws it together if she needs a quick dessert.

Serves 10

29 ounces canned fruit cocktail, drained
1 egg, lightly beaten
1 cup flour
1 cup sugar
1/2 teaspoon salt
1 teaspoon baking soda

Topping:

1 cup brown sugar
3/4 cup chopped walnuts

Preheat oven to 350°F. If using a glass or nonstick pan, preheat oven to 325°F. Butter a 7" x 11" baking pan. In a small bowl, combine drained fruit cocktail and egg. In a medium bowl, combine flour, sugar, salt, and baking soda. Add fruit and egg. Stir to mix well. Pour into pan. Sprinkle brown sugar and walnuts on top. Bake for 35 to 40 minutes.

Nutritional information per serving:

Calories	240
Fat, gm.	2
Protein, gm.	3
Carbohydrate, gm.	53
Cholesterol, mg.	20
Fiber	low

Gingerbread Cake

Remember this great old-fashioned cake that is very easy to make.

Serves 20

1 cup brown sugar
¹/₂ cup shortening
2 eggs
³/₄ cup molasses
2 teaspoons ginger
1 teaspoon cinnamon
2 teaspoons baking soda
¹/₂ teaspoon salt
2³/₄ cups flour
1 cup low-fat buttermilk

1. Preheat oven to 350°F. If using a glass or nonstick pan, preheat oven to 325°F. Butter a 9" x 13" baking pan. In a large bowl, combine sugar and shortening. Beat well. Add eggs and beat again. Add molasses, ginger, cinnamon, baking soda, and salt. Blend well. Stir in flour. Add buttermilk and blend. Spread in pan. Bake for 35 to 40 minutes. Test by touching the middle of the cake lightly with a finger. It should spring back.

2. Serve with whipped cream or a lemon custard sauce.

Nutritional information per serving:

Calories	180
Fat, gm.	6
Protein, gm.	3
Carbohydrate, gm.	29
Cholesterol, mg.	20
Fiber	low

Lazy Daisy Cake

This is the first cake my friend Mary made when she was about eight years old. She got the recipe from her grandmother's cookbook. It is a wonderful dessert but it is also lovely served for a morning brunch or afternoon tea.

Serves 12

¹/₂ cup evaporated fat-free milk
2 tablespoons butter or margarine
2 eggs
1 cup sugar
1 teaspoon vanilla extract
1 cup flour
1 teaspoon baking powder
¹/₄ teaspoon salt

Topping:

¹/₂ cup butter or margarine, melted
³/₄ cup brown sugar
¹/₄ cup evaporated fat-free milk
¹/₂ cup flaked coconut
¹/₂ cup walnuts, optional

1. Preheat oven to 350°F or 325°F if using a glass or nonstick pan. Grease an 8" x 8" baking pan. In a small saucepan, combine milk and butter. Heat until butter has melted. Set aside. In medium bowl, combine eggs, sugar, and vanilla. Beat for 2 minutes or until slightly thick. Combine flour, baking powder, and salt. Add dry ingredients and warm milk mixture to bowl. Mix well. Pour batter into pan. Bake for 25 to 30 minutes or until light brown and the middle of the cake springs back when lightly touched.

2. While cake is baking, prepare topping. In a small bowl, beat together butter, brown sugar, milk, coconut, and nuts. When cake is removed from oven, pour topping over hot cake. Place under the oven broiler for 1 to 2 minutes or until golden brown.

Nutritional information per serving:

Calories	245
Fat, gm.	10
Protein, gm.	3
Carbohydrate, gm.	36
Cholesterol, mg.	55
Fiber	low

Lemon Meringue Pie

If there is one dessert in the world that brings back the best memories of home cooking, it is Lemon Meringue Pie with my mother's flaky tender crust. I can't make a crust anything like hers, so I don't even try.

Serves 8

1 cup sugar
1/3 cup cornstarch
1/4 teaspoon salt
3 eggs, separated
1/3 cup fresh lemon juice
2 teaspoons lemon zest
2 cups water
1 tablespoon butter or margarine
9-inch baked pie crust
1/3 cup powdered sugar

1. Preheat oven to 350°F. In a small saucepan, combine sugar, cornstarch, salt, egg yolks, lemon juice, lemon zest, and water. Cook over medium heat, stirring constantly until mixture comes to a rolling boil and thickens. Add butter. Taste mixture and add an additional tablespoon of lemon juice if desired. Immediately pour into baked pie shell.

2. In a medium bowl, beat egg whites until stiff. Gradually add powdered sugar and beat until glossy and soft peaks form. Pile the meringue over the filling, swirling gently to cover completely. Bake for 10 to 15 minutes or until meringue peaks are lightly browned. Cool before cutting.

Nutritional information per serving:

Calories	275
Fat, gm.	9
Protein, gm.	3
Carbohydrate, gm.	46
Cholesterol, mg.	70
Fiber	0

Maple Nut Pie

This has a creamy soft middle and beautiful nut topping. It isn't quite as rich as the usual pecan pie and it has significantly fewer calories. Serve it in small slices with frozen yogurt.

Serves 10

1 cup maple syrup
1 small box (0.8 ounce) sugar-free vanilla pudding mix (not instant)
3/4 cup evaporated fat-free milk
1 egg
1 tablespoon brandy
1 cup pecans, mixed nuts, or dry-roasted peanuts
8-inch unbaked pie shell

Note: Regular vanilla pudding mix can be substituted for the sugar-free mix but that will increase the calories by 25 per slice.

Preheat oven to 400°F. In a small bowl, combine maple syrup, pudding mix, milk, egg, and brandy. Beat with electric mixer until blended. Stir in nuts. Pour into unbaked pie shell. Bake for 10 minutes. Reduce oven temperature to 325°F and bake for another 35 to 40 minutes or until set in the middle. The pie will appear to be soft but will firm up when cool.

Nutritional information per serving:

Calories	275
Fat, gm.	12
Protein, gm.	6
Carbohydrate, gm.	36
Cholesterol, mg.	20
Fiber	medium

Oatmeal Cake with Coconut Frosting

This has been the most requested birthday cake recipe in my friend Nancy's family for over 50 years. It is exceptionally moist and so, so good.

Serves 20

1 1/4 cups water
1 cup quick-cooking oats
1/2 cup butter or margarine
1 cup sugar
1 cup brown sugar
2 eggs
1 teaspoon baking soda
1 teaspoon cinnamon
1/2 teaspoon salt
1 1/2 cups flour

Frosting:

6 tablespoons butter or margarine
1/2 cup sugar
1/4 cup evaporated fat-free milk
1 cup flaked coconut
1/2 cup chopped nuts
1 teaspoon vanilla extract

1. Preheat oven to 350°F. If using a glass or nonstick pan, preheat oven to 325°F. Butter a 9" x 13" baking pan. In a small saucepan, bring water to a boil and stir in oats and butter. Let stand for 20 minutes. In a large mixing bowl, combine sugar, brown sugar, and eggs. Beat well. Add oatmeal mixture and mix. Add baking soda, cinnamon, and salt. Mix well. Stir in flour. Spoon into pan. Bake for 20 to 30 minutes until set in the middle.

2. When cake has cooled, prepare frosting. In a small saucepan, combine butter, sugar, milk, coconut, and nuts. Bring to a boil over medium heat. Remove from heat and stir in vanilla. Cool slightly and pour over cake. Spread evenly.

Nutritional information per serving:

Calories	240
Fat, gm.	11
Protein, gm.	3
Carbohydrate, gm.	33
Cholesterol, mg.	40
Fiber	low

Orange Zucchini Cake

This reminds me of an old-fashioned moist spice cake. My friend recently served it for her husband's fiftieth birthday party, and guests who say they never eat desserts asked for seconds.

Serves 20

2 cups flour
2 teaspoons baking powder
1 teaspoon baking soda
1 teaspoon cinnamon
2 cups sugar
1 cup Kellogg's All Bran cereal
4 eggs
1 cup canola oil
1/4 cup frozen orange juice concentrate
2 teaspoons orange zest
2 teaspoons vanilla extract
2 cups shredded zucchini
1/3 cup golden raisins, optional

Frosting:

1/4 cup butter or margarine
4 ounces fat-free or low-fat cream cheese
1 1/2 cups powdered sugar
2 teaspoons orange juice

1. Preheat oven to 350°F. Butter a 9" x 13" baking pan. In a large bowl, combine flour, baking powder, baking soda, cinnamon, sugar, and cereal. In another small bowl, beat eggs until fluffy. Add oil, orange juice, orange zest, and vanilla. Beat well. Pour liquids into large bowl with dry ingredients. Beat until smooth. Stir in zucchini. Add raisins if desired. Pour into pan. Bake for 40 minutes or until middle springs back when lightly touched. Cool.

2. Combine frosting ingredients in a small bowl. Beat until light. Frost cake.

Nutritional information per serving:

Calories	270
Fat, gm.	12
Protein, gm.	4
Carbohydrate, gm.	43
Cholesterol, mg.	40
Fiber	medium

Poppy Seed Torte

When I asked my dad for his favorite dessert recipe, without hesitation he replied, "Mother's Poppy Seed Torte." He told me that my mother made it for him on their first date. He said that he asked her for a second date because the dessert was so good and he was hoping she would make it again. Apparently she did, because they have been married for 60 years.

Serves 12

Crust:

1¼ cups graham cracker crumbs
¼ cup brown sugar
4 tablespoons butter or margarine, melted

Filling:

3 egg yolks
3 tablespoons cornstarch
½ cup fat-free milk
12 ounces evaporated fat-free milk
½ cup sugar
1 teaspoon salt
2 tablespoons poppy seeds
2 teaspoons vanilla extract

Topping:

3 egg whites
6 tablespoons sugar

1. Preheat oven to 350°F. In a 7" x 11" baking pan, mix graham cracker crumbs, brown sugar, and butter. Remove ¼ cup of the mixture and set aside for the topping. Press remaining crumbs firmly into the bottom of the pan. Set aside.

2. In a medium heavy saucepan whisk egg yolks until lightly beaten. In a cup, mix cornstarch and fat-free milk. Add to saucepan. Add evaporated fat-free milk, sugar, salt, and poppy seeds. Place over medium heat and cook, stirring constantly, until mixture comes to a boil and thickens. Boil gently for 2 minutes. Remove from stove and add vanilla. Pour into crust.

3. In a medium bowl, beat egg whites until frothy. Add sugar, 1 tablespoon at a time, while beating continuously. Beat until soft peaks form. Spoon over filling. Sprinkle with reserved crumbs. Bake for 15 to 20 minutes or until meringue is lightly browned. Let cool for several hours before serving.

Nutritional information per serving:

Calories	195
Fat, gm.	6
Protein, gm.	5
Carbohydrate, gm.	30
Cholesterol, mg.	65
Fiber	low

Rhubarb Cake

This moist, delicious cake can be made year-round with frozen rhubarb.

Serves 16

1/2 cup shortening
1/2 cup sugar
1 1/2 cups brown sugar
1 egg
1 cup low-fat buttermilk
1 teaspoon salt
1 teaspoon baking soda
1 teaspoon vanilla extract
2 cups flour
3 cups diced frozen or fresh rhubarb

Topping:

1/2 cup brown sugar
1/2 cup white sugar
1 teaspoon cinnamon
1/2 teaspoon nutmeg
1/2 cup chopped nuts, optional
Butter spray

1. Preheat oven to 350°F. If using a glass or nonstick pan, preheat oven to 325°F. Butter a 9" x 13" baking pan. In a large bowl, cream together shortening, sugar, and brown sugar. Add egg and beat well. Add buttermilk, salt, baking soda, and vanilla. Beat well. Stir in flour until well mixed. Stir in rhubarb. Spoon into pan.

2. In a small bowl, mix brown sugar, white sugar, cinnamon, nutmeg, and nuts. Sprinkle over batter. Spray top with butter spray until it is moist. Bake for 30 to 40 minutes or until set in the middle and lightly browned. Do not overbake.

Note: Two 8" x 8" pans can be used in place of the 9" x 13" pan.

Nutritional information per serving:

Calories	220
Fat, gm.	7
Protein, gm.	2
Carbohydrate, gm.	37
Cholesterol, mg.	10
Fiber	very low

Rhubarb Crunch

There are many versions of this rhubarb recipe but my friend Mary claims this is the best.
Make it in two pans and give one to a friend.

Serves 12

6 cups fresh rhubarb, cut into 1-inch pieces
¾ cup sugar
1 box (18 ounces) yellow cake mix
1 cup flaked coconut
1 cup chopped walnuts
½ cup butter or margarine, melted
Butter spray

Note: This recipe can be made without the coconut if you prefer.

Preheat oven to 325°F. Butter a 9" x 13" baking pan. Arrange rhubarb in bottom of pan. Sprinkle with sugar and dry cake mix. Stir to mix. Sprinkle with coconut and walnuts. Pour butter evenly over the top. Spray top with butter spray until the dry cake mix is moistened. Bake for 45 to 55 minutes or until light brown on top and bubbly on the bottom.

Nutritional information per serving:

Calories	340
Fat, gm.	14
Protein, gm.	3
Carbohydrate, gm.	51
Cholesterol, mg.	20
Fiber	low

Rhubarb Custard Pie

This is my mother's recipe. It is very good! It is one of those very easy desserts that can be put together in just a few minutes if you have a refrigerated pie crust on hand.

Serves 8

1 1/2 cups sugar
3 eggs, lightly beaten
1/4 cup evaporated fat-free milk
1/2 teaspoon vanilla extract
1/4 teaspoon salt
3 tablespoons flour
1/4 teaspoon nutmeg
4 cups rhubarb, cut into 1-inch pieces
9-inch unbaked pie crust

Note: To reduce calories and carbohydrates, this recipe works well if you substitute 1/2 of the sugar with Splenda.

Preheat oven to 325°F. In a large bowl, combine sugar, eggs, milk, vanilla, salt, flour, and nutmeg. Mix well. Stir in rhubarb. Pour into unbaked pie crust. Bake at 325°F for 1 1/4 to 1 1/2 hours or until pie is set in the middle.

Nutritional information per serving:

Calories	290
Fat, gm.	8
Protein, gm.	4
Carbohydrate, gm.	51
Cholesterol, mg.	70
Fiber	low

Sour Cream Apple Pie

This is one of Grandmother's best.

Serves 8

1 cup fat-free sour cream
1 egg, lightly beaten
2 tablespoons flour
3/4 cup sugar
3/4 teaspoon cinnamon
1/2 teaspoon salt
1/2 teaspoon vanilla extract
6 medium cooking apples, peeled and sliced
9-inch unbaked pie crust

Topping:

1/3 cup sugar
1/3 cup flour
1 teaspoon cinnamon
2 tablespoons butter or margarine

1. Preheat oven to 400°F. In a large bowl, combine sour cream, egg, flour, sugar, cinnamon, salt, and vanilla. Beat until smooth. Stir in apples. Spoon into unbaked pie crust. Bake for 15 minutes. Reduce heat to 350°F and bake for another 15 minutes.

2. While pie is baking, prepare the topping. In a small bowl, combine sugar, flour, and cinnamon. Cut in butter with a fork until it resembles fine cornmeal. Sprinkle mixture on top of partially baked pie. Bake for another 25 to 35 minutes or until apples are tender.

Nutritional information per serving:

Calories	355
Fat, gm.	10
Protein, gm.	4
Carbohydrate, gm.	62
Cholesterol, mg.	35
Fiber	medium

Strawberries Romanoff

I had this elegant dessert years ago in a French restaurant. I loved it but it seemed so high in calories. I recently met a chef who shared the recipe and I adapted it with fat-free sour cream. Now it not only tastes wonderful, but it is low in calories too.

Serves 4

⅓ cup brown sugar
2 tablespoons brandy
1 cup fat-free sour cream
1 quart fresh strawberries, sliced
Dash nutmeg, optional

In a small saucepan, combine brown sugar and brandy. Place over low heat, stirring constantly, until sugar has melted. Remove from heat and cool to room temperature. In a small bowl, combine sugar-brandy mixture with the sour cream. Cover and refrigerate. When ready to serve, layer strawberries and sour cream mixture alternately in individual glass dessert bowls or large wine goblets. Sprinkle with nutmeg if desired.

Nutritional information per serving:

Calories	135
Fat, gm.	0
Protein, gm.	3
Carbohydrate, gm.	31
Cholesterol, mg.	0
Fiber	high

Wash Day Cake

This easy cake needs no frosting.
It was traditionally made on busy wash days.

Serves 20

1 cup chopped pitted dates
1 1/2 cups water
1 3/4 teaspoons baking soda, divided
1 cup sugar
3/4 cup shortening
2 eggs
1 teaspoon salt
1 teaspoon vanilla extract
1 1/2 cups flour

Topping:
1 cup semisweet chocolate chips
1 cup chopped walnuts

1. Preheat oven to 350°F. If using a glass or nonstick pan, preheat oven to 325°F. Grease a 9" x 13" baking pan. In a small saucepan, combine dates, water, and 1 teaspoon baking soda. Bring to a boil. Reduce heat, and simmer for 10 to 15 minutes or until dates are soft. Cool to room temperature.

2. In a medium bowl, beat sugar and shortening until light and fluffy. Add eggs and beat well. Add ¾ teaspoon baking soda, salt, vanilla, and date mixture. Mix well. Add flour and beat on low speed until well mixed. Pour into baking pan. Sprinkle with chips and nuts. Bake for 25 to 35 minutes or until light brown and the middle springs back when lightly touched.

Nutritional information per serving:

Calories	195
Fat, gm.	8
Protein, gm.	2
Carbohydrate, gm.	29
Cholesterol, mg.	20
Fiber	medium

Index

Mustard
   basic, 253
   and horseradish sauce, 259

N

Noodles
   beef, spinach, and noodle
      casserole, 94
   Sicilian supper, 109
   tuna noodle casserole, 111
   see also Pasta
Nuts, xxiii
   chicken and cashew
      casserole, 97
   green beans with roasted
      peppers and pine nuts,
      211
   maple nut pie, 313
   mushroom nut loaf, 78
   olive nut cheese ball, 16
   orange marmalade-pecan
      bread, 243
   pistachio nut and olive
      tapenade, 18

O

Oatmeal, xix
   butterfingers, 279
   cake with coconut
      frosting, 314
   cherry muffins, 242
   chocolate chip-oatmeal
      cookies, 293
   cranberry chip cookies,
      285
   no-bake chocolate
      oatmeal balls, 290
   oatmeal fudge bars, 291
Oils, xv, xviii
Olives
   mushroom, walnut, and
      olive spread, 15
   olive nut cheese ball, 16
   pistachio nut and olive
      tapenade, 18
Onions
   American onion soup, 54
   carrot, potato, and onion
      gratin, 205
   cooking tips for, xiv, xxx
   onion soup mix, 256
   pie, 192

   rice with green onions and
      mushrooms, 194
   tomato and red onion
      salad, 50
Orange marmalade-pecan
   bread, 243
Orange roughy, citrus-
   marinated, 171
Orange zucchini cake, 315
Organization tips, xiii
Oven baking tips, xxiv
Oven temperatures, xiii

P

Pancakes
   apple, 231
   apple, fancy baked, 274
Pans
   baking, xxii
   cooking, xxvii
   deglazing, xxvi
Parsley dumplings, 193
Parsnips and carrots in lemon
   mustard sauce, 217
Pasta
   cooking tips for, xvi

   fettuccine Alfredo, light,
      75
   with garlic tomato sauce,
      79
   gnocchi, 187
   hamburger and macaroni
      casserole, 101
   linguine carbonara, 104
   salad, 42
   salad, Mexican macaroni,
      77
   salad, shrimp and, 46
   spaghetti pie, 110
   spinach manicotti, 82
   sun-dried tomatoes and
      mushrooms with
      linguine, 84
   turkey tetrazzini, 112
   see also Noodles
Peaches, xxxi
Peanut butter
   butterfingers, 279
   chocolate swirl bars, 284
   cookies, traditional, 294
   corn flake nuggets, 292
Peas, xxx
   chicken and pea pods, 153
   split pea soup, 66

Sausage-stuffed mushrooms, 22
Scallop and shrimp marsala, 178
Sea bass, carrot-crusted, 169
Seafood
chowder, 64
crab cakes, 172
scallop and shrimp marsala, 178
shrimp and artichokes in garlic tomato sauce, 179
shrimp and black bean chili, 65
shrimp and pepper stir-fry, 180
see also Fish
Seasonings
onion soup mix, 256
taco, 257
Serving dishes, xxxi
Serving food, xxxiv
Shellfish. See Seafood
Shepherd's pie, 108
Sherry mushroom sauce, 263
Shrimp
and artichokes in garlic tomato sauce, 179
and black bean chili, 65

cocktail sauce, 264
and pasta salad, 46
and pepper stir-fry, 180
and scallop marsala, 178
Sicilian steak, 141
Sicilian supper, 109
Side dishes, 181–198
Sloppy Joes, 142
Snapper, potato-crusted, 177
Sole, lemon Dijon, 176
Soups
beef barley, 55
chicken, old-fashioned, 62
cooking tips for, xvi–xvii
corn chowder, 58
hamburger, 60
minestrone, 61
onion, American, 54
potato, 63
seafood chowder, 64
split pea, 66
vegetable, 59
wild rice and mushroom, 67
zucchini, 68
see also Stews
Sour cream apple pie, 320
Spaghetti pie, 110

Spinach
and bacon breakfast pizza, 270
and bacon strata, 276
beef, spinach, and noodle casserole, 94
cheese pie, 81
chicken Florentine, 157
with dates, apples, and caramelized walnuts, 31
manicotti, 82
phyllo squares, Greek, 188
salad, raspberry, 43
salad, sweet-and sour, 48
spread, 23
squares, 25
Spreads. See Dips and spreads
Squash
butternut, and apple bake, 204
winter, with maple mustard sauce, 225
Stews
beef, 106
chicken gumbo, 56
chili, 57
shrimp and black bean chili, 65

Storing food, xxxii–xxxiii
Strawberries
kiwi salad with honey raspberry dressing, 47
Romanoff, 321
Stuffings
apple apricot bread dressing, 182
wild rice and mushroom, 197
Sugar cookies, best-ever, 278
Sun-dried tomatoes. See Tomatoes
Swedish meatballs, 144
Sweet potatoes
and apples in orange ginger sauce, 223
casserole, 222

T

Taco cheese pie, 86
Taco seasoning mix, 257
Thawing meats, xxiv–xxv
Tomatoes, xxxi
chili pepper and tomato salsa, 7
Italian spaghetti sauce, 127